VIJÑĀNA BHAIRAVA

The Manual for Self Realization

REVEALED BY

Swami Lakshmanjoo

EDITED BY

John Hughes

Lakshmanjoo Academy

Published by:
Lakshmanjoo Academy

First Edition 2007 (Universal Shaiva Fellowship)
First printing 2012 (Universal Shaiva Fellowship)
Second Edition 2015 (Lakshmanjoo Academy)

Printed in the United States of America

For information, address
Lakshmanjoo Academy
Telephone: 1 (310) 837-0402
Email: office@lakshmanjooacademy.org
http://www.lakshmanjooacademy.org

ISBN 978-0-9816228-4-2 (sbk)
ISBN 978-0-9816228-2-8 (hbk)
ISBN 978-0-9837833-4-3 (ebook)

This pursuit is dedicated to Swamiji
to whom I owe everything.

CONTENTS

Guide to Pronunciation	vii
Preface to Second Edition	ix
Preface to First Edition	xi
Acknowledgments	xv
The Author	xix
Introduction	xxi
Dhāraṇā and Upāya Guide	xxvii
Vijñāna Bhairava	1
Appendix	275
Bibliography	295
Index	299
Publications	312
Free Audio Download	314

GUIDE TO PRONUNCIATION

The following English words exemplify the pronunciation of selected Sanskṛit vowels and consonants. The Romanized Sanskṛit vowel or consonant is first listed and then a English word is given to aid you in its proper pronunciation.

a	as	a in ***A***merica.
ā	as	a in f***a***ther.
i	as	i in f***i***ll, l***i***ly.
ī	as	i in pol***i***ce.
u	as	u in f***u***ll.
ū	as	u in r***u***de.
ṛi	as	ri in mer***ri***ly.
ṛī	as	ri in ma***ri***ne.
e	as	e in pr***e***y.
ai	as	ai in ***ai***sle.
o	as	o in st***o***ne.
au	as	ou in h***ou***se
ś	as	s in ***s***ure.
ṣ	as	sh in ***sh***un, bu***sh***
s	as	s in ***s***aint, ***s***un

Preface to the Second Edition

It has been eight years since the Lakshmanjoo Academy's last publication of Swamiji's translation of the *Vijñāna Bhairava–The Manual for Self-Realization*. I am pleased to introduce our latest edition, which now includes additional footnotes, an elaborate appendix, an index, and free downloadable audio. In this edition, footnotes within quotation marks are Swamiji's own words from published texts and/or the USF archives. All other footnotes are the editor's notes. I am confident that this edition will afford the reader more clarity and understanding of the 112 contemplative practices of the *Vijñāna Bhairava*.

May Swamiji's blessing continue to shine upon you!

John Hughes
Lakshmanjoo Academy
Culver City, California
August 14, 2015

Preface to the First Edition

In this audio study set, the fully Self-realized master, Swami Lakshmanjoo, translates and elucidates 112 paths towards Self-realization, which are revealed by God (Bhairava) to His beloved consort (Bhairavī) in the seminal Kashmir Shaiva text, the *Vijñāna Bhairava*. Having dedicated his whole life to the philosophy and practice of Kashmir Shaivism, Swamiji was uniquely qualified to reveal this oft misinterpreted and misunderstood text.

For more than half a century, scholars and aspirants from all over the world came to study the *Vijñāna Bhairava* under Swamiji's guidance. All have acknowledged Swamiji's invaluable contribution to the clarification of this esoteric text. In his classic, *Zen Flesh, Zen Bones* (1959), Paul Reps dedicated the fourth chapter on "Centering" to Swami Lakshmanjoo[1]. Lilian Silburn first met Swami Lakshmanjoo in 1948. Over a period of ten years she studied a number of text on Kashmir Shaivism under Swamiji's direct guidance. In 1961, she published *Le Vijñāna Bhairava* in French.[2] In 1979, Jaidev Singh studied this text word by word with Swamiji. He dedicated his publication, the *Vijñānabhairava or Divine Consciousness*, with the follow-ing words: "With profound respects to Swami Lakshmanjoo who unsealed my eyes."[3]

---

1 *Zen Flesh, Zen Bones: A Collection of Zen and Pre-Zen Writings,* Paul Reps, Anchor Books, New York, 1957.

2 *Le Vijñāna Bhairava*, Lilian Silburn, Publications de I'Institut de Civilisation Indienne, Editions E. de Boccard, Paris, 1961.

3 *Vijñānabhairava or Divine Consciousness*, Jaideva Singh, Motilal Banarsidass, Delhi, 1979.

In 2002, *Vijñāna Bhairava–The Practice of Centering Awareness*[4] found its way into the market place. This book was compiled from my preliminary transcript of Swamiji's lectures, which was unedited and incomplete. This transcript was unfortunately misappropriated and given to two independent authors for publishing without my consent. Any intelligent reader will see that, by comparison with the present publication it is incomplete and fraught with mistakes.

These revelations of the *Vijñāna Bhairava* were recorded at various times between 1973 and 1984. The recordings include Swami Lakshmanjoo's initial rendering of the verses and the practices they prescribe along with further clarifications and explanations. These additional clarifications were given at the request of some of Swamiji's devotees, who continued to have difficulty understanding certain verses and associated practices. It is because these recordings were made at different times and with different equipment that the audio quality varies throughout.

I have chosen to publish Swamiji's translation and commentary on the *Vijñāna Bhairava* as an audio study set because I am convinced that the subtletites of this divine revelation will be better conveyed by directly listening to the voice of a realized master. The accompanying transcript has been edited for the purposes of clarifying technical terms and concepts as well as for the purposes of making Swamiji's revelation more accessible to the native-English speaker.

The transcript itself has been kept as close as possible to the original spoken word. On a few occasions, where deemed necessary for clarity, I have added additional words within square brackets. Words within rounded brackets are Swamiji's own words. Also, very occasionally a word here or there has been amended for the sake of the flow of the

4 *Vijñāna Bhairava–The Practice of Centering*, Indica Books, Varanasi, 2002.

English. Numerous footnotes have been added to help in the study of this text, all of which are Swamiji's own words unless specified as an "editor's note" or simply a text reference or a literal translation of a Sanskrit word.

To further assist the adept in the comprehension of this text, each *dhāraṇā*, or meditation, has been separated into individual audio tracks. At the behest of Swamiji, each verse has been presented in the transcript in the original *Devanagari* followed by the Romanized transliteration.

The original Sanskrit text used by Swamiji was the *Vijñāna Bhairava*, published in 1918 as Volume 8 in the *Kashmir Series of Texts and Studies* (KSTS). Even though this particular volume contains a commentary, partly by Kṣhemarāja and partly by Shivopādhyāya, Swamiji chose to use it only as a reference for the original verses.

I am sure you will find Swamiji's revelation of the *Vijñāna Bhairava* to be profoundly inspiring and illuminating.

May Swamiji's blessing shine upon you!

John Hughes
Universal Shaiva Fellowship
Culver City, California
September 29, 2007

Acknowledgements for the second edition

First of all, I would like to thank my wife Denise, my son Viresh, my daughter Shanna, George Barselaar, Claudia Dose, Stephen Benson, and Michael Van Winkle, all of whom made the success of this project possible. They all proved to be invaluable in the preparation of the transcript and audios for the publication of this new edition of the Vijñāna Bhairava. George Barselaar and Stephen Benson worked tireless on the first edition, listening over and over to the audio recordings, reading and re-reading the transcript, and making many valuable suggestions. I would like to thank my son Viresh for his masterful editing and additional footnotes in this second edition. His efforts will no doubt give the reader a much greater comprehension of this difficult text. I would also like to thank our very talented graphic designer, Claudia Dose, who provided the beautiful art work for the new cover. My sincere thanks to our audio expert, Michael van Winkle, who tirelessly worked polishing the original audio recordings, many of which were practically inaudible. Lastly I would like to thank my wife Denise who not only worked on the first edition, but made valuable editing suggestions for this second edition.

Swami Lakshmanjoo

SWAMI LAKSHMANJOO

The Author

Swami Lakshmanjoo was born in Srinagar, Kashmir, on May 9, 1907. He was the most recent and the greatest of the long line of saints and masters of the Kashmir Shaiva tradition. From his early childhood, Swamiji spent his life studying and practicing the teachings of this unique and sacred tradition. Having a complete intellectual and spiritual understanding of the philosophy and practice of Kashmir Shaivism, he was a true master in every respect.

Being born with a photographic memory, learning was always easy for him. In addition to possessing a complete knowledge of Kashmir Shaivism, he had a vast knowledge of the traditional religious and philosophical schools and texts of India. Swamiji would freely draw upon other texts to clarify, expand, and substantiate his lectures. He could recall an entire text by simply remembering the first few words of a verse.

In time, his reputation as a learned philosopher and spiritual adept spread. Spiritual leaders and scholars journeyed from all over the world to receive his blessings and to ask him questions about various aspects of Kashmir Shaiva philosophy. He gained renown as a humble devotee of Lord Shiva and as an accomplished master (*siddha*) of the non-dual tradition of Kashmir Shaivism.

Throughout his life, Swamiji taught his disciples and devotees the ways of devotion and awareness. He shunned fame and recognition and did not seek his own glory. He knew Kashmir Shaivism was the most precious jewel and that, by God's grace, those who desired supreme knowledge would be attracted to its teachings. His earnest wish was for Kashmir Shaivism to be preserved and made available to all humankind.

In 1990, during his stay in Nepal, Swamiji translated Abhinavagupta's unique commentaries on the *Paramārthasāra* and the *Bhagavad Gītā*. During his explanation of the sixth chapter of the *Bhagavad Gītā*, Swamiji gave a rare glimpse into the full-ness and glory of his own experience:

> I was smoothly going on with my practice and abruptly *śaktipāta* (grace) came and threw all its force in me. It was *tīvra tīvra* (super-supreme) *śaktipāta*. And then it happened and I was newborn. I became so great. I don't mean to boast but this is what happened. I was newly reborn. And, because I had to become Bhairava, I had to experience all of the states of *yoga*. And it happened, everything happened. I had all experiences; and *cidānanda* also, *jagadānanda*[5] also. Everything happened. You can't imagine the ways of *śaktipāta*.[6]

On the 27th of September, 1991, Swami Lakshmanjoo left his physical body and attained *mahasamādhi*, the great liberation.

5 *Cidānanda* and *jagadānanda* are the final stages of the seven states of *tūrya*, also known as the seven states of *ānanda* (bliss). See Appendix for explanation of the seven states of *ānanda*. See also *Kashmir Shaivism–The Secret Supreme*, 16.113-115.

6 *Bhagavd Gītā–In the Light of Kashmir Śhaivism*, DVD 6.3 (42.01).

INTRODUCTION

Kashmir Shaivism is so rich and detailed in its theology and soteriology that it has been aptly described as "the mystical geography of awareness." It includes a highly developed system of spirituality that emphasizes not only the intellectual understanding of its philosophy but also the direct realization, the direct experience, of its truth.

For the Kashmir Shaiva, the very nature of truth, its defining characteristic, is that it is both limited and unlimited, atomic and universal. The human intellect, however limited, is capable of seizing the reality which transcends and envelops it. Such is the proclamation of God (Bhairava) to His beloved consort (Bhairavī) in this forthcoming text, the *Vijñāna Bhairava.*

Kashmir Shaivism offers many different practical approaches to the realization of the ultimate reality. These approaches vary depending upon the ability of the seeker. In the *Vijñāna Bhairava*, Bhairava sets out one hundred and twelve techniques of spiritual practice to be used by an aspirant eager to realize the divine universal reality. These secret practices are revealed by Bhairava as He answers the questions posed to Him by Bhairavī, the Divine Mother.

The narrative begins with Bhairavī, feigning ignorance, telling Bhairava that, even though She has heard all the various theories and explanations of the nature of reality, She still has doubts and is not completely satisfied. She implores Bhairava, "What is the real essence of the way we have to tread? Please, O Lord, remove My doubts entirely."

Bhairava answers by telling Bhairavī that She has asked the question that is worth asking. He says it is a question–a secret question–that is the real essence of all

Tantras. He then continues by explaining that all the proceses illuminated in the *Tantras* are not meant for great or highly elevated souls, but for those who are not completely developed. He emphasizes that all these processes are just to begin with: "You begin with them and then leave them aside." This is because, in reality, the supreme state is not achieved by the support of the means (*upāya*). These practices are only capable of assisting the aspirant to meet God half-way, and the rest happens automatically by the independent grace of Bhairava. But it is important to undertand that even the mere thought or desire to practice is a sign of God's grace.

All of the means exist within the world, which is bound by time, space, and formation, while the supreme state, the state of Bhairava, is beyond the limitation of space, time, and formation. The state of Bhairava is beyond thought and cannot be perceived by the thought-full mind. Bhairava is the state of unlimited universal subjectivity which can't be found as such. Why? The real state of Bhairava is the state of the knower and therefore, cannot be known; It can't be found because It is the perceiver, not the perceived. When you have a desire to perceive this state, you can only perceive It when It comes down one step lower in the state of Bhairavī, i.e., the state of the known and the world of the means.

So, in answering Bhairavī's question–"What is the real essence of the way we have to tread?"–Bhairava will teach Her one hundred and twelve ways to enter in the universal and transcendental state of consciousness. And, as Swamiji explains, because Bhairavī is Herself the way, all of these ways, these means, reside only in the field of Bhairavī (*śakti*), not in the field of Bhairava.

But what is the relationship of Bhairavī to Bhairava? Is Bhairava superior to His *śakti*, Bhairavī? To answer this, Bhairava tells us in verse eighteen that, "Just as there is no differentiation found between energy and the holder of energy, so also there is absolute unity between Bhairava and Bhairavī." And so, because of the unity of Bhairava and Bhairavī, you can experience the identity between the energy and the holder of energy by entering in the state of energy, Bhairavī. Ignorance, for Kashmir Shaivism, is not the absence of knowledge; rather it is said to be non-fullness of knowledge. The Kashmir Shaiva tells us that knowledge is always present in our life but it is limited differentiated knowledge. He argues that every limited being must have some knowledge because no one could exist without knowledge. On the other hand, real knowledge, which is unlimited, is Self-knowledge. It is undifferentiated (*nirvikalpa*) and identical with consciousness. Being identical with consciousness, it is the essence of reality.

The means (*upāyas*)

The method of traveling from limited individual consciousness to universal God consciousness depends on the ability of the aspirant, and Kashmir Shaivism has revealed three categories of means to achieve this. The first and highest means is called *śāmbhavopāya*. The second means, for aspirants with medium qualifications, is called *śāktopāya*. The third means, called *āṇavopāya*, is regarded as inferior.

Abhinavagupta tells us in his *Tantrāloka* that the aspirant should always try for the highest and best thing first. Failing that, he should try for the next best, and so on. Thus, in the *Tantrāloka*, Abhinavagupta has defined and explained the highest *upāya*, *śāmbhavopāya*, first. His descriptions of *śāktopāya* and *āṇavopāya* follow.

Drawing from the *Mālinīvijaya Tantra*, Abhinavagupta defines *śāmbhavopāya* as that *upāya* wherein the aspirant achieves entry (*samāveṣa*) into supreme consciousness just by the grace of his master, without adopting any process. Swamiji tells us that in this *upāya* you maintain awareness in thought-lessness. You do not use thought (*vikalpa*), *mantra*, or any other aid to meditation. It is also called *icchopāya*, the path of the will.

Śāktopāya is defined as that *upāya* where the aspirant achieves mystical entry (*samāveṣa*) through contemplation of that mental object which cannot be spoken or recited. Swamji says that, in this *upāya,* you maintain awareness in the "organic" world, the world of the five organs of cognition (*jñanendriyas*) and the three internal organs of mind, ego and intellect (*antaḥkāraṇas*). It is also called *jñānopāya*, the path of knowledge.

Āṇavopāya is defined as that *upāya* where mystical entry takes place through concentration on parts of the body (*sthāna prakalpanā*), contemplation (*dhyāna*), recitation (*varṇa*), taking the support of the breath (*uccāra*), and *mantras.*[7] Swamiji says that, in this *upāya,* you maintain awareness in the "elementary" world, the world of the five great elements (*mahābhūtas*). It is also called *kriyopāya*, the path of action.

In Kashmir Shaivism, though the means may be many, the goal is only one–mystical absorption (*samāveśa*) in the *śāmbhava* state, the same reality found in *śāmbhavopāya*. What is the *śāmbhava* state? The *śāmbhava* state is where the *yogi* becomes instantly established in God consciousness. For the Kashmir Shaiva, every absorption in the reality of God consciousness is, in the end, the absorption of the *śāmbhava* state, because in *śām-bhavopāya*, unlike *śāktopāya* and *āṇavopāya*, the *yogi* has nowhere to go. Instead, he only has to be in his own nature. This is real mystical absorption.

What determines which *upāya* the aspirant is qualified for? The secret is the strength of awareness. As Swamiji explains, firm strength of awareness means to possess such power of subjective consciousness that the practitioner's one-pointed subjective awareness is not overshadowed either by objective experience or by thoughts. In the

7 *Tantrāloka* 1.167-169, translation and commentary by Swami Lakshmanjoo, original audio recording, Universal Shaiva Fellowship archives.

experience of the limited subject, the act of thinking or perception typically overshadows the subject, the perceiver, so that one is aware only of the thought or the perception and not the actual perceiver.

Thus, human beings generally live their lives completely in the objective or cognitive worlds. Although we might say, "I am seeing a butterfly", in actual fact, the "I" is eclipsed by the act of seeing and what remains is "seeing a butterfly." In other words, the subject is lost in the act of perception. Because "I-consciousness" is the basis for all thought and perception, it must be present for any thought or perception to take place. Yet it is eclipsed in such a way that, in the act of thinking or perceiving, it is not a part of conscious awareness. As we saw above, in the first two verses of the *Shiva Sutras*, this is the nature of ignorance, i.e., being overshadowed by the world of diversity and not knowing one's real universal nature. Developing strength of awareness means, gaining the ability to think thoughts and experience perceptions without losing Self-awareness.

Śāmbhavopāya

In order to succeed in *śāmbhavopāya*, the *yogi* must possess firm strength of awareness so that he does not need any support to maintain his awareness of Self. Shaiva masters tell us that, in *śāmbhavopāya*, the aspirant has only to continuously maintain the thought-less (*nirvikalpa*) state. For this reason, *śāmbhavopāya* is said to be the most refined *upāya*. Here, the aspirant must reside in the subtlest state of awareness, just at the starting point of any sensation, perception, or thought.

> When you fix your awareness at the very first start, when desire is about to flow out, it has not flown out, it is about to flow out, that is *śāmbhavopāya*.[8]

---

8 *Vijñāna Bhairava*, commentary on v98.

This starting point (*prathamābhāsa*) is found just at the beginning of any sensation, perception, or thought, before it has become determinate. In this *upāya*, the aspirant, by maintaining the thought-less state, resides in this first starting point of perception or thought simply by willing it. This *yogi* has developed such strength of awareness that he has only to will this to happen and it is accomplished. The Kashmir Shaiva points out that, because in *śāmbhavopāya*, the *yogi* has only to maintain thought-lessness, he has nowhere to go and nothing to do. Residing in the thought-less state is the means (*upāya*) and the end (*upeya*), as Swamiji says, "The means exists in the state of the meant." Therefore, in *śāmbhavopāya*, there are no means separate from what is to be achieved. The *yogi* just wills to be there and he is there in his own subjective awareness, maintaining the continuity of thought-lessness.

In this state, the *yogi*, maintaining unbroken thought-lessness, is waiting at the threshold of universal consciousness. Having accomplished this much, there is nothing left for him to do. This state is significant because, up to this point, the *yogi* has depended primarily on self-effort. Swamiji tells us that, from this point onwards, the entry into universal God consciousness is automatic. Kashmir Shaivism holds that it is only by the grace of God (*śaktipāta*), in the form of the grace of the master, that Lord Śiva is revealed. When the disciple, by maintaining thought-lessness, reaches the entrance of the *śāmbhava* state, he is said to be capable of receiving the master's grace.[9] Here, Swamiji explains that it is this grace that carries the disciple to absorption in universal God

9 "*Abhiṣiktaḥ svasaṁvitti devībhirdīkṣitaśca saḥ*. How he achieves without masters and without *śāstras*? For that he [Abhinavagupta] says, his own internal energies of Lord Śiva, *śakti cakra*, have initiated him."–*Tantrāloka* 4.42, translation and commentary by Swami Lakshmanjoo, original audio recording, Universal Shaiva Fellowship archives.

consciousness.[10]

Śāktopāya

It is the nature of the world of particularity and diversity that causes our lives to be filled with a myriad of sensations, perceptions, and thoughts. Each of these *ābhāsa*s, or appearances, has a beginning and an end. Every sensation, perception, and thought that comes into being, exists for some time, and then comes to an end. This, Shaivism teaches, is the nature of existence. Every moment of our lives is filled with this flux of creation, preservation, and destruction.

For the contemplative, the most important thing to bear in mind is the momentary gap or junction between the end of one sensation, perception, or thought and the beginning of another. Within the gap itself shines the universal undifferentiated reality of God, which is the eternal substratum and life of the differentiated universe.

Unlike *śāmbhavopāya*, *śāktopāya* requires the suport of cognition and action. In *śāktopāya*, the aspirant achieves absorption in God consciousness by concentrating on the supreme Being as found in the junction between any two successive thoughts or any successive two actions. As the junction exists everywhere, any thought or action is fit for this practice, e.g., while raising your arm and putting it down, between two steps, between the waking state and the dreaming state, between the dreaming state and the state of deep sleep, between the outgoing breath and the incoming breath. Between every successive set of cognitions or actions, a gap or junction exists and is observable. In this practice, the aspirant has to maintain an uninterrupted and continuous awareness of the junction (*sandhi*). The Shaiva masters call this process "centering" (*madhyam dhyātvā*):

10 *Kashmir Shaivism, The Secret Supreme* 5.34.

> *Madhyam dhyātvā*: concentrate on that center, and while concentrating on that center, be established in that center . . . and in making yourself established in that center, the reality of God consciousness is revealed.[11]

Through developing this intensity of awareness, the *yogi* will be able to maintain unbroken awareness, for it is only by maintaining unbroken awareness in a chain-like manner that the *yogi* will be able to discover the reality of the gap. Without this intensity of awareness, the aspirant will not be able to achieve the purpose of *śāktopāya*, and would then have to resort to *āṇavopāya*. On the other hand, for the capable practitioner of *śāktopāya*, even the practices that belong in *āṇavopāya* can be utilized.

Swamiji tells us that the goal of the *śāktopāya* aspirant is to develop an ever-increasing firmness of awareness, making himself capable of receiving the *guru's* grace. When the *yogi* reaches this state, he is said to be in that state that is described as "being at the feet of the *guru*."[12] This aspirant, being established in the fullness of God consciousness, is now fit to achieve absorption in universal God consciousness. When this *yogi* receives the grace of the *guru* in *śāktopāya*, he reaches that state of mystical absorption, which is one with the supreme mystical absorption (*samāveśa*) existing in the *śāmbhava* state.

Āṇavopāya

Āṇavopāya, which is considered inferior to the other two *upāyas*, is so named because it is the means concerned with *aṇu*, the individual soul. In *āṇavopāya*, the aspirant needs support and help from all sides to focus, maintain, and strengthen his awareness. We have seen how the *śāktopāya* aspirant, who has developed more strength of awareness, needs the support of two successive cognitions or actions in

---

11 *Vijñāna Bhairava*, commentary on v61.

12 *Kashmir Shaivism, The Secret Supreme* 5.35.

order to become established in the universal center. In *śāmbhavopāya*, the aspirant has developed such strength of awareness that he needs only to will to seize the universal center of thoughtless-ness, and it takes place. So, the *āṇavopāya* aspirant needs every support, the *śāktopāya* aspirant needs some support, and the *śāmbhavopāya* aspirant needs no support.

In *āṇavopāya*, the aspirant needs the help of many different processes to aid him in maintaining and strengthening his awareness. He may employ concentration on breathing (*uccāra*), concentration on experience through a particular sense organ (*karaṇa*), meditative contemplation (*dhyāna*), or concentration on some particular place (*sthāna prakalpanā*). All of these various practices may be undertaken together or separately as an aid to developing awareness.

Uccāra, concentration on the breath, is a fundamental practice in *āṇavopāya*. In *uccāra*, the aspirant concentrates on the flow of the breath and, in particular, on the point between the outgoing and incoming breath and the point between the incoming and outgoing breath.

In *karaṇa*, the aspirant maintains one-pointedness through his senses. The sense of sight, however, is the most important. For example, the aspirant may go on gazing at a particular object without blinking his eyes. In this process, he should try to maintain an unbroken chain of awareness. When that perception vanishes, as it will when he enters into the vastness of the center, this practice is complete.

Meditative contemplation (*dhyāna*) is another practice in *āṇavopāya*. There are many different forms of *dhyāna*. To meditate on the lotus in your heart, or on the meaning of a *mantra* such as "*so'ham*" or "*Śiva*" are forms of *dhyāna*. In this practice, the aspirant concentrates on these sounds, locations, or forms, while thinking and reflecting upon their meaning. It is said that contemplation on the meaning of spiritual words is a higher form of contemplation than the contemplation of an object with form. Anytime an aspirant uses *mantras* in his practice, it is considered *dhyāna*, and it is not uncommon to find *dhyāna* combined with *uccāra* and *karaṇa*, as in the practices of *cakrodaya* and *ajapā gāyatrī*, which are described below.

Sthāna prakalpanā means, concentration on some particular place. In the lower, ordinary form of *sthāna prakalpanā*, the aspirant must concentrate on different points in the body. In Kashmir Shaivism, there are three main places for concentration: between the eyebrows, the pit of the throat, and the heart. In the higher, more refined practice of *sthāna prakalpanā*, the aspirant must see the vastness of this universe represented in the span of a single breath. Swamiji explains that, in this higher form of *āṇavopāya*, the aspirant must discover where each aspect of reality is found in the span of one breath. The "reality" that Swamiji is describing here is said to encompass the realm of the gods (*devās*), the locations of the protectors of the world (*lokapālās*), the astronomical locations, and including but not confined to the location of the dawn, sunset, midnight, and so on. All of these points and positions are to be located and concentrated on in the span of one single breath.[13]

Of the countless practices that are found in *āṇavopāya*, there are two practices that stand out as most typical: *cakrodaya* and *ajapā gāyatrī*. Both of these practices incorporate *uccāra*, concentration on breath, *dhyāna*, contemplation with *mantra*, and *karaṇa*, which here refers to one-pointedness through the sense of sight. Furthermore, depending on the advice of the aspirant's master, *sthāna prakalpanā* may also be included.

In the practices of *cakrodaya* and *ajapā gāyatrī*, *uccāra* (concentration on the breath) functions as the central element. In both of these practices, the *yogi* follows the movement of the breath, seeking to become aware of the center between the outgoing and incoming breath, and the center between the incoming and outgoing breath, while

13 *Kashmir Shaivism, The Secret Supreme* 5.38.

also maintaining awareness of the flow of the breath in the total breathing cycle. However, here, predominance is given to the beginning point and the ending point of the breathing cycle.

These two practices, however, differ in one important respect. In *ajapā gāyatrī*, the *yogi* maintains a slow and silent movement of the breath, while, in *cakrodaya*, he maintains a slow movement of the breath along with the sound of breathing. In both of these practices, along with breathing, the aspirant mentally repeats the *mantra* given to him by his master.

The aspirant in these practices must endeavor to maintain full awareness in the center between the two breaths. Swamiji specifies that this awareness must be lively and enthusiastic–indeed, it should be "continually fresh, new, and filled with excitement." Certainly, the practice should not become routine-like. The *yogi* should be excited by his practice.[14]

Through the strengthening of awareness in *āṇavopāya*, the aspirant will enter into this center between the two breaths. At this point, his practice will become *śāktopāya*, and eventually he will enter into the mystical absorption (*samāveśa*) of *śāktopāya*. Finally, the *yogi* will attain the mystical realization of *śāmbhavopāya*.

It is important to realize that, although there are different *upāyas*, all of these *upāyas* lead the *yogi* to the same state of transcendental consciousness. The difference in the *upāyas* is that *āṇavopāya* takes longer, *śāktopāya* is a shorter way, while *śāmbhāvopāya* is the quickest. Although the means are different, the end to be achieved is one.[15]

In his revelation of this *Vijñāna Bhairava*, Swamiji identifies and explains the means (*upāya*) associated with each of the one hundred and twelve practices that are taught to the Goddess, Bhairavī.

---

14 *Self Realization in Kashmir Shaivism* 2.42.

15 *Self Realization in Kashmir Shaivism* 2.40.

Mokṣa

One might ask whether *śāmbhava samāveśa*, the mystical absorption in the state of Śiva, is equivalent to *mokṣa*, liberation. In fact, it is not. It certainly must exist if *mokṣa* is to occur, but it is not its defining characteristic. Abhinavagupta tells us in his *Tantrāloka* that "*Mokṣa* only exists when your being becomes absolutely independent (*svatantrātmaka*)."[16] What is this "independence" that Abhinavagupta specifies as the neceśary condition of *mokṣa*? We have seen above that it is repeatedly declared that the essential characteristic of Lord Śiva is his independence. It is explained that Lord Śiva created this universe by means of his independence. Śiva's independence means complete unbridled freedom–freedom to will, freedom to know, freedom to do.

According to Abhinavagupta, a *yogi* can only be said to be liberated when he possesses this absolute independence (*svātantrya*). For a *yogi* to be independent, nothing must be able to limit him or overshadow his Universal consciousneś. This means that this *yogi* must experience the same state of Universal consciousness, the same absolute independence, in the external world as he does in the mystical absorption of the *śāmbhava* state. From the Trika Shaiva point of view, until he attains this state, he cannot be said to be absolutely independent or to have attained complete *mokṣa* (liberation).

Swamiji, in discussing the supreme mystical absorption of *śāmbhava*, explains how the *yogi's* internal mystical trance becomes fused with and transforms his external experience (*vyutthāna*). He tells us that this proceś begins when the *yogi* is experiencing the state of internal mystical awareneś, when he is relishing the fullness of his internal God consciousneś (*nimīlanā samādhi*). At that moment he

16 *Tantrāloka* 1.31, translation and commentary by Swami Lakshmanjoo, original audio recording, Universal Shaiva Fellowship archives.

is pulled out of the internal world into the world of external experience (*unmīlanā samādhi*). His eyes open and he experiences the world. But this external experience is different; it is now filled with the oneness of universal God consciousness. He may experience a chair, but the experience of this chair is filled with universal God consciousneś. He may see a tree, and the experience of the tree is filled with universal God consciousness. Everywhere he looks, whatever he sees is filled with universal God consciousness. Then again, his eyes close and he is drawn inside. And again, after a few moments, his eyes open and he is drawn outside experiencing the world filled with the oneness of God. He cannot stop this process. Even though the *yogi* may try to stop this process, he cannot. This proceś of going from inside to outside, back inside, and again outside is automatic and continues for some time. This is the proceś known as *krama mudrā*.

> *"One moment you are inside experiencing the bliss of the rise of* cit kuṇḍalinī *and then the next moment you breathe out and your eyes are open and you are experiencing the world filled with ecstasy. This process of coming out and remaining in continues and, each time it occurs, it is filled with more and more ecstasy. This proceś is called* krama mudrā." [17]

In clarifying this process, Swamiji tells us that this *yogi* experiences the fusing of his inner and outer worlds in the oneneś of God consciousneś. He says that the *yogi's* I-consciousneś, his universal I-consciousneś, is diluted in consciousness-of-this, consciousneś of the external world, and consciousness-of-this is diluted in I-consciousneś. Here, the fullneś of I-consciousneś absorbs "this-ness," external objectivity, and produces the oneness of internal mystical trance (*samādhi*) and external experience (*vyutthāna*). The nature of this *yogi* and the external world become one, and

17 *Vijñāna Bhairava,* commentary on v28, footnote 57 (see also *Kashmir Shaivism, The Secret Supreme* 17.120).

the *yogi* experiences them as being completely united, one with the other. There is absolutely no difference between them.

The process of *krama mudrā* results in the absolute oneness of universal Consciousness and the outer world, and this absolute oneness is the state of absolute independence. The *yogi*, in this state, experiences that the internal world of mystical trance and the external world are absolutely the same. This independence and absolute oneness gives rise to the state of *jagadānanda* (universal bliss).[18]

To explain the state of *jagadānanda*, Abhinavagupta says, "My master Śambhunātha described *jagadānanda* as the state that is completely unencumbered, where bliss (*ānanda*) is found shining, where it is universally strengthened by the supreme I-consciousness of God, and where the six limbs of yoga–*bhāvanā, dhāraṇā, dhyāna, pratyāhāra, yoga,* and *samādhi*–are no longer used or required."[19]

This aspirant, whose being has become absolutely independent (*svatantrātmaka*) and who possesses the state of *jagadānanda*, is said to be a *jīvan mukta*, a being who is liberated while living. In his *Bodhapañcadaśikā*, Abhinavagupta tells us that when the aspirant attains real knowledge of reality, which is the existent state of Lord Śiva, that is final liberation.[20] What is this real knowledge? Real knowledge exists when the aspirant comes to understand that this whole objective universe of diversity and duality is just a magic trick, the play of Lord Śiva.

> *"The Lord himself is the great magician. He has placed this trick before us . . and, although we are undifferentiated, it seems that we are differentiated from each other."* [21]

18 *Self Realization in Kashmir Shaivism*, 5.112-113.

19 *Self Realization in Kashmir Shaivism*, 5.113.

20 *Self Realization in Kashmir Shaivism* 1.31.

21 *Vijñāna Bhairava*, commentary on v102.

That does not mean, however, that it is a trick that creates an unreal world. For the liberated Trika Shaiva *yogi*, the world does not disappear, as the teachers of *Advaita Vedānta* proclaim. Nor is the goal of the Shaiva the *Sāṁkhyā* world-oblivion of *kaivalya* (isolation). For the Shaiva, this objective world, being Lord Śiva's creation, is just as real as Lord Śiva. The trick lies in the fact that, by Śiva's play, he causes the limited individual to experience this world of diversity as the only reality. Real knowledge exists when the aspirant becomes one with universal God consciousness, which is the same as attaining perfect Self-knowledge. In possessing real knowledge, he knows that the world of differentiation is not actually different from Śiva, the supreme reality.

The cycles of bondage and liberation are both one with Lord Śiva. It is only his trick that we think that some souls are bound in ignorance while others are elevated. As only Lord Śiva exists, there is not any second thing that could cover or bind him. It is only his play that we think that this covering of diversity actually exists as a separate reality. There is not a second being or reality. His trick, therefore, is our trick. Why? Because we are Lord Śiva. We have concealed ourselves in order to find ourselves. This is his play, and therefore it is our play.

Anupāya

The ultimate reality is clearly illuminated by the concept of *anupāya*. The Sanskrit word *an-upāya* literally means "no-*upāya*." We have already seen that, in Kashmir Shaivism, there are three *upāyas*: *śāmbhava*, *śākta*, and *āṇava*. In addition to these three *upāyas*, another called *anupāya* is also mentioned. As the name implies, *anupāya* is not actually an *upāya*, for in *anupāya* there are no means. The one who resides in *anupāya* has only to observe that nothing is to be done. Just to "be" is enough. In *anupāya*, the aspirant experiences that everything is filled with his own God consciousness. In fact, *anupāya* is the unexplainable reality of the liberated aspirant. In *anupāya*, the *yogi* is filled with the realization that they were never ignorant, and are therefore not now liberated. They know that nothing was lost and nothing is gained. What could they have been ignorant of and what are they liberated from? They experience that it was their own play, their own trick, that they appeared ignorant before and appear liberated now. They truly know that they are Śiva and that this world is their own divine playground.

Verse	Dhāraṇā	Upāya	Page
24	1	*āṇavopāya*	32
25	2	*śāktopāya*	34
26	3	*śāmbhavopāya*	36
27	4	*āṇava – śākta*	37
28	5	*āṇava – śākta*	41
29	6	*āṇava – śāmbhava*	44
30	7	*āṇavopāya*	49
31	8	*āṇavopāya*	53
32	9	*śāktopāya*	55
33	10	*śāktopāya*	58
34	11	*śāktopāya*	60
35	12	*śāmbhavopāya*	62
36	13	*āṇavopāya*	64
37	14	*āṇavopāya*	66
38	15	*śāktopāya*	68
39	16	*āṇava – śāmbhava*	70
40	17	*śāmbhavopāya*	72
41	18	*śāmbhavopāya*	74
42	19	*āṇava – śāmbhava*	76
43	20	*āṇava – śāmbhava*	80
44	21	*āṇava – śāmbhava*	82
45	22	*śāktopāya*	84
46	23	*śākta – śāmbhava*	85
47	24	*śāktopāya*	87
48	25	*śākta – śāmbhava*	88
49	26	*śāktopāya*	89
50	27	*śāktopāya*	90
51	28	*āṇava – śāmbhava*	92
52	29	*śākta – śāmbhava*	95
53	30	*śāktopāya*	96
54	31	*āṇava – śākta*	98
55	32	*āṇava – śāmbhava*	101
56	33	*śākta – śāmbhava*	107
57	34	*śāktopāya*	108
58	35	*śākta – śāmbhava*	110
59	36	*śāmbhavopāya*	111
60	37	*śāmbhavopāya*	113
61	38	*śāktopāya*	114
62	39	*śāktopāya*	116

Verse	Dhāraṇā	Upāya	Page
63	40	*śāktopāya*	119
64	41	*āṇavopāya*	121
65	42	*śāktopāya*	122
66	43	*śāktopāya*	123
67	44	*āṇava – śāmbhava*	125
68	45	*śāktopāya*	131
69 & 70	not dhāraṇās		136
71	46	*śākta – śāmbhava*	138
72	47	*śāktopāya*	140
73	48	*śāktopāya*	141
74	49	(not listed)	144
75	50	*śāmbhavopāya*	145
76	51	*śāktopāya*	148
77	52	*śāmbhavopāya*	150
78	53	*āṇava – śākta – śāmbhava*	157
79	54	*āṇava – śākta*	158
80	55	*śāmbhavopāya*	160
81	56	*āṇavopāya*	163
82	57	*śākta – śāmbhava*	165
83	58	*śāktopāya*	166
84	59	*śāmbhavopāya*	168
85	60	*śāktopāya*	169
86	61	*āṇava – śāmbhava*	170
87	62	*śāktopāya*	175
88	63	*śāktopāya*	177
89	64	*śāktopāya*	179
90	65	*āṇava – śākta*	180
91	66	*śāmbhavopāya*	183
92	67	*śāktopāya*	186
93	68	*āṇava – śāmbhava*	187
94	69	*śāktopāya*	188
95	70	*śāktopāya*	189
96	71	*śāmbhavopāya*	190
97	72	*śāktopāya*	191
98	73	*śākta – śāmbhava*	193
99	74	*śāktopāya*	195
100	75	*śāktopāya*	197
101	76	*śāmbhavopāya*	198
102	77	*śāktopāya*	200

Verse	Dhāraṇā	Upāya	Page
103	78	*śāktopāya*	203
104	79	*śāktopāya*	204
105	80	*śāktopāya*	205
106	not dhāraṇā		207
107	81	*śāktopāya*	208
108	82	*śāmbhavopāya*	209
109	83	*śākta – śāmbhava*	210
110	84	*śākta – śāmbhava*	211
111	85	*śāmbhavopāya*	212
112	86	*śāktopāya*	213
113 & 114	87 & 88	*śāmbhavopāya*	214
115	89	*śāktopāya*	216
116	90	*śāmbhavopāya*	217
117	91	*śāktopāya*	218
118	92	*śāmbhavopāya*	220
119	93	*śāktopāya*	222
120	94	*śāktopāya*	224
121	95	*śāmbhavopāya*	225
122	96	*śāktopāya*	226
123	97	*śāktopāya*	228
124	98	*śāktopāya*	229
125	99	*śāktopāya*	231
126	100	*śāktopāya*	232
127	101	*śāmbhavopāya*	233
128	102	*śākta – śāmbhava*	234
129	103	*śākta – śāmbhava*	236
130	104	*śāktopāya*	238
131	105	*śāmbhavopāya*	240
132	106	*śāktopāya*	242
133	107	*śāmbhavopāya*	243
134	108	*śāmbhavopāya*	245
135	109	*śāktopāya*	247
136	110	*śākta – śāmbhava*	249
137	111	*śāktopāya*	250
138	112	*śāmbhavopāya*	252

Vijñāna Bhairava

The *Vijñāna Bhairava* is one chapter in the *Rudrayāmala Tantra*. And another chapter in the *Rudrayāmala Tantra* is the *Parātriṁśikā*.[1] This chapter[2] is from the Bhairava point of view. These are not Rūdra *śāstras* nor Śiva *śāstras*.[3] These are Bhairava *śāstras*–monistic, pure monistic.

You already know there are three *upāyas*, three means. One is superior, the other is medium, and the third one is inferior. The inferior one is called "*āṇavopāya*", the medium is called "*śāktopāya*", and the superior is called "*śāmbhav-opāya*".[4]

---

1 Commonly translated as "The Thirty Verses on the Supreme", "Abhinavagupta has changed this name to *Parātrīśikā*. *Parātrīśikā* is the supreme energy which is the kingdom of three energies, the explanation of three energies (*parā*, *parāparā*, and *aparā*). This is the kingdom of three energies here." *Parātriśikā Vivaraṇa,* with the commentary of Abhinavagupta, translation and commentary by Swami Lakshmanjoo (original audio recording, USF archives, Los Angeles, 1982-85).

2 The *Vijñāna Bhairava*.

3 Rūdra *śāstras* are mono-*cum*-dualistic, the Śiva *śāstras* are dualistic, and the Bhairava *śāstras* are purely monistic.

4 "The word "*upāya*" in Kashmir Shaivism is used to indicate the means to enter into Universal God Consciousness from individual consciousness. . . . It is important to realize that though there are different *upāyas*, all lead you to the state of one transcendental consciousness. The difference in these *upāyas* is that *āṇavopāya* will carry you in a long way, *śāktopāya* in a shorter way, and *śāmbhavopāya* in the shortest way. Although the ways are different, the point to be achieved is one." *Kashmir Shaivism–The Secret Supreme*, Swami Lakshmanjoo, ed. John Hughes, (Universal Shaiva

Śāmbhavopāya is just to maintain awareness in thought-lessness. When you maintain awareness in the organic world[5], that is *śāktopāya*. When you maintain awareness in the elementary world[6], that is *āṇavopāya* (that is breath, breathing, *mantra*, recitation of *mantra*, and all these–these are called *āṇavopāya*).

When you are just in a concentrative mood–that is being in the organic world, without the recitation of *mantra*, without breathing exercises–that is *śāktopāya*. When you are maintaining awareness in thought-lessness, that is *śāmbhavopāya* (superior, supreme). [In *āṇavopāya*], you have to put the adjustment of other sources also: sources of breath, sources of mind–everything is there. This is *āṇavopāya*. In *śāktopāya*, there is only mind, the functioning of the mind. In *śāmbhavopāya,* there is not mind also. In *śāmbhava*, you have to discard the functioning of the mind. It is not mind, it is just to dive in the un-minded state. That is *śāmbhavopāya*. If you put only the mind, not other sources, that will be *śāktopāya*. If you put adjustment of the breath, adjustment of a *mantra,* adjustment of all those things (worship, *pūjā*), that is *āṇavopāya.*[7]

Fellowship, Los Angeles, 1985-2003), 5.33-40. For a detailed explanation of the *upāyas*, see Introduction (pp.xxix-xli).

5 Swamiji uses the word "organic" to refer to the five organs of cognition (*jñānendriyas*: smell, taste, sight, touch, and hearing), in the sense of the energy of seeing and the energy of hearing, etc., along with the three internal organs (*antaḥkaraṇas*: mind, ego, and intellect).

6 Swamiji uses the word "elementary" to refer to the five great elements (*pañca mahābhūtas*–earth, water, fire, air, and ether).

7 "*Śāmbhavopāya* is also called *icchopāya*, as it is the means which exists in *icchā śakti*. The means which exists in *jñāna śakti* is *śāktopāya* and is called *jñānopāya. Āṇavopāya* is called *kriyopāya* because it is the means which is found in *kriyā śakti*." *Kashmir Shaivism–The Secret Supreme*, 5.33-40.

"[Lord Śiva's] energies are the means; [His] energies have become the *upāyas*. The energy of His will is explained as *śāmbhavopāya*, the energy of knowledge is *śāktopāya*, and the energy of action is *āṇavopāya*. The energy of action is breathing exercises, reciting *mantras*, reciting *ślokas* (hymns), and *pūjā* (worship). All

And you have to see [for] yourself which way is *śāmbhavopāya*, which way would be *āṇavopāya*, and which would be *śāktopāya*. That you have to see [for] yourself in this book.[8]

Actually these processes are meant for masters. These are not meant for students. This is a book for masters.

JOHN: Training guide.

SWAMIJI: Training guide, yes. How to teach people, in which way.[9]

---

these are in action, in the world of action. So, all these things are included in *āṇavopāya* and they will carry you to the state of Lord Śiva. And [the energy of] knowledge, this is *śāktopāya*. Perceiving, middle-ing, centering, all these are in the world of *śāktopāya*. They will also carry you to the state of Lord Śiva. And [the energy of] will is the first start of each and every action. That is *śāmbhavopāya*. That will carry you to Śiva's state." *Tantrāloka* of Abhinavagupta, translation and commentary by Swami Lakshmanjoo (original audio recording, USF archives, Los Angeles, 1972-1981), 1.70.

8 "As long as there is the question of speaking something, we have to speak of one hundred and twelve ways; but, at the same time, we have to know that we have to cross the cycle of one hundred and twelve ways in the end." *Vijñāna Bhairava*, Swami Lakshmanjoo, (additional audio recordings, USF archives, Los Angeles 1980).

9 "Be attached to your own practice. It will carry you to *śāktopāya* and *śāmbhavopāya* by its own way. There are a thousand ways, and the way that has been selected by your master is the best, is the divine way, for you." Ibid. See Introduction for a detailed explanation of the *upāyas* (means).

श्रीदेव्युवाच
श्रुतं देव मया सर्वं
  रुद्रयामलसंभवम् ।
त्रिकभेदमशेषेण
  सारात्सारविभागशः ॥ १ ॥
अद्यापि न निवृत्तो मे
  संशयः परमेश्वर ।

śrīdevyuvāca

śrutaṁ deva mayā sarvaṁ
  rudrayāmalasaṁbhavam /
trikabhedamaśeṣeṇa
  sārātsāravibhāgaśaḥ // 1 //
adyāpi na nivṛtto me
  saṁśayaḥ parameśvara / 2a

[Devī[10] speaks]: O Lord, I have already heard the essence of the three-fold school of thought *aśeṣena*, entirely, that has come out from the *Rudrayāmala Tantra*, or has come out with the union of Bhairavī and Bhairava (that is *rudrayāmala saṁbhavam*).

You can translate it in both ways: the outcome from the union of two energies (the Lord and Pārvatī) or [from the] *Rudrayāmala Tantra*.

By finding out the reality of thought as Trika[11] (that is

---

10 The Goddess, Bhairavī.

11 Kashmir Śaivism is known as the pure Trika system. The word "Trika" means "the threefold science of man and his world." In the idea of Trika, there are three energies: *parā* (supreme), *aparā* (lowest), and *parāparā* (combination of the lowest and the highest). These three primary energies represent the threefold activities of the world. In the thought of Trika, therefore, it is admitted that this whole universe and every action in it, whether spiritual, physical,

sārāt sāra vibhāgaśa; *vibhāgaśaḥ*, by finding out the reality of thought as Trika), [although] I have already heard it from Your lips, still My doubts are not cleared. *Adyāpi na nivṛtto me saṁśayaḥ*, O Lord, My doubts are not entirely removed. What is the reality of thought in all the schools of Trika, that also I have heard from You, but still My doubts are not entirely removed.

किं रूपं तत्त्वतो देव
शब्दराशिकलामयम् ॥ २ ॥
किं वा नवात्मभेवेन
भैरवे भैरवाकृतौ ।
त्रिशिरोभेदभिन्नं वा
किं वा शक्तित्रयात्मकम् ॥ ३ ॥
नादबिन्दुमयं वापि
किं चन्द्रार्धनिरोधिकाः ।

---

or worldly, is existing in these three energies. The Trika philosophy is meant for any human being without restriction of caste, creed, or color. Its purpose is to enable you to rise from individuality to universality. The Trika system is comprised of four sub-systems: the Pratyabhijñā system, the Kula system, the Krama system, and the Spanda system. These four systems, which form the one thought of the Trika system, all accept, and are based on, the same scriptures.
These scriptures, which in Śaivism are called *āgamas*, are the ninety-two *āgamas* of Śaivism, the monistic Bhairava *śāstras* which are supreme (*parā*) and which are sixty-four in number; the mono-dualistic Rūdra *śāstras* which are medium (*parāparā*) and which are eighteen in number; and the dualistic Śiva *śāstras* which are inferior (*aparā*) and which are ten in number." *Kashmir Shaivism–The Secret Supreme*, 19.129.

चक्रारूढमनच्कं वा
किं वा शक्तिस्वरूपकम् ॥४॥

kiṁ rūpaṁ tattvato deva
śabdarāśikalāmayam / / 2b / /

kiṁ vā navātmabhedena
bhairave bhairavākṛitau /
triśirobhedabhinnaṁ vā
kiṁ vā śaktitrayātmakam / / 3 / /

nādabindumayaṁ vāpi
kiṁ candrārdhanirodhikāḥ
cakrārūḍhamanackaṁ vā
kiṁ vā śaktisvarūpakam / / 4 / /

O Lord (*deva*), what is the real essence of the way we have to tread (*kiṁ rūpaṁ tattvato deva*)?

This is one sentence, an exclusive sentence.

O Lord, what is the real essence of the way we have to march, we have to tread?

Tattvato means "in reality, the real essence."

Is the way of that to tread on the fifty letters[12] and return? Is this the way of *śabda rāśi kalā*, the way we have to make the journey from '*a*' to '*kṣa*' and return from '*kṣa*' to '*a*' again? Is this the way? [Pārvatī] puts this question: *Kiṁ śabda rāśi kalāmayam tattvam*? Or, *kiṁ vā navātma bhedena*, or is it *navātma bheda*, is it the journey of the nine states? The journey from one state to the second, from the second to the third, from the third to the fourth, from the fourth to the fifth, to the sixth, to the seventh, to the eighth, to the ninth, and then back again to the first, is this the way?

The nine states are [to be explained now]. The first state is *prakṛti*. The original source of the material world is *prakṛti*. *Puruṣa* is the individual soul who treads on that material world (this is the second). The third is the

12 *Śabda rāśi*.

kañcukas, the five *kañcukas*, the five coverings of *puruṣa*–the five *kañcukas*.[13] You have not to go in the depth of the letters here. [These are the] *kañcukas*: *kalā, vidyā, rāga, kāla,* and *niyati*. Then the fourth point is *māyā*. *Māyā* is the personified will of the supreme will.

There is a difference between *prakṛti* and *māyā*. *Prakṛti* is the original source of the material world, māyā is the personified will of the supreme Lord, the supreme Self. This is the difference between *māyā* and *prakṛti*. Otherwise, the function of *prakṛti* is just like the function of māyā. Only, the personified will of the supreme Self is *māyā* where[as] the original source of the material world is *prakṛti*. *Prakṛti, puruṣa*, the *kañcukas*, and *māyā*–these are four.

Then you have to tread again in the pure state of knowledge, that is *śuddhavidyā*. The pure state of knowledge and action, that is *īśvara*. Establishment in knowledge and action, that is *sadāśiva*. And the universal energy is Śakti and its holder is Śiva.

These are the nine states. This is *navātma bheda*. This is *navātma bheda* when you keep before you the theory of states.

When you keep before you the theory of [letters], then those [letters] are respectively: *'h', 'r', 'kṣ', 'm', 'l', 'v', 'y', 'ṇūṁ*[14]'. These are *navātma bheda* from the mantric point of view. You have to tread on this field of mantra, the mantra field.

And [with regard to] states, [you must tread] the field of states from *prakṛti* to Śiva and back to *prakṛti* with His glory. When you tread from *prakṛti*, you are not glorified. When you return from Śiva, you are glorified with garlands and with Śaivism and with Śiva-thought and everything–everything comes with you.

---

13 *Kalā* (limited action), *vidyā* (limited knowledge), *rāga* (limited desire), *kāla* (limited time), and *niyati* (limited place). See also *Kashmir Shaivism–The Secret Supreme*, 1.7-8.

14 Or *ṇa* plus '*ūṁ*'. The *ṇūṁ* of the *Navātma mantra* consists of "*ṇa*" plus "*ūṁ*", i.e., two syllables, which when separated make up the total of nine (*nava*) syllables of the *mantra*. [*Editor's note*]

Is this the way of *navātma*, . . .

Bhairave means "in the Bhairava *āgama*[15]". *Bhairavā kṛtau* [means] "for entering in the state of Bhairava". "*Bhairavā kṛtau*" is *naimittikī saptamī*[16].

. . . *bhairavā kṛtau*, for entering in the formation of Bhairava? Or, *triśiro bheda bhinnam vā kiṁ vā śakti trayātmakam*, or just as in the *Triśirobhairava* [*Tantra*][17] it is said, "You must tread on the three energies from *parā*, *parāparā*, and *aparā*, and then return again"?

From *aparā* to *parāparā*, from *parāparā* to *parā*, from *parā* to *parāparā*, and then from *parāparā* to *aparā* again, this is the reality of the journey in Shaivism.

Is that the way (this is the asking of Devī[18]), or *nāda bindumayaṁ vāpi kiṁ candrārdha nirodhikāḥ*, is this the way to travel: from *nāda* to *bindu*, from *bindu* to *ardhacandra*, from *ardhacandra* to *nirodhikāḥ*, from *nirodhikāḥ* to *nādānta*, then *śakti*, then *vyāpinī*, and then *samanā*? Is this the way? Or, if this is [not] the way, then You tell Me clearly what is the real way I have to travel.

> *Nāda* means–first you have to begin traveling, begin the journey, from *nāda*–*nāda* means '*a*', '*u*', and '*ma*' (*a-kāraśca, u-kāraśca, ma-kāraḥ*). This is *nāda*.[19]
>
> Then *bindu*. One-pointed perception in the movement of breath while reciting this mantra, '*auṁ*', that is *bindu*.
>
> Then *ardhacandra*. *Ardhacandra* is that state of movement of *auṁ-kāra* where there is no breath, without breath. *Ardhacandra* is without breath. Breath stops

15 "*Āgama* means that which has come out from above, from the original source that is Śiva." *Spanda Saṁdoha* of Kṣemarāja, translation and commentary by Swami Lakshmanjoo (original audio recording, USF archives, Los Angeles, 1981),

16 The seventh or locative case.

17 "The *Triśirobhairava* [*Tantra*] is [also] a Bhairava *āgama*, so this will teach you the same course of the journey." *Vijñāna Bhairava*, additional audio (USF archives).

18 The Goddess Bhairavī.

19 "This [process] applies to every *mantra*; ['*auṁ*'] is just an example." *Vijñāna Bhairava*, additional audio (USF archives).

there.

Then *nirodhikā*, the establishment of the stoppage of breath. In *ardhacandra*, there is an apprehension of breathing again, but in the *nirodhikā* state, there is no question of the breathing way. *Nirodhikā* is the complete establishment of breathless-ness.

Then comes the state of *nādānta*, entrance in the soundless state of sound. This is the soundless state of sound. *Nādānta* means, when you enter in that sound which is soundless, soundless sound.

Then the establishment of '*ahaṁ*' is Śakti in the state of supreme oneness–*vyāpinī* and *samanā*.

Is this the way?

Vā (or) *cakrārūḍham anackaṁ vā kiṁ vā śakti svarūpakam*, or you have to travel on that universal energy which is moving in such a velocity that moveless-ness takes place (that is *anackam*).

Anackam means "without movement". *Cakrā rūḍham* means "in the wheel of movement", *anackam*, without movement.

That energy, that *svarūpa*[20] of energy, is that the way to make yourself established in that state?[21]

---

20 Lit., self (*sva*) form (*rūpa*), Swamiji often uses the word "*svarūpa*" in the sense of "nature".

21 Additionally, Swamiji notes that, "[*Cakrā rūḍham anackaṁ vā*] is not a separate question. This is regarding the same course; this is one course of *mantra*, recitation of *mantra*, starting with gross and ending with nothing, ending with 'automatic'. [After *nirodhikā*], then it will be *anackaṁ*, *cakrā rūḍham anackaṁ*: *cakrā rūḍham śakti svarūpakam* and *anackaṁ śakti svarūpakam*. *Cakrā rūḍham* is the first state of that, the first subtlest state, after *nirodhikā*, and the last one is *anackaṁ*, which cannot be [recited]. There is no recitation. It goes on within one's own nature. It is the intensity of movement in such velocity that it appears without movement. [Then] it will go to *nādānta*, *cakra rūḍham*; *anackaṁ* will go in the cycle of *śakti*. *Śakti* is that *kiṁ vā śakti svarūpakam*, energy, it is just energy. [This *mantra*] takes the formation of energy afterwards (*śakti svarūpakam*). And onwards also [to] *vyāpinī*, *samanā*, and

She puts these questions before Lord Śiva.

JOHN: There are so many words in Shaivism that have a different meaning than their ordinary meaning. *Anacka* means "without vowels" literally, isn't it?

SWAMIJI: Yes.

JOHN: And you have translated this as "movement-less movement".

SWAMIJI: Yes.

JOHN: Can you say to us why this word means "movement-less"?

SWAMIJI: Movement, because it is *spanda*[22]; "movement-less" because there is no *vikalpa*, there is no thought.

JOHN: Yes, but why does the word "*anackam*", which usually means "no vowels", why is it in our Shaivism it means "movement-less-ness"?

SWAMIJI: For instance, you have to utter '*ka*'. For instance, for some time, just say '*ka*'. You cannot utter '*ka*' if there is not an '*a*' in the end. '*A*' is found in the class of '*ac*'[23]. "*Aiuṇ ṛlik eoñ aiauc*"[24]–that is "*ac*" ("*ac*" is vowels). So when there are no vowels, you can't utter it. So it is why he says, "*anackam*".[25]

JOHN: But you have translated this as "movement-less wheel of movement".

SWAMIJI: Because there is no movement, you can't utter it.

When you recite '*ka*' without '*a*', it is just practice, it is just one-pointedness. It does not move in the outside circle of the uttered letters.

She has risen in the wheel, She is moving in the wheel–the *śakti*–but in the movement also, She is not moving at

---

unmanā." *Vijñāna Bhairava*, additional audio (USF archives).

22 Lit., vibration. In Kashmir Shaivism, *spanda* is synonymous with *svātantrya śakti* (the energy of absolute freedom) and *vimarśa śakti* (the energy of Self-awareness).

23 The set of vowels.

24 The first four *sūtras* of the *Aṣṭādhyāyī*, Pāṇini's classical text on Sanskrit grammar, which denote the vowels from '*a*' to '*au*'.

25 That is, without (*an*) vowels (*ac*).

all. That is *anacka*.

But it cannot be without movement because then it will be *jaḍa*[26], you will have to nominate it as *jaḍa*, just like a rock. It is not a rock. It is all-consciousness.

So, there is some movement, and you cannot observe that it is moving. In movement, it is not [moving]; in the movable, it is not moving. *Spanda* and *aspanda*–in *spanda*, it is *aspanda*; in *aspanda*, it is *spanda*–both.[27]

JOHN: And that's what this is? This *cakrā rūḍham* is to enter into the movement-less quality of letters?

SWAMIJI: Yes, *cakrā rūḍham* means, in other words, [that] in all the *mātṛkā cakra*[28], you'll find in each and every letter the same state–in the cycle of *mātṛkā cakra*.

JOHN: So, in the movement of these letters, the movement is what?

SWAMIJI: It is immovable-movement.

JOHN: Immovable-movement.

JAGDISH: So these *cakras* are *mantras* or other states?

SWAMIJI: *Cakra* is *mātṛkā cakra*. *Mātṛkā cakra* is the collection of all letters from '*a*' to '*kṣa*'. It is not *ṣaṭ cakra* here.[29]

[Devī's question continued]: *Cakrārūḍham* . . .

JAGDISH:. . . *anackaṁ vā*.

SWAMIJI: . . . *kiṁ vā śakti svarūpakam*, what is the *svarūpa* of *śakti* in that *cakra*–*cakrārūḍham anackaṁ*.

JOHN: So, She is saying, "Is the nature of *śakti* to be found in this . . . ?"

SWAMIJI: No. *Śakti* is *bas*[30], the means. *Śakti* is the pathway on which you have to tread. Because later on He will

---

26 Inert, insentient.

27 "It is the intensity of movement in such velocity that it appears without movement." *Vijñāna Bhairava*, additional audio (USF archives).

28 The collection of all letters.

29 *Ṣaṭ cakra* refers to the six (*ṣaṭ*) *cakras* in the body.

30 Swamiji often uses this Hindi word, which means "that is all" or "enough".

say, "*śaivī mukham ihocyate*".[31] *Śaivī* means *śakti*; *mukham* is the pathway. It is said that the pathway is *śakti*. You have to sentence your mind to Lord Śiva through that pathway (Pārvatī *śakti*[32]). Not Pārvatī who is residing in Kailash.[33]

JOHN: Oh, She wants to know what is the pathway in this *cakrārūḍham*, in this movement-less wheel of movement.

SWAMIJI: Yes, yes.

JAGDISH: And *śakti svarūpam* . . .

SWAMIJI: *Kiṁ vā śaktisvarūpaka.*

JAGDISH: . . . means?

SWAMIJI: The *svarūpa* of *śakti*. Is this the *śakti*, that *anacka*? Is this the formation of *śakti*?

JAGDISH: Or . . . ?

SWAMIJI: If She is *cakrārūḍham*, if She is *anacka*, or if She is only *śakti*, only energy, the embodiment of energy.[34] This is the question of Devī.

परापरायाः सकलम्
अपरायाश्च वा पुनः ।
पराया यदि तद्वत्स्यात्
परत्वं तद्विरुध्यते ॥५॥

parāparāyāḥ sakalam
aparāyāśca vā punaḥ /
parāyā yadi tadvatsyāt
paratvaṁ tadvirudhyate / / 5 / /

There are three energies. In fact, these *śaktis* are three-fold, triple *śaktis*–one is *parā*, another is *parāparā*, and the

---

31 See verse 20.

32 *Spanda*, *svātantrya śakti*, *vimarśa śakti*.

33 Mount Kailash is known as the earthly residence of Lord Śiva and Pārvatī.

34 "*Cakrārūḍham* is *spanda*, *anackam* is *aspanda*. *Śakti svarūpam* is only energy." *Vijñāna Bhairava*, additional audio (USF archives).

third is *aparā*.[35]

[Devī]: *Parāparāyāḥ sakalam aparāyāśca vā punaḥ* (*sakalam* means "in the cycle of functioning[36]"), if *parāparā* is existing in the cycle of functioning or [if] in *aparā* also the cycle of functioning is continuous, what lies in *parā* then?[37] *Parāyā yadi tadvatsyāt*, if *parā* also holds the [same] cycle of functioning, how *parā* will be called supreme?

This is another question.

> Because *sakala rūpa* means, that which has *kalanā*. *Kalanā* means, that which can be observed, that which can be perceived, that which can be heard, that which can be seen, that which can be touched. When there is sensation, any sensation, wherever there is sensation, that is *sakala rūpa*.[38]
>
> When there is no sensation, only the supreme existence of God consciousness, that is *parā*.[39] It is without sensation, because sensation remains only there where the sensation is felt by the feeler. God consciousness is not felt, it is your own Self.
>
> Because, for instance, you are John. You don't feel John

---

35 As explained in the *Triśirobhairava Tantra*: *parā* (supreme), *parāparā* (medium), and *aparā* (inferior).

36 That is, affected by the elements of the material world.

37 "If the *sakala rūpa* (functioning) of *parā* is just like the *sakala rūpa* of *parāparā* or just like the *sakala rūpa* of *aparā*, then where is the supremacy of *parā* found then?" *Vijñāna Bhairava*, additional audio (USF archives).

38 *Sakala* literally means, consisting of parts, divisible, material. "*Sakala* is where there is some sensation–it may be in form, it may be in space, it may be in time. Only these three things exist: space, time, and form."

"In *rūpa*, there are two things to be noted: *mantra* and form. By '*sauḥ*' you can feel that when you are rising. It is that state where you are rising from up to down. That is the particular state of the formation of that *mantra*. And '*sauḥ*' is the *mantra*. Its *mantra* is '*sauḥ*' and its state is that movement of rising down." Ibid.

See Appendix for an explanation of the *mantra* '*sauḥ*'.

39 "It has no space, it has no time, it has no form in the state of *parā* because [*parā*] is your own Self." Ibid.

every now and then because it is your own nature, it is your own *svarūpa*. You can feel Jagdish, you can feel Jeremy, you can feel all others, but you cannot feel yourself always. Why? Because it is your own self. This is the case with *parā* also. In *parā*, the Self is already in the state of knower-ship, not the known. The Self is not known in the state of *parā*. Knowledge resides only in *parāparā* and *aparā*. In the *parāparā* state, knowledge resides, and in *aparā* also, knowledge is . . .

JOHN: So there is sensation in *parāparā*?

SWAMIJI: You can feel the state of God consciousness in *parāparā* and in *aparā*. You cannot feel the state of God consciousness in *parā*–it is your own Self.

śāntiṁ no labhate mūḍho yataḥ śamitum icchati /[40]

Śānti, that duffer *yogi* does not achieve the absolute peace of God consciousness, because he wants it! As long as the urge is there, it is useless. As long as it becomes your nature, then it is right. It must become your nature, it must not become your [desired] object.

That is what we feel in the state of *parā*.

Parāyā yadi tadvat syāt, if, in *parā* also, You will explain that it is felt, *paratvam tad virudhyate*, where is *paratva*[41] there? *Paratva* is finished, *paratva* is absolutely vanished, it is nowhere to be found. This supreme state of God consciousness is nowhere. Then *paratva* is as good as *parāparā* or *aparā*.

This is the question of Devī.

न हि वर्णविभेदेन
देहभेदेन वा भवेत् ।
परत्वं, निष्कलत्वेन,
सकलत्वे न भावयेत् ॥ ६ ॥

40 From the *Aṣṭāvakra Saṁhitā*, 18.39.

41 The suffix "*tva*" denotes "the quality of", i.e., the quality of *parā*.

na hi varṇavibhedena
dehabhedena vā bhavet /
paratvaṁ, niṣkalatvena,
sakalatve na bhāvayet[42] / / *6* / /

This is a misunderstanding of Pārvatī. She wants to clarify it.

Na hi varṇa vibhedena deha bhedena vā bhavet, paratvaṁ. Paratvaṁ cannot exist when there is *varṇa vibheda* or *deha bheda*, the differentiated-ness of letters or the differentiated-ness of bodies. As long as differentiated bodies are concerned and differentiated *varṇa mala* is concerned (the cycle of letters is concerned), *paratva* is not found. *Paratva* cannot exist when there is differentiated-ness in *varṇas* (letters) or bodies (bodies means *svarūpa*).[43]

Varṇa vibhedena, deha bhedena, paratvaṁ na bhavet. If *paratva* will be accepted there, then it won't be *niṣkala*, you can't nominate it as *niṣkala*[44]. *Paratva* is *sakala, paratva* becomes *sakala,* when there is differentiated-ness of *varṇas* and differentiated-ness of bodies (*svarūpas*). *Sakalatve na ca bhavet*, if there is *sakalatva, paratva* won't be accepted there in *sakala. Sakala* cannot be *niṣkala* and *niṣkala* cannot be *sakala.*[45]

This is a misunderstanding of Pārvatī. But, in fact, *sakala* can be *niṣkala* and *niṣkala* can be *sakala* because of our theory of that pathway of traveling when we reach that *ahaṁ*

---

42 Swamiji corrected "*sakalatve na tad bhavet*" to read "*sakalatve na bhāvayet*".

43 "*Varṇa vibheda* means, by the process of *mantras. Deha bheda* means, by the process of states, forms. [Devī observes that] *paratvaṁ*, the attainment of the supreme state of the Lord, is not possible by the process of *mantras* or by the process of formations." *Vijñāna Bhairava*, additional audio (USF archives).

44 Undifferentiated, indivisible; the condition of Brahman, the Absolute. Swamiji also defines *niṣkala* as "without any thought", viz., *nirvikalpa.*

45 "*Parāparā* and *aparā* reside in *sakala rūpa*, while *parā* will reside in *niṣkala.*" *Vijñāna Bhairava*, additional audio (USF archives).

and *ma-ha-a*.[46]

प्रसादं कुरु मे नाथ
निःशेषं छिन्धि संशयम् ।

prasādaṁ kuru me nātha
niḥśeṣaṁ chindhi saṁśayam / 7a

O Lord, do this favor to Me (*prasādaṁ*, do this favor). *Prasādaṁ kuru*, do this favor to Me, O Lord: *niḥśeṣam chindhi saṁśayam*, *niḥśeṣam* (entirely), please remove *saṁśayam* (my doubts). Please remove all of my doubts entirely. Do this favor to me, O Lord.

भैरव उवाच

bhairava uvāca

Now, you must put "*bhairava uvāca*" [because] it is

46 "This two-fold process [of *ahaṁ* and *ma-ha-a*] is meant by Lord Śiva to equalize inside and outside, equalize the lowest and the topmost. This will be adjusted to *krama mudrā*. *Krama mudrā* is automatic, it is not to be done–it appears. You are not doing [it]. It is not your choice. It is not anybody's choice. It appears like that. It happens. *Krama mudrā* is the real point [and] for this is this two-fold way of *ahaṁ* and *ma-ha-a*. The pathway is through *sauḥ* and *piṇḍanātha*." Ibid. See Appendix for an explanation of *krama mudrā*, and *sauḥ mantra*.

"It may be in *ahaṁ bhāva* or in *ma-ha-a bhāva,* [they are] one and the same thing from the Shaiva point of view. When you digest this whole, along with Śiva, in the individual, that is *ahaṁ bhāva*. We are situated in *ahaṁ bhāva* at present. And when [the individual] is digested in the supreme nature of God consciousness, that is *ma-ha-a bhāva*. *Ma-ha-a* is the introverted course and [*ahaṁ*] is the extroverted course. [They are] one and the same thing. You may be an individual, no worry; you may be universal, no worry. There is no difference, not even the slightest difference, between the individual soul and Lord Śiva from the Trika point of view." *Parātriśikā Vivaraṇa* (USF archives), introductory verse 3.

omitted.[47]

साधु साधु त्वया पृष्टं
तन्त्रसारमिदं प्रिये ॥७॥
गूहनीयतमं भद्रे
तथापि कथयामि ते ।

sādhu sādhu tvayā pṛṣṭaṁ
tantrasāramidaṁ priye / / 7b / /
gūhanīyatamaṁ bhadre
tathāpi kathayāmi te / 8a

O dear, O dear Pārvatī (*priye*, O dear Pārvatī), You have asked Me that [which] was worth to be asked for (*sādhu sādhu tvayā pṛṣṭaṁ*), because this is the essence of all *Tantras* (*tantra sāram idaṁ priye*). The question You have put before Me is the essence of all *Tantras* (*tantra sāram idaṁ priye*).

Gūhanīyatamaṁ bhadre, O Devī, although it is to be concealed–You must conceal this, it is worth concealing, hiding; it must not be exposed because it is a secret–even then, I will explain it, I will expose this secret to You.

यत्किञ्चित्सकलं रूपं
भैरवस्य प्रकीर्तितम् ॥८॥
तदसारतया देवि
विज्ञेयं शक्रजालवत् ।

yatkiñcitsakalaṁ rūpaṁ
bhairavasya prakīrtitam / / 8b / /

47 "*Bhairava uvaca*" (Bhairava speaks) was omitted from the original text: *Vijñāna Bhairava with the commentary partly by Kṣemarāja and partly by Śivopādhyāya,* ed. Pandit Mukunda Rāma Śāstrī. *KSTS* 8, Bombay, 1918.

tadasāratayā devi
vijñeyaṁ śakrajālavat[48] / *9a*

Whatever forms, any form of the Lord, [be they] in the divided formation of *mantras* and forms or in the undivided formations of *mantras* and forms, whatever formation [of the Lord] You find explained in all *Tantras*, *tad asāratayā devi vijñeyaṁ śakra jālavat*, that is all bogus. That is written only for writing only, not to be understood; it is not worth understanding. It is only deception or delusion. It is deception, *tat asāratayā*, because it has no sense, it has no meaning in the background.

For instance, *śabda rāśi* (the fifty-fold journey), or the nine-fold journey[49], or the three-fold journey[50], or the eleven-fold journey[51], all these are bogus. It has no essence in it.

Tad asāratayā devi, that has no essence there. You must know that this is only deception or delusion and nothing else. Not only this much.

मायास्वप्नोपमं चैव
गन्धर्वनगरभ्रमम् ॥९॥

māyā svapnopamaṁ caiva
gandharvanagarabhramam // *9b* //
[not recited in full]

This is only *māyā*. This is the expansion of *māyā*. All these states and all these processes are just like a dream. Or, *gandharva nagara bhramam*, just like a wrong conception, just like an imaginary city in the sky.

---

48 Although some readings have "*indra jālavat*" (the net of Indra), Swamiji preferred "*śakra jālavat*", which he said conveys the same meaning since Śakra is another name for the god, Indra.

49 *Navātma bheda*.

50 *Triśiro bheda*.

51 *A-u-m-bindu, ardhacandra, nirodikā, nāda, nādānta, śakti, vyāpinī,* and *samanā* are the 11 phases of sound. The 12th sound *unmanā* is not included since it is supreme (*parā*) and the actual state of God consciousness.

There is a wrong conception when you feel that there is an imaginary *nagara* (city) in the sky. That is *gandharva nagara*.

Then the question arises there: Why are these ways put in the *Tantras* then? What is the fun in putting them in these Bhairava *āgamas*?

ध्यानार्थं भ्रान्तबुद्धीनां
क्रियाडम्बरवर्तिनाम् ।
केवलं वर्णितं पुंसां
विकल्पनिहितात्मनाम् ॥ १० ॥

dhyānārthaṁ bhrāntabuddhīnāṁ
kriyāḍambaravartinām /
kevalaṁ varṇitaṁ puṁsāṁ
vikalpanihitātmanām[52] */ / 10 / /*

Bhrānta buddhīnām, whose intellect is always astray, scattered, and those people who are established in the commencement of actions only (*kriyāḍambara vartinām*; *āḍambara* means "commencement"), . . .

[For example], Śrīkaṇṭha[53] has now commenced *havan* of Caṇḍi and all these. All these are bogus, it has no value. He has collected so much money, thousands, and he will spend there–finished. It is *kriyāḍambara*.

. . . for those, these ways are written in the *Tantras*–for those people. *Kevalaṁ varṇitāṁ puṁsāṁ*, this is told for those people, whose mind is always established in thoughts, in differentiated thoughts (*vikalpa nihitātmanām*).

तत्त्वतो न नवात्मासौ
शब्दराशिर्न भैरवः ।

52 Swamiji corrected "*nihatātmanām*" to read "*nihitātmanā*".

53 In reference to a Kashmiri brahmin who was performing a *havan* at that time.

न चासौ त्रिशिरो देवो
न च शक्तित्रयात्मकः ॥ ११ ॥

tattvato na navātmāsau
śabdarāśirna bhairavaḥ /
na cāsau triśiro devo
na ca śaktitrayātmakaḥ / / 11 / /
[not recited]

Tattvato na navātmāsau, in fact, [Bhairava] is not the nine-fold way. It is not the fifty-fold way. This Bhairava is not *śabda rāśi*, this is not the collection of the fifty-fold way (treading the journey from '*a*' to '*kṣa*' and return again). *Na cāsau triśiro devaḥ*, this *Deva* is not the holder of the three-fold energies (*parā*, *parāparā*, and *aparā*).

नादबिन्दुमयो वापि
न चन्द्रार्धनिरोधिकाः ।
न चक्रक्रमसंभिन्नो
न च शक्तिस्वरूपकः ॥ १२ ॥

nādabindumayo vāpi
na candrārdhanirodhikāḥ /
na cakrakramasaṁbhinno
na ca śaktisvarūpakaḥ / / 12 / /
[not recited in full]

It is neither *nāda*, *bindu*, *candra*, *ardhacandra*, *nirodhikā*, *śakti*, *vyāpinī*, *samanā*, all these. [Bhairava] is not existing [in these]. *Na cakra krama saṁbhinna*, this is not the establishment of that moving wheel which is without movement–not even that. *Na ca śakti svarūpakaḥ*, it is not the *svarūpa* of universal energy. It is something else.

Then what is that?

अप्रबुद्धमतीनां हि
एता बालबिभीषिकाः ।
मातृमोदकवत्सर्वं
प्रवृत्त्यर्थमुदाहृतम् ॥ १३ ॥

aprabuddhamatīnāṁ hi
etā bālavibhīṣikāḥ /
mātṛmodakavatsarvaṁ
pravṛttyarthamudāhṛtam // 13 //

Etā, these ways established in the *Tantras* are *bāla vibhīṣikā*, just for diverting ignorant boys from bad actions.

You terrify those boys by saying that, "If you do such and such action, this ghost will eat you. Don't do this! This ghost, he will eat you just now. Don't do this action. Keep quiet."

DEVOTEES: [laughter]

SWAMIJI: This is *bāla vibhīṣikā*. And this terrifying process is functioned for whom? Not for great souls, highly elevated souls, [but] for those who have *aprabuddhamatīḥ*, whose intellect is not developed, [not] well-developed.

Or, *mātṛ modaka vat sarvaṁ pravṛttyartham udāhṛtam*, [if] you have to take a dose of medicine, a medicine dose which is not sweet, it is sour, it is not tasteful, you do not like to take it, then what does your mother do? She puts something sweet in your mouth first and [then] says, "Take [the medicine] now." Just as a mother directs her son for doing something good by giving him some sweets first (*mātṛ modakavat sarvaṁ*, that is the *modaka*, the sweet offering of a mother), *pravṛttyartham udāhṛtam*, just to begin with, these processes are just to begin with, but not to dive in those processes. These processes are nothing! You have not to tread on those processes. It is just to begin with (*pravṛttyartham udāhṛtaṁ*; the meaning of *pravṛttyartham udāhṛtam* is, it is just to begin with). You begin and, leave them aside, and then go on the right path.

JOHN: Well then why, if it is not unspeakable, do we say that this is all bogus, this, all this talk, these theories, this law, this way, this way, so many fifteen-fold ways, thirty . . . ? Why do we always say, "This is bogus, there is no path, there is no . . ."?

SWAMIJI: We don't say this is bogus. Why should we say it is bogus?

JOHN: Doesn't Lord Śiva just say here in the beginning that it is bogus, all these theories?

JAGDISH: *Etaḥ bāla vibhīṣikāḥ.*

SWAMIJI: Yes, in that state, because there are means. Actually, [Bhairava] is not achieved by the support of means, in the actual way of understanding.

JAGDISH: It is only *pravṛttyartham*.

SWAMIJI: *Pravṛttyartham. Mātṛ modakavat sarvaṁ pravṛttyartham udāhṛtam*, you just have to take this dose of the mixture, and mother wants you to take that dose of the mixture, which is very . . .

DENISE: Terrible taste.

SWAMIJI: . . . terrible taste, and she first gives you one piece of candy to taste, and then this [medicine]. So this is that candy, these means.

JOHN: But what's the terrible medicine?

SWAMIJI: The exact medicine is that medicine where you have to do nothing. It is terrible, you can't do that. You have to digest it with these *upāyas*, these means, with some support in the beginning, and that support is these one hundred and twelve ways. There is no way to achieve that, actually. One hundred and twelve ways are just in place of sugar candy.

What is the right path? He puts that now.

दिक्कालकलनोन्मुक्ता
देशोद्देशाविशेषिणी ।
व्यपदेष्टुमशक्यासा-
वकथ्या परमार्थतः ॥१४॥

अन्तः स्वानुभवानन्दा
विकल्पोन्मुक्तगोचरा ।
यावस्था भरिताकारा
भैरवी भैरवात्मनः ॥ १५ ॥

तद्वपुस्तत्त्वतो ज्ञेयं
विमलं विश्वपूरणम् ।

dikkālakalanonmuktā
deśoddeśāviśeṣiṇī /
vyapadeṣṭumaśakyāsāv-
akathyā paramārthataḥ / / 14 / /

antaḥ svānubhavānandā
vikalponmuktagocarā /
yāvasthā bharitākārā
bhairavī bhairavātmanaḥ / / 15 / /

tadvapustattvato jñeyaṁ
vimalaṁ viśvapūraṇam / 16a

This state of Bhairava is beyond the limitation of space, time, and formation. It has no space, It has no time, It has no form–It is beyond that, beyond these three (*dikkāla kalana unmuktā*). *Deśa uddeśa aviśeṣiṇī*, there is no *uddeśa* or *deśa*, [there is no] nomination of the seat of Lord Śiva.

> Do you know where Lord Śiva resides? In Śiva-loka. Śivaloka is the residence of Lord Śiva in the heavens, and the residence of Lord Śiva in this universe is [Mount] Kailasha. He lives on the top of Kailasha. This is all humbug!

Dikkāla kalana unmuktā, there is no *deśa* (neither space, nor time, nor form) and there is no *uddeśa* (nomination of his particular place)–*deśa uddeśa aviśeṣiṇi*.

Vyapadeṣṭum aśakyāsau, this state is, in fact, indescribable, It can't be described. *Akathyā paramārthataḥ*, in reality, It can't be told. *Antaḥ*, internally It happens; It is filled with your own ecstasy, your own *ānanda*. It is beyond the apprehension of *vikalpa* (*vikalpa unmukta gocara*), beyond thought.

Yāvasthā bharitākārā bhairavī bhairavātmanaḥ, that state, which is filled, always filled, always full, that state of Bhairavī, [which] is that full state of Bhairava, is, in reality, to be known as absolutely pure, and absolutely filled with universal existence (*viśva pūraṇam*).[54]

That state is not the object of *vikalpas*, It can't be perceived by *vikalpas* (thoughts). You can't perceive It through the mind. [It is] *vikalpa unmukta gocara*, It is not *vikalpa gocara* as you are *vikalpa gocara* to me. With *vikalpas*, I can understand you, but you can't understand That state through *vikalpas*. *Vikalpa unmukta gocara*, It has gone above the cycle of becoming the object of *vikalpas–vikalpa unmukta gocara*. [Bhairavī] has gone above [becoming] the object of thoughts. You can express It but you cannot feel It just like we feel in this-ness, objectivity. For instance, you have the information of the *Tantrāloka*. If you have the information of the *Tantrāloka* and you need the *Tantrāloka* book to explain–you take the support of the *Tantrāloka* book and you explain the words of the *Tantrāloka*–that is *vikalpa sahita gocara*. It is not *vikalpa unmukta gocara* because it is in that state of subjectivity, which is attached to objectivity. This [state of Bhairavī] must be in *pramiti bhāva* (that is *vikalpa unmukta gocara*).

JOHN: *Pramiti bhāva*.

SWAMIJI: *Pramiti bhāva* is the state of that pundit, that scholar, who does not take the support of the *Tantrāloka*. I will show you, I will make you understand more vividly. For instance, I understand, I know, the *Tantrāloka*. For the time being, I know the *Tantrāloka* [but] I have no

54 "*Bharitākārā* means, the state (*āvasthā*) of fullness. *Bharitākārā* is the qualification of Bhairavī, and it belongs to Bhairava. This state, which is of Bhairavī, belongs to Bhairava." *Vijñāna Bhairava*, additional audio (USF archives).

books. I don't remember any *śloka* (verse) in my mind. In my mind, I don't remember any *śloka*, but whenever somebody asks me [about] some *śloka*, *bas*, [the explanation] comes out. Where was that *śloka* residing in my brain? Where? In the *nirvikalpa* state. That is *pramiti bhāva*.[55] That state is of Pārvatī. That state is of that Universal Consciousness where there are no objects of *vikalpa*. [On the other hand], this is the object of *vikalpas*, when you take the support of a book.

एवंविधे परे तत्त्वे
कः पूज्यः कश्च तृप्यति ॥ १६ ॥

evaṁvidhe pare tattve
kaḥ pūjyaḥ kaśca tṛpyati / / 16b / /

When you put this thing in your view, *evaṁ vidhe*, in this supreme essence of transcendental truth, who is to be worshiped and who is the worshiper? *Kaḥ pūjyaḥ*, who is to be worshiped? *Kaśca tṛpyati*, who is the worshiper?

एवंविधा भैरवस्य
यावस्था परिगीयते ।
सा परा, पररूपेण
परादेवी प्रकीर्तिता ॥ १७ ॥

evaṁvidhā bhairavasya
yāvasthā parigīyate /
sā parā pararūpeṇa
parādevī prakīrtitā / / 17 / /

55 "*Pramiti* [*bhāva*] is that state where subjective consciousness prevails without the agitation of objectivity. The state of *pramiti* is without any object at all. In other words, when he is residing in his own nature, that subjective consciousness is the state of *pramiti*." *Kashmir Shaivism–The Secret Supreme*, 11.81. See Appendix for an explanation of *pramiti, pramātṛ, pramāṇa* and *prameya bhava*.

This state of Bhairava that is already sung in the body of the *Tantras, yāvasthā parigīyate* (*parigīyate*, sung), that state is in Its supreme way (*pararūpena*), [and It] is the state of Bhairavī (*parā devī*).

In other words, the real state of Bhairava is the state of Bhairavī. Whenever you explain, whenever you find out, what is the real state of Bhairava, you can't find it out because the real state of Bhairava is, in fact, the real state of the knower. It can't be found [because] It is the [finder]. The real state of Bhairava is the perceiver, It is not perceived. You can't perceive that state. When It is perceived, when there is a desire in you to perceive It, you can perceive It [only] when It comes down in the state of Bhairavī. So that is the way. When you tread on the level of Pārvatī, then you are treading on the path. This is the journey we have to do, the journey we have to do in the field of Pārvatī, not in the field of Bhairava [where] there is no journey. He is the knower of everything, so It can't be found, that state cannot be found. That state can only be found when It comes down one step lower at the state of Pārvatī.

So, now, here we will describe one hundred and twelve ways to enter in the universal and transcendental state of consciousness. One hundred and twelve ways will be explained in this book, and those one hundred and twelve ways will reside only in the field of Pārvatī. It can't reside in the field of Bhairava because Pārvatī is the way.

This is what he puts down [as] the foundation stone for entering in the consciousness of the one hundred and twelve ways.

Evaṁvidhā bhairavasya yāvasthā parigīyate, this state of Bhairava, which is sung in the *Tantras*, is really the supreme state of the Goddess, Pārvatī (*sā parā pararūpeṇa*, in Its supreme way is *parā devī prakīrtitā*).

But is there any difference of supremacy? Is there a difference of supreme-ness between Lord Śiva and Pārvatī? This is what he explains now.

शक्तिशक्तिमतोर्यद्वत्
अभेदः सर्वदा स्थितः ।

अतस्तद्धर्मधर्मित्वात्
  परा शक्तिः परात्मनः ॥ १८ ॥

śaktiśaktimatoryadvat
  abhedaḥ sarvadā sthitaḥ /
atastaddharmadharmitvāt
  parā śaktiḥ parātmanaḥ / / 18 / /

Just as between energy and the holder of energy there is no differentiation at all to be found–always there is *abheda*, there is unity, unity between energy and the holder of energy (*śakti* and Śiva), there is no differentiated-ness–in the same way, *tat dharma dharmitvāt* (*tat dharma* means, all the aspects of Lord Śiva–*tad dharma*; *tat* means Lord Śiva, of Lord Śiva), all the aspects of Lord Śiva are held by Pārvatī Herself (*tat dharma dharmitvāt*).

"*Dharmi*" is the holder of all aspects. *Dharmi*, who is *dharmi*? Pārvatī. *Tat dharma*, all the aspects of Lord Śiva are held by Pārvatī.

So, *parā śakti parātmanaḥ*, that supreme energy is the energy of the supreme Lord. There is no difference in any case.

न वह्नेर्दाहिका शक्तिः
  व्यतिरिक्ता विभाव्यते ।
केवलं ज्ञानसत्तायां
  प्रारम्भोऽयं प्रवेशने ॥ १९ ॥

na vahnerdāhikā śaktiḥ
  vyatiriktā vibhāvyate /
kevalaṁ jñānasattāyām
  prārambho'yaṁ praveśane / / 19 / /

Because, when there is a fire (for instance, there is a fire), its energy is *dāhikā*[56], [and *dāhikā's*] energy is *pācikā*[57] [and]

56 Burning.

prakāśikā[58]. All these energies are owned by fire, but those energies–lightening, giving light, burning, heating, all these energies are produced from fire–but these energies are undifferentiated with fire. From fire, these energies are not different from fire. That is what he says: *na vahner*, from fire, *dāhikā śakti*, the energy of burning, burning energy, is not *vyatiriktā* (separated) *vibhāvyate* (found), it is not found that it is separated.

Kevalaṁ jñāna sattāyāṁ prārambho'yaṁ praveśane, it is just to enter in that state of fire, i.e., to put a kettle on it or to put fuel on it (*dāhikā*, *prakāśikā*, and *pācikā*). It is just to enter in the state of fire, i.e., to put fuel and to put that kettle [on it].

So, [in the same way], it is just to enter in the *jñāna sattā*[59] of Lord Śiva. You have to enter in the *jñāna sattā* of Lord Śiva, and [although] you are maintaining the *nāvatma mantra* and all these [processes], these are nothing. [They are] only *prārambha*, just to begin with.

शक्त्यावस्थाप्रविष्टस्य
निर्विभागेन भावना ।
तदासौ शिवरूपी स्यात्
शैवी मुखमिहोच्यते ॥२०॥

śaktyāvasthāpraviṣṭasya
nirvibhāgena bhāvanā /
tadāsau śivarūpī syāt
śaivī mukhamihocyate / / 20 / /

When you enter in the state of energy and leave your individual state (you have not to enter in the state of energy for always), you have to throw off the individual state and enter in the energy to enter in the universal state in the end. Because, unless you [throw] off your individuality,

57 Cooking.

58 Illumination.

59 Knowledge or intelligence (*jñāna*) of Being or existence (*sattā*).

universality will not rise, universality won't take place.

So you have to enter in the state of energy first (*śakti avasthā praviṣṭasya*), then afterwards, *yadā nirvibhāgena bhāvanā bhavet*, when you feel that undifferentiated-ness comes in your consciousness–undifferentiated between energy and the holder of energy–*tadāsau śivarūpī syāt*, at that very moment, this *sādhaka*[60], his *bhāvanā*[61] becomes one with Lord Śiva.

So, the path is Śakti, the path is not Śiva (*śaivī* means Śakti). Energy is *mukham*, the path is *iha*, here, *ucyate*, explained. Energy is the real path you have to tread.

यथालोकेन दीपस्य
किरणैर्भास्करस्य च ।
ज्ञायते दिग्विभागादि
तद्वच्छक्त्या शिवः प्रिये ॥२१॥

yathālokena dīpasya
kiraṇairbhāskarasya ca /
jñāyate digvibhāgādi
tadvacchaktyā śivaḥ priye / / 21 / /

O dear Pārvatī, just like with the light of your candle or torch (*dīpasya ālokena*, by the light of your torch, or candle, or by the rays of the sun), all the differentiated points of *deśa* (space) are known, are understood, in the same way, Śiva is being understood by Śakti, by His energy. Energy is the means by which you can understand and enter in the state of Lord Śiva.

---

60 Aspirant.

61 Contemplation, meditation, in continuity; when you sentence your mind with awareness to one point.

श्रीदेव्युवाच

देवदेव त्रिशूलाङ्क,
    कपालकृतभूषण ।
दिग्देशकालशून्या च
    व्यपदेशविवर्जिता ॥ २२ ॥

यावस्था भरिताकारा
    भैरवस्योपलभ्यते ।
कैरुपायैर्मुखं तस्य
    परादेवी कथं भवेत् ॥ २३ ॥

यथा सम्यगहं वेद्मि
    तथा मे ब्रूहि भैरव ।

śrī devī uvāca

devadeva triśūlāṅka
kapālakṛtabhūṣaṇa /
digdeśakālaśūnyā ca
vyapadeśavivarjitā / / 22 / /

yāvasthā bharitākārā
bhairavasyopalabhyate /
kairupāyairmukhaṁ tasya
parādevī kathaṁ bhavet / / 23 / /

yathā samyagahaṁ vedmi
tathā me brūhi bhairava /

O Lord of lords, O [You who are] glorified by *triśūla*[62]

62 The trident, Lord Śiva's weapon.

(*triśūlāṅka*) and *kapāla kṛta bhūṣaṇa*, glorified with the skull bone, You are glorified with the skull bone (*kapāla kṛtabhūṣaṇa*), . . .

[These are] *āmantraṇam*[63], calling Lord Śiva.

. . . that state which is beyond space, beyond time, and *vyapadeśa vivarjitā*, and that state which cannot be named, nominated, that state of Bhairava, which is always known as full (*bharitākārā*), *kairupāyairmukhaṁ tasya, parādevī kathaṁ bhavet*; *tasya mukhaṁ kairupāyair*, [the *yogi's*] *mukhaṁ*, journey, *kairupāyair bhavati* (*tasya mukhaṁ kairupāyair bhavati*), his journey, *kairupāyair*, with what means can [that journey] be adopted (*kairupāyair tasya mukhaṁ bhavati*)? *Parādevī kathaṁ bhavet*, how can *parā devī* take place? *Parādevī svarūpam kathaṁ bhavet, sākṣātkāratayā prāpnuyāt*[64]? *Yathā samyak ahaṁ vedmi*, put that way before me, O Lord, by which way I could understand it.

Now, one hundred and twelve ways will be explained.[65]

---

63 Vocative case.

64 Attainment (*prāpnuyāt*) of the evident or intuitive perception or realization (*sākṣātkāra*).

65 Up to verse 23, the traditional commentary is by Kṣemarāja, the principle disciple of Abhinavagupta. From verse 24 onwards, Kṣemarāja's commentary appears to have been lost, although, in his various writings, *Śiva Sūtra Vimarśinī*, etc., he includes many of the later verses of the *Vijñāna Bhairava*. The commentary after verse 23 is by Śivopādhāya, though Swamiji added that, "Śivopādhāya was just a Śaivite-*cum*-Vedāntist. He was not an actual Śaivite, not a pure Śaivite." *Vijñāna Bhairava*, additional audio (USF archives).

Dhāraṇā[66] 1

श्रीभैरव उवाच

ऊर्ध्वे प्राणो ह्यधो जीवो
विसर्गात्मा परोच्चरेत् ।
उत्पत्तिद्वितयस्थाने,
भरणाद्भरिता स्थितिः ॥ २४ ॥

śrī bhairava uvāca

ūrdhve prāṇo hyadho jīvo
visargātmā paroccaret /
utpattidvitayasthāne
bharaṇādbharītā sthitiḥ / / 24 / /

Ūrdhve means "from upwards".

The movement from upwards (i.e., from the heart to *dvādaśānta*[67]) is *prāṇaḥ* (*prāṇaḥ* means, the outgoing breath). *Adhaḥ*, from *dvādaśānta* to *hṛdaya* (the heart) is *jīvaḥ* (*jīvaḥ* means, the in-going breath).

The outgoing breath is represented by '*sa*' and the ingoing breath is represented by '*ha*'. So '*sa*' and '*ha*', *visargātmā parā uccaret utpatti dvitaya sthāne*; *utpatti dvitaya sthāne*, [these are] two starting points. From the heart, there is one starting point, and from *bāhya dvādaśānta*, there is another starting point (that is *utpatti dvitaya*, two starting points). There, *visargātmā parā uccaret*, this supreme energy, which is full of *visarga*[68], appears. And by this process, *bharaṇāt bharitā sthitiḥ*, *bharitā sthiti, bhairavasya sthitiḥ syāt*, one becomes

66 Contemplation.

67 A technical term in Kashmir Shaivism, literally meaning "twelve finger spaces." In this case, it refers to *bāhya dvādaśānta*, the starting point of breath outside (*bāhya*) the body, twelve finger spaces from the center of the eyebrows.

68 The vowel, '*aḥ*', which is represented by a colon in the Sanskrit alphabet, literally means "emission" or "flow".

one with Bhairava, *bharaṇāt*, because of its fullness.

This *upāya*, this means, is connected with *āṇavopāya*. It can't be *śāktopāya* or *śāmbhavopāya*. It is *āṇavopāya* because it is functioning in the objective field of consciousness.

Ūrdhve, you have to take the breath [out] from the heart to *dvādaśānta*, and take it in from *dvādaśānta* to the heart again, and recite *prāṇa* and *jīva*. "Recite *prāṇa*" means, recite '*sa*', the letter '*sa*', and "recite *jīva*" [means, recite] the letter '*ha*'. And, in these *utpatti dvitaya*, in these two starting points, you have to recite *visarga* and '*ṁ*'-*kāra*. The *visarga* of '*sa*' will be recited in the outward *dvādaśānta*, and the '*ṁ*'-*kāra* of '*ha*' will be recited in the heart. When you take your breath inside, [the recitation of '*ha*'] will end in '*ṁ*'[69]. When you take it out, [the recitation of '*sa*'] will end in *visarga*–'*saḥ*'. And, in these two starting points, if you concentrate, you will become one with Bhairava because of its fullness.

This is *āṇavopāya*.

69 '*Haṁ*'.

Dhāraṇā 2

Now next.

मरुतोऽन्तर्बहिर्वापि
 वियद्युग्मानिवर्तनात् ।
भैरव्या भैरवस्येत्थं
 भैरवि व्यज्यते वपुः ॥२५॥

maruto'ntarbahirvāpi
 viyadyugmānuvartanāt /[70]
bhairavyā bhairavasyettham
 bhairavi vyajyate vapuḥ / / *25* / /

Antar bahir, internally or outwardly (*vāpi* means "or"), internally or outwardly, *marutaḥ*, this energy of breath, when [it] is followed by two voids by returning back to two ethers, *viyat yugma ānuvartanāt*, by maintaining the uninterrupted awareness there–[that] means "*bhairavyā*", by means of Bhairavī (Bhairavī means, uninterrupted awareness)–when You maintain uninterrupted awareness in these two voids (internally and externally; there is an internal void and an external void), *itham*, by this way of treading on this process (*itham*, by this way), *bhairavasya vapuḥ vyajyate*, the formation (*svarūpa*) of Bhairava is revealed (*vyajyate*).

"*Bhairavi*" is *āmantraṇam*.[71]

O Bhairavī, O Pārvatī, here, You have not to recite '*so*'[72] or '*ham*'. It is without the recitation of '*sa*' and '*ha*'. It is only awareness that functions here.

It is why this is *śāktopāya*. This can't be *āṇavopāya* because you have to maintain awareness only, no recitation of *mantra*. Only you have to [inhale] and [exhale] breath and

70 Swamiji preferred "*anuvartanāt*" to "*anivartanāt*".

71 Vocative case.

72 That is, '*saḥ*'. According to the Sanskrit rules of phonological processes that occur at word boundaries (*sandhi*), *visarga* ('*aḥ*') followed by a voiced consonant becomes an '*o*'.

see where are these two voids.[73]

DEVOTEE: Between going out and coming in?

SWAMIJI: Between going out and coming in. Here[74] and in the heart.

JOHN: In *āṇavopāya*, there is an object.

SWAMIJI: Because [there is an] object [and] there is *mantra* also.

JOHN: But there is not an object here.

SWAMIJI: There is no object. It is why it is called here *śāktopāya*.

---

73 Swamiji emphasized that these are two "voids", not two "gaps".

74 Referring to the external point, *bāhya dvādaśānta*. See footnote 67.

Dhāraṇā 3

न व्रजेन्न विशेच्छक्ति-
मरुद्रूपा विकासिते ।
निर्विकल्पतया मध्ये
तया भैरवरूपता ॥ २६ ॥

na vrajenna viśecchaktir
marudrūpā vikāsite /
nirvikalpatayā madhye
tayā bhairavarūpatā / / 26 / /

Now He goes to the more subtle process.

Madhye nirvikalpatayā, when You establish onepointedness in the central path, the central vein (*suṣumnā*; *madhye* means, in *suṣumnā*, in the central vein), when You maintain one-pointedness in that central vein (*nirvikalpatayā*)–then what happens?–*marut rūpā śakti*, this energy of breath neither goes out nor enters in (*na vrajet na viśet*) because *madhye vikāsite*, this central vein is *vikāsite,* it is already illuminated. And by this process, *bhairava rūpatā bhavati*, one becomes one with Bhairava.

This is *śāmbhavopāya*. This is not *śāktopāya*. It is more than *śāktopāya* because there is only *nirvikalpi bhāva*[75] and one-pointedness in that central vein, no recitation of *mantra* and no objective field of consciousness.

---

75 The state (*bhāva*) of thought-lessness (*nirvikalpa*).

Dhāraṇā 4

कुम्भिता रेचिता वापि
पूरिता वा यदा भवेत् ।
तदन्ते शान्तनामासौ
शक्त्या शान्तः प्रकाशते ॥२७॥

kumbhitā recitā vāpi
pūritā vā yadā bhavet /
tadante śāntanāmāsau
śaktyā śāntaḥ prakāśate / / 27 / /

This is a practice with a little effort, what you call "*haṭha yoga*".

When You take Your breath inside, when it reaches the point of the heart, just [retain it] for a while, and take it out afterwards–after stopping there, take it out afterwards–and when it reaches at the point of *dvādaśānta* outside, then stop, just wait, don't take it in again rapidly–just wait.

This is what He says here.[76]

Pūritā sati prāṇa śakti kumbhitā, when You leave out this energy of breath outside, stop it outside for a while (it is not to stop it forever; just stop it for half a minute or one fourth of a minute), that is *kumbhakā*[77] there. *Kumbhakā* is not to stop it with full force.

GANJOO: As long as one can.

SWAMIJI: As long as one can, easily. You have to begin this practice while taking the breath outside first, and then take it in again and stop [it] in the heart.

JOHN: What does it mean, "stop in the heart"?

SWAMIJI: Don't leave it–hold it.

JOHN: For some time.

SWAMIJI: You have to hold it. Hold it just for ten seconds

---

76 "This practice is not accompanied by *mantra*." *Vijñāna Bhairava*, additional audio (USF archives).

77 Retention of breath.

and then leave it again.

JOHN: You keep doing this back and forth.

SWAMIJI: Yes, you have to do it in each and every breath, in each and every breath.

JOHN: For some time.

SWAMIJI: [Until] the Supreme is revealed. It is not only for some time. This is a complete process.

JOHN: You mean, all day, every day, do this.

SWAMIJI: Yes, do this for six hours a day. It is not harmful. It is not a harmful practice. You have to hold it only for ten seconds outside and ten seconds inside with each and every breath. *Recitā satī kumbhitā, pūritā satī kumbhitā, yadā bhavet prāṇa śakti. Tadante*, in the end, what happens? *Śāntanāma asāu śāntaḥ*, the state of *sadāśiva* . . .

Śānta nāma means, the state of *sadāśiva*[78]; *śānta* means, *śa-vargasya antaḥ–sa-kāraḥ*. *Sa-kāra* is the representative letter of *sadāśiva*[79] (*śa-vargasya antaḥ śānta*, *śānta nāma*).

. . . *śānta nāma*, the state which is nominated as *sadāśiva*, which is *śāntaḥ*, which is appeased, . . .

Śāntaḥ means . . . [this] next "*śāntaḥ*"[80] does not mean this is *śa-vargasya antaḥ*. *Śāntaḥ* means, the appeased state, full of peace, appeased, *śāntaḥ*. "*Śāntanāma*" means *sadāśiva*, the state of *sadāśiva* which is *śāntaḥ* (*śāntaḥ* means, absolutely appeased, calm).

. . . that is *prakāśate*, revealed, *tadante*, in the end, *śaktyā*, by this way of *prāṇa śakti*, by this process of *prāṇa śakti*, this way.

You have to take [the breath] out and hold it for some time, [then] take it in and hold it in the heart for some time, and go on practicing like this. And in the end, what will happen? The state of *sadāśiva*, which is the completely appeased form of *svarūpa*, will be revealed by this practical *prāṇā śakti*, energy

---

78 See appendix for a list of the 36 elements.

79 *Śānta* (*śa-antaḥ*) in the third line of the verse means, *śa-vargasya antaḥ*, the last letter in the class of letters beginning with *śa*, i.e., *śa*, *ṣa*, and *sa*. In the theory of *mātṛkā,* the letter '*sa*' represents the pure element known as *sadāśiva*.

80 Swamiji is referring to the second occurrence of the word "*śāntaḥ*" that appears in the last line of the verse.

of *prāṇa*.

So, it is *āṇavopāya* sentenced to *śāktopāya*. Because, as long as there is *kumbhakā*, that is *āṇavopāya*. You have to hold the breath, so you have to be aware of holding breath then. There is mind, there is the functioning of the mind there. [The mind] is not dead there, so there is *āṇavopāya*. And when you reach that appeased state of *sadāśiva*, then it is *śāktopāya*. So, it is *āṇavopāya* sentenced to *śāktopāya*.

DEVOTEE: What is the difference here between the experience of *sadāśiva* and the experience of Śiva or Bhairava?

SWAMIJI: *Sadāśiva* is Bhairava, but Bhairava is that state of *sadāśiva* which is when you don't return in this body. *Sadāśiva* is as good as Śiva, but in the body. As long as the body is there, that is Bhairava's state of *sadāśiva*. Śiva means the state which is of Bhairava only, in the solo way. "Solo" is just only Śiva. The not-solo state of Śiva is *sadāśiva*.

DEVOTEE: He is in *sadāśiva*.

SWAMIJI: He is in the *sadāśiva* state. It can't be above *sadāśiva*.

dehapāte tu paramaśiva bhaṭṭāraka eva bhavati /[81]

After leaving this physical frame, then he becomes one with that Śiva, solo.

JOHN: But can you experience this Śiva in this life?

SWAMIJI: Yes, yes, but it is *sadāśiva*.

JOHN: But why would he be in *śāktopāya* only then? That's what I don't understand. If that is highest state . . . ?

SWAMIJI: Because there is *kumbhakā*, you have to hold the breath.

JOHN: But after gaining that *sadāśiva,* there is no more holding breath then?

SWAMIJI: Then it is *śāktopāya*.

---

81 *Parāprāveśikā* of Kṣemarāja, translation and commentary by Swami Lakshmanjoo (original audio recording, USF archives, Los Angeles, 1980). See *Self Realization in Kashmir Shaivism–The Oral Teachings* of Swami Lakshmanjoo, ed. John Hughes (State University of New York Press, Albany, 1995), 3.69.

JOHN: But why wouldn't that be *śāmbhavopāya*?

SWAMIJI: *Śāmbhavopāya* it can't be because it has come by holding the breath.

JOHN: But they're both realization?

SWAMIJI: Yes, both realization. As long as there is holding of the breath, it is an inferior way of process. And, by that inferior way, he goes to that supreme way, and that will be only *śāktopāya*. From *āṇavopāya*, you cannot fly to *śāmbhavopāya*.[82]

JOHN: But I thought that you also, after leaving *śāktopāya,* must pass through *śāmbhavopāya*; that *śāktopāya* is not the end.

SWAMIJI: No, *śāktopāya* is not the end.

JOHN: It is end?

SWAMIJI: No, it is not the end.

JOHN: You must go through *śāmbhavopāya*?

SWAMIJI: Yes, it will go. After reaching that *śāktopāya*, then he will automatically go in *śāmbhavopāya* in the end.

---

82 This comment applies specifically to this *dhāraṇā*.

Dhāraṇā 5

आ मूलात्किरणाभासां
सूक्ष्मात् सूक्ष्मतरात्मिकाम् ।
चिन्तयेत्तां द्विषट्कान्ते
शाम्यान्तीं, भैरवोदयः ॥२८॥

ā mūlātkiraṇābhāsāṁ
sūkṣmāt sūkṣmatarātmikām /
cintayettāṁ dviṣaṭkānte
śāmyantīṁ, bhairavodayaḥ // 28 //

Bas. After "*śāmyantīm*", you should put a comma.

Ā mūlat (*mūlāt* means *mūlādhāra*[83]), right from *mūlādhāra* (*ā mūlāt*: *ā*, right from, *mūlāt*, *mūlādhāra*), *tām cintayet,* you should realize Her nature, realize the nature of the Goddess, *parā*.

How?

Kiraṇābhāsāṁ, just like filled with varieties of rays–*kiraṇābhāsāṁ*. *Sūkṣmāt sūkṣmatarātmikām*, first it is gross, then it becomes subtle, then it becomes subtler, subtler, subtler, subtlest, in the end it becomes subtlest (that is "*sūkṣmāt sūkṣmatarātmikām*"). And you should *cintayet*[84], you should find out *tāṁ*, that *śakti*, *śakti* of *parā śakti*.

You should not refer to *prāṇa kuṇḍalinī*, *cit kuṇḍalinī*, or *śakti kuṇḍalinī* here.[85]

---

83 "*Mūlādhāra* is that part of the body where sexual excitement takes place. The rectum is not the place for that–it is *mūlādhāra*, it is above the rectum." *Tantrāloka* 15.77, (USF archives).

84 Swamiji explained that "*cintayet api*" does not mean "meditated upon" in the sense of *dhyāna* or *bhāvana*. He said, "You must be aware there also; when you achieve that state of *kuṇḍalinī*, you have to be aware. You [must] be there, you make yourself present there. You don't ignore your awareness. You just be aware of what it is going on." *Vijñāna Bhairava*, additional audio (USF archives).

85 See Appendix for detailed explanation of *kuṇḍalinī*. See also *Kashmir Shaivism–The Secret Supreme*, 17.117-124.

You should *cintayet*, find out, *tām*, that *śakti*, *dviṣaṭkānte śāmyantīm*, at the point of *dviṣaṭkānte* (*dvādaśānta*; *dviṣaṭkānte* means *dvādaśānta*), . . .*

JAGDISH: *Ūrdhva dvādaśānta*? Which one is this?

SWAMIJI: There is nothing, no question of *ūrdhva dvādaśānta* or other *dvādaśānta*. Any *dvādaśānta* will do. When it rises from *mūlādhāra cakra*, there are so many *dvādaśāntas*. It may rest in *nabhi*[86], it may rest in the heart, it may rest in the throat-pit.

*. . . *bhairava udayaḥ*, [the rise of Bhairava] is absolutely vividly found there.

It is not always that it must go to *brahmarandhra*.[87] In fact, the state of *brahmarandhra* is held everywhere in all the *cakras*. That is what He refers [to] in this *dhāraṇā*: *ā mūlat kiraṇābhāsāṁ*; *kiraṇābhāsāṁ*, just like flowing of rays up, above.

GEORGE: Is he saying to hold that in *mūlādhāra* or that's just giving the concept that it's to be held everywhere?

SWAMIJI: No, *mūlādhāra* is the point; *mūlādhāra*, how you reach *mūlādhāra*. You cannot reach *mūlādhāra* just while talking. You have to meditate, meditate in continuity, and then your breath goes down in the central vein, in the pathway of the central vein, then it touches *mūlādhāra*.[88] From that *mūlādhāra* is the appearance of *parā śakti*. And that *parā śakti* takes the formation of sometime in *prāṇa kuṇḍalinī*, sometime *cit kuṇḍalinī*, and sometime *parā kuṇḍalinī*. That is another thing, that is another question. But you have to understand that this is *parā śakti*, *parā śakti* rising from *mūlādhāra*. Then there is no breath. And the more it rises, the more it becomes subtle. It becomes more

---

86 The navel.

87 Lit., the opening (*randhra*) of Brahma, which is situated at the top of the skull.

88 "When you stop your breathing, then what happens next is that your breath immediately rushes down in the central vein. Your breath is 'sipped' down and you actually hear the sound of sipping. The gate of the central vein (*madhya nāḍī*) opens at once and your breath reaches down to that place called *mūlādhāra*, which is near the rectum." *Kashmir Shaivism–The Secret Supreme*, 16.112. See also *Self Realization in Kashmir Shaivism*, 5.106-107.

subtle, so breath has no room there to exist. Breath has already stopped at the time of going inside, in the pathway of the central vein (*suṣumnā*). And when you find, when you experience, this *parā śakti* rising from *mūlādhāra* just like the fountain of *kiraṇa* (rays), rays of *cit* (consciousness), if it rests at *nābhī*, *bhairava udayaḥ*, you will find the state of Bhairava existing; or [at] the heart, you will find the state of Bhairava; or [at] the throat pit, [you will find the] Bhairava state; [at] this [*bhrūmadhya*[89], you will find the] Bhairava state; and at the top also[90], [you will find] the Bhairava state. This is one technique found in this.

JAGDISH: What *upāya* is this, sir?

SWAMIJI: It is *āṇavopāya* mixed with *śāktopāya*. *Āṇavopāya* in the beginning. *Āṇavopāya* will end in this sipping course [down] to the *mūlādhāra*[91]–that is *āṇavopāya*. From that [point onwards], it is *śāktopāya*. It is not *śāmbhavopāya*. *Śāmbhavopāya* begins from *krama mudrā*. It is just like opening and closing, opening and closing, opening and closing, automatically.[92]

---

89 Between the two eyebrows.

90 *Brahmarandhra*.

91 *Mūlādhāra* is a *cakra* at the base of the spine near the rectum. It is the resting place of *kuṇḍalinī*.

92 "You experience the rising flow of *cit kuṇḍalinī* as filling the whole channel from *mūlādhāra* to *brahmarandhra*. Here again you abruptly breathe out and your eyes are open. This lasts for only a moment and then you are again inside, without breathing, experiencing the rise of *kuṇḍalinī*. Then again you breathe out and again your eyes are open and for a moment you feel that the outside world is full of ecstasy and bliss. This happens again and again. One moment you are inside experiencing the bliss of the rise of *cit kuṇḍalinī* and then the next moment you breathe out and your eyes are open and you are experiencing the world filled with ecstasy. This process of coming out and remaining in continues and, each time it occurs, it is filled with more and more ecstasy. This process is called *krama mudrā*." *Kashmir Shaivism–The Secret Supreme*, 17.120.

Dhāraṇā 6

Now, this is a *cakrodaya*[93]:

उद्गच्छन्तींतडिद्रूपां
प्रतिचक्रं क्रमात्क्रमम् ।
ऊर्ध्वं मुष्टित्रयं यावत्
तावदन्ते महोदयः ॥२९॥

udgacchantīṁ taḍidrūpāṁ
praticakraṁ kramātkramam /
ūrdhvaṁ muṣṭitrayaṁ yāvat
tāvadante mahodayaḥ / / 29 / /

This is the pathway of *āṇavopāya*.

Udgacchantīṁ taḍit rūpāṁ (it is another technique), another technique is *tadit rūpam* (*taḍit rūpāṁ*, just like lightening), when you feel that it is just like lightening, and it is rising from *mūlādhāra*. *Prati cakra*, and it is *prati cakraṁ kramāt kramam*, it rests again and again, again in each and every *cakra* (in the navel *cakra* it rests, here, here, etc.). It shoots upwards (*udgacchantīṁ*), it takes the formation of shooting. It shoots upwards just like the streak of lightening (*taḍit rūpāṁ*). And it shoots–it does not shoot straight from *mūlādhāra* to *brahmarandhra*–it shoots *prati cakraṁ*, in a successive form.

This is the formation of *prāṇa kuṇḍalinī* again.

Sometimes it shoots straight from *mūlādhāra* to *ūrdhva dvādaśānta*. It is there *cit kuṇḍalinī*. Sometimes it shoots from *mūlādhāra*, *prati cakraṁ kramāt kramam*, [in a] successive way up to each and every wheel in the body. For instance, it shoots from the *mūlādhāra cakra* to the *cakra* of the navel. And from the navel it shoots again to heart. [From the heart] it shoots again to throat. From the throat it shoots again to *bhrūmadhya*, and from *bhrūmadhya* it shoots again

93 *Cakrodaya* is used here in the sense of rising (*udaya*) through the *cakras*.

to *brahmarandhra.*

Prati cakraṁ kramāt kramam muṣṭitrayaṁ (*muṣṭitrayaṁ* means *dvādaśānta*[94]), all these are shooting in the span of *dvādaśānta.* Because, from *mūlādhāra* to the navel, this is the span of *dvādaśānta*, twelve finger spaces. Twelve finger spaces is from *mūlādhāra* to the navel, from the navel to the heart is twelve finger spaces, from the heart to the throat is twelve finger spaces, from the throat to [*bhrūmadhya*] is twelve finger spaces, and from [*bhrūmadhya*] to [*brahmarandhra*] is twelve finger spaces. So all these spaces, the span of spaces, are called *dvādaśānta.* And this *dvādaśānta* is called *ūrdhva dvādaśānta* in the end. *Ūrdhvaṁ muṣṭitrayaṁ yāvat*, it rises only *muṣṭitrayaṁ* (*dvādaśāntā*; *ūrdhvan* means *ūrdhva dvādaśānta* here). When, [in] the end (*ūrdhva dvādaśānta*), it rises, it reaches, [to] the state of *ūrdhva dvādaśānta* (*ūrdhva dvādaśānta* is *brahmarandhra*), *tāvat ante mahodayaḥ*, there the *sādhaka* experiences the great rise (*udayaḥ*; *udayaḥ* means, the state of the divine nature). *Ūrdhvaṁ muṣṭitrayaṁ yāvat tāvad ante*, there, in the end, *mahodayaḥ*, the supreme bliss of Lord Śiva shines.

DEVOTEE: Is it more usual in the rise of *prāṇa kuṇḍalinī* to get as far as *bhrūmadhya cakra* only, and then unusually to go on to *sahasrāra*[95]?

SWAMIJI: No, if it is functioned properly, then it will go to *sahasrāra.*

DEVOTEE: You said that *prāṇa kuṇḍalinī* takes place when there is desire also for *siddhis.*

SWAMIJI: Yes.

DEVOTEE: Otherwise *cit kuṇḍalinī.*

SWAMIJI: Otherwise *cit kuṇḍalinī.*

DEVOTEE: So under what circumstances would the rise of *prāṇa kuṇḍalinī* take place and then go on from *bhrūmadhya* to *sahasrāra cakra*?

SWAMIJI: No, when it rises from *mūlādhāra cakra* to each and every *cakra*, it shoots upwards, then eight great powers

94 *Muṣṭitrayam* literally means three (*trayaṁ*) fists (*muṣṭi*), which is equal to twelve finger spaces (*dvādaśānta*).

95 Lit., thousand-spoked, a kind of cavity said to be found in the top of the head and to resemble a lotus reversed (fabled as the seat of the soul).

are possessed by that *sādhaka / yogi.*[96]

DEVOTEE: But it says, that is when it goes to *bhrūmadhya cakra*.

SWAMIJI: No, when it goes from each and every *cakra*.

DEVOTEE: If it only gets to *bhrūmadhya cakra*?

SWAMIJI: No, it can't be. It won't go only to *bhrūmadhya cakra*. Or it will go straight from *mūlādhāra* to *ūrdhva dvādaśānta*, then no powers [are attained].

DEVOTEE: It is not only *bhrūmadhya*.

SWAMIJI: No, not *bhrūmadhya*. You have misunderstood there. It is not *bhrūmadhya* only. When [it rises to] *bhrūmadhya cakra*, it has to go through all these other *cakras* (from *mūlādhāra* to the navel, from the navel to the heart, from the heart to the throat, the throat to *bhrūmadhya*).

JOHN: But can it stop? It can stop at *bhrūmadhya* though.

SWAMIJI: It is not in [the *yogi's*] power. It can't be stopped. He can't stop, the *sādhaka* cannot stop.

JOHN: But the rise could stop, the rise could stop at any point.

SWAMIJI: Yes, yes, when there is some defect.

JOHN: It could stop here, it could stop here.

SWAMIJI: It can stop, it can stop by itself, and the *sādhaka* will get perturbed, worried what has happened.

DENISE: Why? Because of some defect?

SWAMIJI: Because of some defect of this process. There has been some defect in the process of this practice. When the process is quite clean and flawless, then he will go straight to *bhrūmadhya*, and from *bhrūmadhya* to *sahasrāra*.

JOHN: You said in one lecture that if the *sādhaka* still had desires for worldly attainments and that it would stop at *bhrūmadhya cakra* and stop there.

SWAMIJI: Yes. It will not start from *bhrūmadhya*, it will

---

96 They *yogic* powers are: *aṇimā* (the power to make one's body extremely small), *mahima* (the power to make one's body infinitely large), *garima* (the power to become infinitely heavy), *laghima* (the power to become weightless), *prāpti* (the power to be anywhere), *prā-kāmya* (the power to achieve any desire), *īśtva* (the power to possess absolute sovereignty), and *vaśitva* (the power to subjugate).

end in *bhrūmadhya*.

JOHN: End there, end there . . .

SWAMIJI: It will end in . . . it doesn't go up then if there is more flaw, more flaw, . . .

JOHN: Yes, more flaw.

SWAMIJI: . . . more defect in the processes. More defect, more attachment for worldly pleasure.

JOHN: Then that *sādhaka* would have lots of power but no realization.

SWAMIJI: No realization. Realization won't happen.

DEVOTEE: So he would not be in *śuddhadhva*[97] when he experienced *bhrūmadhya cakra*.

SWAMIJI: No.

DEVOTEE: What level of consciousness is he at? When *kuṇḍalinī* has risen that far, he is already . . . ?

SWAMIJI: This will end in *mantra pramātṛ bhāva*, not *mantreśvara bhāva*.[98]

DEVOTEE: He will fall from this?

SWAMIJI: He won't fall. He will never fall!

DEVOTEE: He has partial enlightenment.

SWAMIJI: One who has entered in the path of *kuṇḍalinī*, he will never fall. He is always on the path. He will never fall, but he won't gain anything.

GANJOO: He won't gain the reality.

SWAMIJI: He won't gain in this life, anything.

DENISE: Even by further practice he won't gain anything?

SWAMIJI: Further practice, if he does. It is never [too] late. In the twenty-eighth [verse, the *yogi*] feels the divine nature

---

97 *Śuddhadhva* here refers to the three pure elements (*śuddha tattvas*) above *māyā*: *śuddhavidyā*, *īśvara*, and *sadāśiva*.

98 The perceivers (*pramātṛs*) of the pure elements/states of *śuddhavidyā*, *īśvara*, and *sadāśiva*, are known as *mantra*, *mantreśvara*, and *mantra maheśvara*, respectively. Here, Swamiji is indicating that this particular rise of *prāṇa kuṇḍalinī* will end in *mantra pramātṛ bhāva* (the state of *śuddhavidyā*), not *mantra maheśvara bhāva* (the state of *sadāśiva*). See Appendix for an explanation of the seven *pramātṛs* (perceivers). See also *Kashmir Shaivism–The Secret Supreme*, 8.53.

in each and every *cakra*. Here, [in this verse], he experiences [the divine nature] in the end.

JAGDISH: In the twenty-ninth.

SWAMIJI: Twenty-ninth, yes.

JOHN: But the question is, is this *śāktopāya* sentenced to *śāmbhavopāya*, or is this *āṇavopāya*?

SWAMIJI: No, this is *āṇavopāya* sentenced to *śāmbhavopāya.*

JOHN: *Āṇavopāya* sentenced to *śāmbhavopāya.*

SWAMIJI: *Śāmbhavopāya.* Because *mahodayaḥ*[99] will rest in *śāmbhavopāya*, and this succession will be of *āṇavopāya.*

99 The great (*mahā*) rise (*udaya*) of the supreme bliss of Lord Śiva.

Dhāraṇā 7

क्रमद्वादशकं सम्यग्
द्वादशाक्षरभेदितम् ।
स्थूलसूक्ष्मपरस्थित्या
मुक्त्वा मुक्त्वान्ततः शिवः ॥३०॥

kramadvādaśakaṁ samyag
dvādaśākṣarabheditam /
sthūlasūkṣmaparasthityā
muktvā muktvāntataḥ śivaḥ / / 30 / /

Now, there is a successive way of *āṇavopāya*. This is a successive way of *āṇavopāya*, complete *āṇavopāya*–successive way of *āṇavopāya*.

There are twelve parts of these successive states (*krama dvādaśakam*), that is, twelve-fold *kramas*, twelve-fold successive processes. And that twelve-fold is (in the commentary you will see[100]): one is *janmāgra*, *mūla*, *kanda*, *nābhi*, *hṛt*, *kaṇṭha*, *tālu*, *bhrūmadhya*, *lalāṭa*, *brahmarandhra*, *śakti*, *vyāpinī*. These are the twelve-fold successive points.

When one rises from *janmāgra* (*janmāgra* means *meḍhra kanda*; *meḍhra kanda* is the opening of the rectum), *mūla*[*dhāra*] is higher than that, *kanda* is higher than that (where one gets conceived, in that womb[101]), higher than that is the navel, higher than that is the heart, higher than that is the throat, then the palate, then *bhrūmadhya*, then *lalāṭa* (the forehead), then *brahmarandhra*, then *śakti* (after *brahmarandhra*, there is *śakti*; *śakti* means that force which breaks that *randhra*[102] and penetrates that *randhra* to move outside [in] the universal sphere of ether), then, when one

100 Śivopādhyāya's commentary.

101 "These are all three together, [*janmāgra*, *mūlādhāra*, and *kanda*], one over another." *Vijñāna Bhairava*, additional audio (USF archives).

102 Opening.

enters in that universal ether, there is *vyāpinī*[103]. These are the twelve-fold successive *kramas*, successive stages. And [in] these successive stages, you must put in these [the corresponding vowel from the] twelve vowels (*dvādaśa ākṣara bheditam*), the twelve *svaras*, *śānta varjam*[104], but not *ṛ*, *ṛī*, *ḷ*, and *ḷī* (without *ṛ*, *ṛī*, *ḷ*, *lī*, only the twelve vowels for these twelve states[105]), *sthūla sūkṣma para sthityā*, by processing it for functioning [with] the grossness of [inferior] awareness, [with] medium awareness, and [with] supreme awareness (subtle awareness). The grossness of awareness is *dhyāna*, medium awareness is *spanda mānatā*, and subtle awareness is *jyoti rūpatā–dhyāna*, *spandana*, and *jyoti rūpatvaṁ*. *Muktvā muktvā*, after leaving the *dhyāna* of these twelve, you go in its movement[106], and after establishing one's consciousness in that movement, you leave that movement and establish yourself in the flame[107] of these twelve successive states, then one becomes one with Śiva. So, this is the ascending process.

JOHN: What does it mean to insert these letters in these vowels? What does it mean to insert these *svaras* in these vowels–these twelve *svaras*?

SWAMIJI: You see, these states must be converted into vowels first.

JOHN: How do you convert them?

SWAMIJI: Because these states are gross. For instance, there is the rectum. Don't go to the grossness of this state, go to the letter '*a*'. This is '*a*', [but] '*a*' has no meaning there, so it will come into that subtleness. When you enter in those subtle twelve movements of these twelve states, you have to put *dhyāna* first, and then *spanda mānatā*, and [then] *jyoti rūpatā*. It is a kind of *laya cintanā* (to put one in another, one in another, one in another[108]), and in the end, *antataḥ śivaḥ*, in the end only Śiva will be revealed.

---

103 Pervasion.

104. The *śānta bijas* (*ṛ*, *ṛī*, *ḷ*, and *ḷī*) are to be *varjam* (excluded).

105 The twelve *svaras* (vowels) are: *a-ā-i-ī-u-ū-e-ai-o-au-ṁ-ḥ*.

106 *Spanda mānatā*.

107 *Jyoti rūpatā*.

108 *Laya cintanā* means to absorb grosser awareness into subtler awareness.

So it is a successive way of *āṇavopāya*. It is an inferior way of *āṇavopāya*, because it is a successive way. You have to see *janmāgra* and recite its *mantra* '*a*', you have to see *mūla*[*dhāra*] and recite '*ā*', [and so forth], and, in the end, you will go to '*aḥ*' (*visarga*), [which corresponds with] *vyāpinī*. And then you have to take *dhyāna* of these, then *spanda mānatā,* and then *jyoti rūpatā*.

JOHN: How do you function these three?

SWAMIJI: *Dhyāna* means, first with breath. You see, when there is breath, it is gross.

JOHN: In and out, in and out.

SWAMIJI: Then it is like that. [Then] this movement of the in-going breath and the out-coming breath takes the form of *spanda mānatā.*[109] You can understand it when you practice it. You can't understand it without practice.

JOHN: But what is the flash in *jyoti*, this burning in the fire of . . . ?

SWAMIJI: That is fire. That is realization. After that, realization takes place.

DEVOTEE: When he experiences *spanda mānatā*, is it already an automatic process?

SWAMIJI: It is automatic.

DEVOTEE: This is *citta pralaya*[110], in the moving of the breath?

SWAMIJI: It is about [to be] *citta pralaya*. It is not *citta pralaya* yet. *Citta pralaya* will come in *jyoti rūpatā*.

JOHN: Burned in that.

SWAMIJI: When he enters in *jyoti rūpatā*, then [it is *citta pralaya*].

DEVOTEE: But in *citta pralaya*, the two breaths are drawn down.

SWAMIJI: They have not drawn, they are moving, [but] only in one point.

DEVOTEE: They are waiting.

---

109 Vibration.

110 Lit., the dissolution (*pralaya*) of thought (*citta*). For a further clarification of *citta pralaya*, see *Kashmir Shaivism–The Secret Supreme*, 3.26-27.

SWAMIJI: They are waiting.

DEVOTEE: This is like *nirodhikā*.

SWAMIJI: *Nirodhikā*[111]. They are moving without any span of space. It is only due to concentration, the power of concentration. When there is not the power of concentration, then the breath will go up to the thirty-sixth finger space. There is one-pointedness developed by and by, this is the power of one-pointedness that the [span of] breath becomes shorter and shorter, and shorter and shorter–the in-going breath and the out-coming breath. It goes shorter and shorter, and in the end, it moves only on one point. That is *spanda mānatā*. And afterwards, what happens? *Jyoti rūpatām*, then shines forth that reality of Lord Śiva.

DEVOTEE: Is that the rise of *kuṇḍalinī*, that *jyoti rūpatā*?

SWAMIJI: This is not *kuṇḍalinī*. This is not *kuṇḍalinī*, *kuṇḍalinī* is finished. *Kuṇḍalinī* is finished in the twenty-ninth *śloka*. This is the thirtieth *śloka*. It is another way.

DEVOTEE: You mean, there can be the attainment of realization without the movement of *cit*?

SWAMIJI: It is not necessary that always there must be *kuṇḍalinī*, the rise of *kuṇḍalinī*. Without the rise of *kuṇḍalinī*, realization takes place.

---

111 *Nirodhikā* is the complete establishment of breath-lessness. See verse 4.

Dhāraṇā 8

तयापूर्याशु मूर्धान्तं
भङ्क्त्वा भ्रूक्षेपसेतुना ।
निर्विकल्पं मनः कृत्वा
सर्वोर्ध्वे सर्वगोद्गमः ॥३१॥

tayāpūryāśu mūrdhāntaṁ
bhaṅktvā bhrūkṣepasetunā /
nirvikalpaṁ manaḥ kṛtvā
sarvordhve sarvagodgamaḥ / / 31 / /

This is the way of *āṇavopāya* without succession. The former was the way of *āṇavopāya* with succession. This is the way of *āṇavopāya* without succession.

Tayā[112], by that energy of *prāṇa* (breath), you must fill your body up to *brahmarandhra*, and then, after having suspended the *prāṇa śakti*, after having suspended the moving of breath by *bhrūkṣepa setunā*, . . .

[In this practice], you have to concentrate on the center of the eyebrows. That [concentration] is there [like] a "mound" or a "bank"[113]. *Bhrūkṣepa* means *bhrū bhedana*, just to put one-pointedness between the two eyebrows.

. . . when you put that one-pointedness between the two eyebrows, while you are moving your breath inside and outside–then what happens?–by putting your one-pointedness between these two eyebrows, *mūrdhāntam āpūrya*, you fill your whole body up to the *brahmarandhra* with this breath, and *bhaṅktvā*, after doing that, the movement of *prāṇa śakti* is suspended, suspended for the time being, and after it is suspended (the *prāṇa śakti*, when it is suspended), then you must see that your mind becomes absolutely un-

---

112 "*Tayā* refers to *khecarī*, which is the subtlest state of breath." *Vijñāna Bhairava*, additional audio (USF archives). For more on *khecarī*, see commentary on verse 77.

113 *Setu* literally means, a binding, who or what binds or fetters; a bridge, a mound, or a bank (e.g., the bank of a river).

minded (*nirvikalpaṁ manaḥ kṛtvā*). Then *sarva urdhve*, in that supreme state of Lord Śiva, *sarvagodgamaḥ* (*sarvagodgamaḥ* means, all-pervadingness shines), he becomes all-pervading in that supreme [state].

This is the way of *āṇavopāya* because you have to practice with breath.[114] As long as there is a breathing exercise, it is *āṇavopāya*. It can't be *śāktopāya*, it can't be *śāmbhavopāya*.[115] It is not *kumbhakā*, it is one-pointedness. You have to stop your breath by one-pointedness. You have not to stop the breath by holding it. If you hold your breath, that is *kumbhakā*. If your breath is held automatically by one-pointedness, it is this practice.

GANJOO: By concentration.

SWAMIJI: Concentration not; only concentration won't do.

JOHN: Strength of awareness.

SWAMIJI: Strength of one-pointedness. [To John]: How is . . . ?

JOHN: . . . *manas*[116] made *nirvikalpa*?

SWAMIJI: By one-pointedness (*bhrūkṣepa setunā*). He has put that *bhrūkṣepa setunā*, you have to keep your mind attentive between these two eyebrows, just [by] one-pointedness. Don't let it move even for half a second (that is *bhrūkṣepa setunā*). It becomes *setu*, it stops, it rejects, the breath. It rejects breath, it doesn't allow breath to move onwards. It is why He has called it "*setu*". *Bhrūkṣepa*[117] is *setu*, [like] a mound.

GANJOO: Bund.

SWAMIJI: Bund.[118]

---

114 Breathing here is normal, not extra hard.

115 "When there is only voidness, concentration on voidness, that will be *śāktopāya*, always; when there is concentration on breath, it will be *āṇavopāya*; and when there is only awareness of one-pointedness, that is *śāmbhavopāya*." *Vijñāna Bhairava*, additional audio (USF archives).

116 The mind.

117 One-pointedness between the two eyebrows.

118 An embankment or causeway.

Dhāraṇā 9

शिखिपक्षैश्चित्ररूपै-
मण्डलैः शून्यपञ्चकम् ।
ध्यायतोऽनुत्तरे शून्ये
प्रवेशो हृदये भवेत् ॥ ३२ ॥

śikhipakṣaiścitrarūpair-
maṇḍalaiḥ śūnyapañcakam /
dhyāyato'nuttare śūnye[119]
praveśo hṛdaye bhavet / / 32 / /

Śikhipakṣair (*śikhipakṣair* means, the wings or feathers of a peacock), just like the wings or feathers of a peacock (you see, the feathers of a peacock are filled with various colors, multicolored; *citra rūpair* means, with various formations), in the same way, *maṇḍalaiḥ* (*maṇḍalaiḥ*[120] means, the five-fold organs of the senses[121]), the five organs of the senses are just like the wings or feathers of a peacock.

JOHN: *Jñānendriyas*?

SWAMIJI: *Jñānendriyas.*[122]

What you have to do with these five-fold organs when the five-fold organs are functioning on their own objects? What you have to do is to think that that object that is perceived by the eye, or the object perceived by the ear, or the object perceived by the nose, or the skin, touch, or the tongue, all

119 Swamiji said to place a comma after "*dhyāyataḥ*".

120 Lit., with the circles.

121 On another occasion, Swamiji also interpreted the five voids (*śūnya pañcakam*) as the voids between the five states of consciousness: wakefulness, dreaming, deep sleep, *turya*, and *turyātīta*: "These five voids represent just the state of God consciousness, because the state of God consciousness is the life of all these five states. When you concentrate on one [void] wholeheartedly, it will make a circle (*maṇḍala*) and take you to the same goal." *Vijñāna Bhairava*, additional audio (USF archives).

122 The organs of knowledge.

these objects, you must know that it is only *śūnya*, only void. It has nothing in it. It is only a void. *Śūnya pañcakam dhyāyataḥ*, you must concentrate on all these just like *śūnya*, five-fold voids.[123] *Anuttare śūnye hṛdaye praveśo bhavet*–then what happens?–you enter in that supreme heart which is full of voidness, and that supreme heart is Lord Śiva Himself. *Śikhipakṣaiścitrarūpair maṇḍalaiḥ śūnyapañcakam dhyāyataḥ*. [The *yogi*] *anuttare śūnye hṛdaye praveśaḥ bhavet*, he enters in that *anuttara*[124], the supreme heart, *śūnya*.

It is absolutely pure *śāktopāya*.

DEVOTEE: How can he see with the ear?

SWAMIJI: You have not to see with the ear, you have to hear with the ear. You have to see with the eyes, you have to hear with the ears, smell with the nose, taste with the tongue, touch with the skin. You must concentrate simultaneously on [the void while experiencing each of] these five, that it is nothing, it is only a void and nothing else. Then, you have to forcibly concentrate that these are nothing, [that] these objects are nothing–"What I see is nothing, what appears to me is nothing, what I hear is nothing, what I touch and what I get [as] the sensation of smell, it is nothing, it is only *śūnya*." It is only seeing as energy–just seeing only, hearing only, *bas*, not to analyze that. When I see Denise, *bas*, I see Denise, I don't see the formation of Denise. I see only, it is

---

123 "The theory of *śūnya pañcakam* is to understand that, 'The whole universe is my Self'. The essence of *śūnya pañcakam*, it is not that, 'I am in the body', 'I am down below my body', 'I am on the top of my body', 'I am in the center of my body', 'I am in the right side of my body', 'I am on the left side of my body'. This is not *śūnya pañcakam*. [*Śūnya pañcakam* means], the totality of universality, to feel the Universal *svarūpa* everywhere. That is Universal." *Vijñāna Bhairava*, additional audio (USF archives).

124 Though it appears only once in the verses of the *Vijñāna Bhairava*, the word "*anuttara*" is a very important term in Kashmir Shaivism. In this verse, *anuttara* means, the supreme heart of Lord Śiva. In other texts of Trika, *anuttara* is used variously to signify Parabhairava, *svātantrya*, the supreme Self, and the unparalleled state of consciousness represented by the first Sanskrit letter, '*a*'. See also *Shiva Sutras–The Supreme Awakening*, Swami Lakshmanjoo, ed. John Hughes (Universal Shaiva Fellowship, Los Angeles, 2002), 95-96.

only seeing. There it ends. And when I feel smelling, there ends that. At the time of that sensation of smelling, you must end it there. You must not go further, You must not go beyond that so that you will [avoid being] entangled in the world of the senses.

JOHN: This is like blades of grass, seeing the blades of grass, but you don't see singularly, you just . . . ?

SWAMIJI: Just like that, yes. Simultaneously you have to concentrate.

GANJOO: All the five.

SWAMIJI: All the five. Then you will enter in that supreme state of the heart, the supreme state of Lord Śiva.

Dhāraṇā 10

ईदृशेन क्रमेणैव
यत्र कुत्रापि चिन्तना ।
शून्ये कुड्ये परे पात्रे
स्वयं लीना वरप्रदा ॥ ३३ ॥

īdṛśena krameṇaiva
yatra kutrāpi cintanā /
śūnye kuḍye pare pātre
svayaṁ līnā varapradā / / 33 / /

By adopting this means (*īdṛśena krameṇa*), *yatra kutrāpi cintanā*, wherever you will put this one-pointed thought of awareness–you may put it on voidness, you may put it on some wall, you may put it on some consciousness of your favorite disciple[125]–*svayaṁ līnā varapradā*, this giver of boons, that energy of Lord Śiva, is revealed there, there and then. It is revealed in that voidness, which has been practiced. It is revealed in that wall, which has been practiced. It is revealed in that heart of the disciple, and that disciple will be also illuminated at once.

Dhyāna[126] is more gross than *cintanā*[127].

saṁketānādare śabda-
niṣṭhamāmarśanaṁ paṭhiḥ /
tadādare tadarthastu
cinteti paricarcyatām / /[128]

125 "*Pare pātre*" means, any disciple. He may be pure or impure. Although Śivopādhyāya interpreted *pare* as *nirmala* (pure), Swamiji said that this interpretation is not correct.

126 Meditation.

127 One-pointed reflection.

128 *Tantrāloka* of Abhinavagupta, 4.103.

> When *saṁketa*[129] is put aside and you concentrate on that *śabda*[130] (that is *dhyāna* and *pāṭha*[131]), *tadādare tadarthastu cinteti paricarcyatām*, just to maintain that, you have to do that concentration of that one-pointedness–that is *cintanā*. So *cintanā* is more subtle than *dhyāna*.[132]

Śūnye kuḍye pare pātre, [the *yogi*] may concentrate this one-pointedness on any void–voidness of the sky, or *kuḍye* (on some wall), or *pare pātre* (on some heart of a disciple)–[then] this *varapradā*, this giver of boons (*varapradā*; *pradā* means, giver of *vara*, boons), the boon-giver, the energy of Lord Śiva, *svayaṁ līnā*[133], *sphurati*, It is revealed.

This is also *śāktopāya* because you have to concentrate on something. When you have to concentrate on something (it may not be with *mantra* or with breath or with anything), when you have to concentrate on something, it becomes *śākta*. It will be automatically *śāktopāya*. It can't be *śāmbhavopāya*.

---

129 Conventional meaning or linguistic indication.

130 Here *śabda* is used in the sense of a sound, word or *mantra* used for meditation.

131 Recitation.

132 "One-pointedness is held by both *dhyāna* and *cintanā*, but *dhyāna* is gross while *cintanā* is subtler." *Vijñāna Bhairava*, additional audio (USF archives).

133 Having absorbed (*līna*) oneself (*svayam*) in the concentration of one-pointedness.

Dhāraṇā 11

कपालान्तर्मनो न्यस्य
तिष्ठन्मीलितलोचनः ।
क्रमेण मनसो दार्ढ्यात्-
लक्षयेल्लक्ष्यमुत्तमम् ॥ ३४॥

kapālāntarmano nyasya
tiṣṭhanmīlitalocanaḥ /
krameṇa manaso dārḍhyāt
lakṣayellakṣyamuttamam / / 34 / /

What you have to do next in this next practice?

Tiṣṭhan mīlita locanaḥ, you have to sit in some posture with your eyes closed (*tiṣṭhan mīlita locanaḥ*, sit in some posture and keep your eyes absolutely closed).

Kapālāntar mano nyasya, put your mind, establish your mind, fix your mind, in the skull of your *brahmarandhra*, in this skull. *Kapāla antar*, in the skull, in the vacuum of the skull, you must put your mind.

And what you have to do? In that skull–it is not just only to put your mind inside that skull–you have to see that there is fire shining all around–in your *kapāla*, in that skull. In the vacuum of the skull, there is fire going on, shining, flaming, flames of fire.

This way, when you think *krameṇa* (successively), *manso dārḍhyāt*, when the mind becomes fully established in this way of process, *lakṣayet*, he observes *uttamam lakṣayam*, the supreme aimed consciousness of Lord Śiva.

Lakṣyam means, aimed, supreme aimed, aimed consciousness. That is *lakṣyam. Lakṣyam* is the goal that is aimed at. That supreme aimed thing is being revealed.

This *upāya* is *śāktopāya*, complete *śāktopāya*.

JOHN: What is this flame in the head, this fire, this illumination in one's body? Is that imagination?

SWAMIJI: It's not imagination.

JOHN: Is that *vikalpa*[134]?

SWAMIJI: No, it is not imagination. That is fire. There is the fire of *cit* (consciousness). There is the fire of *cit* (consciousness) that is produced in *ūrdhva kuṇḍalinī*, *dhāman* of *cit kuṇḍalinī*.[135] *Lakṣayet lakṣyam uttamam* is That! The supreme target of Lord Śiva is revealed.

134 Thought.

135 "When *cit kuṇḍalinī* rises from *mūlādhāra cakra* and becomes firmly established in *brahmarandhra*, it is nominated as *ūrdhva kuṇḍalinī*. This is the abode (*dhāman*) of *cit kuṇḍalinī*. It is here that the experience of *krama mudrā* takes place." *Vijñāna Bhairava*, additional audio (USF archives). See Appendix for an explanation of *kuṇḍalinī* and *krama mudrā*.

Dhāraṇā 12

मधयनाडी मध्यसंस्था
बिससूत्राभरूपया ।
ध्यातान्तर्व्योमया देव्या
तया देवः प्रकाशते ॥३५॥

madhyanāḍī madhyasaṁsthā
bisasūtrābharūpayā /
dhyātāntarvyomayā devyā
tayā devaḥ prakāśate / / 35 / /

Madhya nāḍī (*madhya nāḍī* means, the central vein), the central vein *suṣumnā*, which is *madhya saṁsthā*, situated in the central path, and this *madhya nāḍī* should be concentrated [upon] just like taking the formation of (*ābha* means "just like") *bisa sūtra* (*bisa sūtra* means "the fiber of a lotus"), just like the fiber of a lotus, so tiny and subtle. Contemplate on that central vein that it is so minute, going from bottom to top, in the form of that fiber of a lotus, lotus fiber. You have to concentrate, not with your mind, *antar vyomayā devyā dhyātā sati*, you have to concentrate by this *madhya nāḍī. Madhya nāḍī* is to be concentrated [upon] by this *madhya nāḍī*.[136]

This is complete *śāmbhavopāya*.

JOHN: To have awareness of this *madhya nāḍī* by this *madhya nāḍī*, what does that mean?

SWAMIJI: When you reach *madhya nāḍī*, your individual body won't reach, your individual consciousness won't reach there. *Madhya nāḍī* will reach there. *Madhya nāḍī* is realized by *madhya nāḍī*, not by any other agency. There is no other agency than *madhya nāḍī*. In *madhya nāḍī*, . . .

JOHN: What is *madhya nāḍi*?

SWAMIJI: That central path.

136 "There is no concentrating point. It is only *madhya nāḍī*, the central vein (*suṣumnā*). *Suṣumnā* is so subtle, it can't be existing in the objective field, it can't remain in the objective field." *Vijñāna Bhairava*, additional audio (USF archives).

JOHN: A state of consciousness?

SWAMIJI: State of consciousness. That state of consciousness is realized by that consciousness of that state. It is not realized by another agency. There is no other agency working there. So this is *śāmbhavopāya*. This can't be *śāktopāya* in *śāmbhavopāya*.

JOHN: What *pramātṛ bhāva*[137] is this?

SWAMIJI: *Parā pramātṛ bhāva*, supreme *parā pramātṛ bhāva*.[138]

Tayā devyaḥ prakāśate, bas, devaḥ, the Lord, is revealed by that *devyā*[139] (*tayā devyā; tayā devyā devaḥ prakāśate*), by *antar vyomayā*.[140] *Devyāḥ dhyātā sati devaḥ prakāśate.*

---

137 Subjective state, viz., the seven perceivers. For more on the seven perceivers, see *Kashmir Shaivism–The Secret Supreme*, Chapter 8.

138 "The beginning of *parā pramātṛ bhāva* state begins from *śuddhavidya* and ends in *sadāśiva*. So, *sadāśiva*, *īśvara*, and *śuddhavidya* are one, in one state. That is the span of *parā pramātṛ bhāva*." *Tantrāloka* 4.169-179, (USF archives).

139 Divine power, i.e., *madhya nāḍi*.

140 Lit., inner (*antar*) space (*vyoma*).

Dhāraṇā 13

Now, it is pure *āṇavopāya*:

करुरुद्धदृगस्त्रेण
भ्रूभेदाद्द्वाररोधनात् ।
दृष्टे बिन्दौ क्रमाल्लीने
तन्मध्ये परमा स्थितिः ॥ ३६ ॥

kararuddhadṛgastreṇa
bhrūbhedāddvārarodhanāt[141] /
dṛṣṭe bindau kramāllīne
tanmadhye paramā sthitiḥ / / *36* / /

Kara ruddha dṛg astreṇa, *ruddha dṛk astreṇa*, by closing all the openings of the head, . . .

I mean, the eyes, the two nostrils, the two ears, and one mouth. You have to close them by your own hand. The thumbs will go in the ear [Swamiji demonstrates].

JEREMY: Forefingers [on the] eyes, second fingers [on the] nostrils, . . .

SWAMIJI: Upper lips and lower lips.

JEREMY: . . . upper lips, lower lips, [with] the last two fingers. Thank you, sir.

SWAMIJI: This way you have to close, but before closing these openings, you have to maintain awareness first of one-pointedness. When you have completed that one-pointedness, then you must close them at once. Because if you close them without maintaining that one-pointedness, you will only get suffocation of breath and you will die.[142] So you have to maintain awareness by continuity of *abhyāsa* (practice).

JOHN: In *āṇavopāya*?

SWAMIJI: In *āṇavopāya*, yes.

How you have to maintain awareness? *Bhrū bhedāt*, by

141 Swamiji corrected "*bhrū bhedām*" to read "*bhrū bhedāt*".

142 The retention of breath must be automatic, viz., *Dhāraṇā* 8.

piercing the center of the eyebrows. "Piercing" means, just contemplating between the two eyebrows. When you contemplate between the two eyebrows, afterwards you close all the openings of your head by your hands. *Dvāra rodhanāt*, by closing all openings (*dvāra* means, these openings; *rodhanāt* means, by closing), and then what you will feel and experience? You will feel *tāraka prakāśa* in front of you–*bindu prakāśa*.[143] *Dṛṣṭe bindau kramāt līne*, and that *bindu*, that *tāraka prakāśa*, will get subsided. In succession, it will get subsided, *tan madhye*, and then you will find yourself in *paramā sthitiḥ*, in the supreme *sthitiḥ*[144] of Lord Śiva. You will enter in *samādhi*.[145]

Kara ruddha dṛg astreṇa. *Kara*, by hands, *ruddha*, closing, *dṛg astreṇa*, by these *dṛk* (*dṛk* means, not only the eyes, *dṛk* means, all the openings)–by doing what process?–*bhrū bhedāt*, by centering, by concentrating, between two eyebrows, *dṛṣṭe bindau kramāt līne*, successively you will find that *tāraka prakāśa* is fading away. And when it has faded away completely, then you will find yourself situated in that state of Paramaśiva.

This is *āṇavopāya*, pure *āṇavopāya*.

143 A star-like (*tāraka*) point (*bindu*) of light (*prakāśa*).

144 Establishment.

145 "This is *nimīlanā samādhi*, not *unmīlanā*." *Vijñāna Bhairava*, additional audio (USF archives). See Appendix for an explanation of *nimīlanā* and *unmīlanā samādhi*.

Dhāraṇā 14

धामान्तः क्षोभसंभूत-
सूक्ष्माग्नितिलकाकृतिम् ।
बिन्दुं शिखान्ते हृदये
लयान्ते ध्यायतो लयः ॥३७॥

dhāmāntaḥ kṣobhasaṁbhūta-
sūkṣmāgnitilakākṛtim /
binduṁ śikhānte hṛdaye
layānte dhyāyato layaḥ / / 37 / /

Dhāmāntaḥ (*dhāma* means, the pupil of the eye by which we see, perceive form), you must agitate it with pressing, like this [Swamiji demonstrates]. When you agitate the pupils of the eyes by pressing them with the fingers, . . .

This is also *āṇavopāya*. It can't be *śāktopāya* because there are so many things to be done.[146]

. . . *dhāmāntaḥ* (*dhāma* means that pupil), *antaḥ*, inside, *kṣobha saṁbhūta*, when you agitate it by pressing–what do you find?–*sūkṣmāgni tilakā kṛtim*, you will find a subtle formation of a flame before you, before your eyes. The subtle formation of a flame takes place before you. *Binduṁ*, and that *bindu*, that one-pointed flame, when you concentrate on that one-pointed flame, which has come out from the agitation of these two pupils of the eyes, . . .

These are called "pupils"?

DEVOTEE: Eyeballs.

SWAMIJI: Eyeballs.

DEVOTEE: Because it is the whole eye, isn't it?

SWAMIJI: Yes.

. . . *śikhānte hṛdaye dhyāyataḥ*, when you concentrate on that flame, when you meditate on that *bindu* of flame in *dvādaśānta* and in the heart . . .

---

146 This is *āṇavopāya* because of *sthāna*, *karaṇa*, and the putting of pressure on the eyeballs.

Śikhānte means, in *dvādaśānta*, *ūrdhva dvādaśānta*.

DEVOTEE: Above the head.

SWAMIJI: Above head.

DEVOTEE: Top of the *śikhā*.[147]

SWAMIJI: Top of the *śikhā*, yes. *Śikhānte* and *hṛdaye* (in the heart here, between the two breasts).

. . . when you concentrate on that *bindu* in these two places[148], *layānte*, and when, in the end, *layānte*, when that concentration is over, or that concentration is perfect, *layaḥ* (*layaḥ* means, absorption in Śiva), you are absorbed in Śiva, in the state of Śiva.

JOHN: Same as *samāveśa*?

SWAMIJI: *Samāveśa*. *Layaḥ* means *samāveśa*.[149]

---

147 The *śikhā* is a lock of hair on the crown of the head. In this verse *śikhānte* refers to the small knot tied at the end (*ante*) of the lock of hair, which is traditionally 12 finger spaces (*ūrdhva dvādaśānta*) above the crown of the head.

148 Swamiji says that one has to concentrate on the heart and on *dvādaśānta* simultaneously, and that this practice has nothing to do with the awareness of breath.

149 *Samāveśa*: absorption, penetration.

Dhāraṇā 15

It is now *śāktopāya*, the thirty-eighth one.

अनाहते पात्रकर्णे-
ऽभग्नशब्दे सरिद्द्रुते ।
शब्दब्रह्मणि निष्णातः
परं ब्रह्माधिगच्छति ॥३८॥

anāhate pātrakarṇe-
'bhagnaśabde sariddrute /
śabdabrahmaṇi niṣṇātaḥ
paraṁ brahmādhigacchati / / 38 / /

That sound which is un-struck is called *anāhata.*

[You must] *pātra karṇe.*[150] *Pātra karṇe* means, [to meditate on the un-struck sound] which is heard in your own ears, the sound which does not come from outward sources, which is heard only in your ears–*pātra karṇe.* That is *pātra karṇe* (*pātraṁ karṇau yasya*).

Or, if you can't meditate on the *anāhata* sound, [then] when any sound is produced without a break (*abhagna śabde*). *Abhagna śabde* means, that sound which has no breakage. The sound of a waterfall, it is without breakage–that is *abhagna śabde.* To that [point], He explains, to make it clear. He says, *sariddrute*, just like the *vega* (the flow) of *sarit* (a stream), which is flowing in great speed, great velocity. That is *sarit drute. Śabda brahmaṇi*, that is *śabda brahma*, that is that sound which is one with Brahman.

And, in that *śabda brahmaṇi*, whoever is *niṣṇātaḥ*, whoever has taken a bath, taken a dip (*niṣṇātaḥ*; *niḥśeṣaṇa snāta, niṣṇātaḥ*), *paraṁ brahmādhi gacchati*, he is sentenced to *paraṁ brahma*, he enters in the state of *paraṁ brahma.*

This is *śāktopāya* because there is no *mantra.* There is nothing of that sort to be done–no *mantra*, no recitation, no breathing exercise. It is only just to concentrate on the

150 Place your hands cup-shape (*pātra*) over your ear (*karṇa*).

continuity of that sound, waterfall, or *anāhata śabda*, [but] not both. *Anāhata* or a waterfall.

For instance, you put [your] fingers on [your] ears, you'll find *anāhata dhvani*[151]. Or, you put your hands just like a ball, cup shape [over your ears], you'll feel that sound, the continuity of that sound. Just contemplate on that sound.[152]

This is *śāktopāya*, pure *śāktopāya*.

151 Unstruck (*anāhata*) sound (*dhvani*).

152 "It is more than '*oṁ*', it is *anāhata*. I have tried my best to explain this sound. You close your ears [with your hands] and see. [Hear] it there. '*Mmmmmm*' it will go. It is not by touch, it is not produced by touch, it is just sound with bliss, it is a blissful sound." Swami Lakshmanjoo, trans., *Bhagavad Gita–In the Light of Kashmir Shaivism* (Universal Shaiva Fellowship, Los Angeles 2013).

Dhāraṇā 16

Now, He will explain another way of process, which is *āṇavopāya* and sentenced to *śāmbhavopāya*. That is the thirty-ninth *śloka*.

प्रणवादिसमुच्चारात्
प्लुतान्ते शून्यभावनात् ।
शून्यया परया शक्त्या
शून्यतामेति भैरवि ॥ ३९ ॥

praṇavādisamuccārāt
plutānte śūnyabhāvanāt /
śūnyayā parayā śaktyā
śūnyatāmeti bhairavi / / 39 / /

Bhairavi, O Pārvatī, *praṇavādi samuccārāt, . . .*

There are three kinds of *praṇavas–Vedic praṇava*, *Śiva praṇava*, and *Māyā praṇava*. *Vedic praṇava* is *'oṁ'*, *Śiva praṇava* is *'hūṁ'*, *Māyā praṇava* is *'hrīṁ'*. *'Hrīṁ'* is called *Māyā praṇava* from our Shaiva point of view, and *'hūṁ'* is called *Śiva praṇava*, and *'oṁ'* is called *Veda praṇava*. Just recite these, any of these. You may recite *'oṁ'*, you may recite *'hūṁ'*, or you may recite *'hrīṁ'* (*Veda praṇava*, *Śiva praṇava*, or *Māyā praṇava*).

. . . *praṇavādi samuccārāt*, You must recite it in this way–*plutānte*[153]. You must not recite just like *'oṁ'*–not like that. *Plutānte*, You must end it in *pluta*: *'Oooooooooooooṁṁṁ'*, like this [Swamiji demonstrates]. In the same way, You must recite *'hūṁ'* and You must recite *'hrīṁ'*. Any of these *mantras* You may recite. When You recite it, in the end, You must concentrate on the voidness of that sound, where this sound merged in the end. The sound is finished afterwards, and there You must concentrate, there You must contemplate.

Śūnya bhāvanāt parayā śūnyayā śaktyā, and, by that supreme awareness of voidness, [the *yogi*] enters in the

153 Prolated or lengthened.

transcendental void state of Śiva. *Śūnyatāmeti bhairavi*, he enters in the transcendental state of Lord Śiva, transcendental void state, voidness.

Praṇavādi samuccārāt plutānte śūnya bhāvanāt. Only there is a touch of *āṇavopāya* in the beginning, just to start with, but in the body of this process, it is all pure *śāktopāya*.[154]

154 This *dhāraṇā* has a touch of *āṇavopāya* at the beginning because a *mantra* is to be recited first.

Dhāraṇā 17

यस्य कस्यापि वर्णस्य
पूर्वान्तावनुभावयेत् ।
शून्यया शून्यभूतोऽसौ
शून्याकारः पुमान्भवेत् ॥४०॥

yasya kasyāpi varṇasya
pūrvāntāvanubhāvayet /
śūnyayā[155]*, śūnyabhūto'sau*
śūnyākāraḥ pumānbhavet / / 40 / /

At the beginning of uttering any *mantra* ('*oṁ*' or '*sauḥ*[156]' or any *mantra*, whatever is found in your thought in Shaivism), at the beginning of utterance of the *mantra*[157], or at the end of uttering this *mantra*, when you are going to recite the *mantra* and when the recitation is over, at these two places, . . .

When you are just [about] to recite–you are not reciting [as

155 Swamiji suggested to add a comma after "*śūnyayā*". This results in the understanding that, *śūnya śaktya anubhāvayet*, that *śakti* is the means. As has already been explained, these processes are all based on Śakti (Bhairavī), these processes are not based on Śiva (Bhairava). As it has been said, *śaivī mukham ihocyate*, *śakti* is the means. This is true even in *śāmbhavopāya*.

156 In Kashmir Shaivism, the seed (*bīja*) *mantra* '*sauḥ*' is the supreme *mantra*. It is above all other *mantra*s including the *mantra*s '*ahaṁ*', '*oṁ*', and '*so'haṁ*'. The entire universe consisting of the thirty-six elements resides in the *mantra* '*sauḥ*'. This supreme *mantra*, which is both universal and transcendent, is the essence of Trika. '*Sauḥ*' is not a *mantra* for recitation. '*Sauḥ*' is perceived in *samādhi*, only in the state of *jagadānanda*. See Appendix for an explanation of *sauḥ*. See also *Self Realization in Kashmir Shaivism*, 3.66-69).

157 "It is not to be recited. It just just to think that you will recite, it is just to hold the energy of reciting the *mantra*." *Vijñāna Bhairava*, additional audio (USF archives).

yet], you have [yet] to recite, you are going to recite–there, at that place, or, [when] the recitation is over, at that place, that is *pūrvāntau–pūrvakāle antakāle ca–purvāntau*, at the beginning and at the end, you must *anubhāvayet*, contemplate on that, that nothingness.

In the beginning of uttering any *mantra*, what is there? Nothing? There is some force only, there is some energy.[158]

And, by maintaining awareness on the void (that is *śūnyayā), śūnyayā*, by maintaining the awareness of voidness, this person who is reciting, who does this process, *asau*, that person becomes *bhavet śūnyākāraḥ*, his *svarūpa*, his formation, becomes the embodiment of voidness, and that is Lord Śiva. That is the state of Lord Śiva. That is *viśvottīrṇā avasthā*.[159]

This is *śāmbhavopāya*.

---

158 This energy is *icchā prasāra*, the initial flowing of *icchā*, the energy of will.

159 The transcendental (*viśvottīrṇā*) state (*avasthā*).

Dhāraṇā 18

तन्त्र्यादिवाद्यशब्देषु
दीर्घेषु क्रमसंस्तितेः ।
अनन्यचेताः प्रत्यन्ते
परव्योमवपुर्भवेत् ॥४१॥

tantryādivādyaśabdeṣu-
dīrgheṣu kramasaṁsthiteḥ /
ananyacetāḥ pratyante
paravyomavapurbhavet / / 41 / /

Take those string instruments, e.g., a *sitar*, or *vina*, or that violin . . .

DENISE: With string.

SWAMIJI: . . . with string (that is also a string instrument). For instance, when you play on that string, this sound should not be stopped. Do you understand? For instance, this is a *sitar*, [and] when I do like this [Swamiji demonstrates], you should not do like this and stop the sound [by putting your hand across the strings]. You should let the sound . . .

JEREMY: Prolong.

SWAMIJI: . . . prolong as long as it can. That is *dīrgheṣu krama saṁsthiteḥ*; *krama saṁsthiteḥ*, in succession, it must be long. This sound must travel on a long pathway.

GEORGE: Continuum.

SWAMIJI: Continuum: "'*Hmmmmmmmmmmmmm*'–like this.

Dīrgheṣu krama saṁsthiteḥ ananyacetāḥ, now, the *sādhaka* –what he has to do?–he has to just put uninterrupted awareness on that sound–when that sound absorbs, his mind also absorbs, along with this sound.

JOHN: The sound disappears, you mean.

SWAMIJI: Disappears. Because it will disappear–that sound.

GEORGE: And his mind disappears also.

SWAMIJI: His mind also disappears, and *para vyoma vapur*, he becomes one with Lord Śiva (*cidākāśa*[160]).

It is *śāmbhava*.

JAGDISH: What is "*pratyante*", sir?

SWAMIJI: *Pratyante*, in the end.

JAGDISH: In the end of that . . .

SWAMIJI: In the end of that fading away of that sound.

JAGDISH: It ends in *śūnya*, in the end.

SWAMIJI: Not *śūnya*. *Paravyoma . . . paravyoma*, supreme [void], supreme God consciousness.

It is *śāmbhavopāya*.[161]

---

160 The ether (*ākāśa*) of consciousness (*cit*).

161 "In these sounds [of stringed instruments], you will find separate sounds, but if you go into the depth of this hearing, you will see that collectively one sound is proceeding from the instrument, one collective sound. This can be heard by anyone, [but] only the man with awareness can rise with the sound. It can be heard by anybody but you have to maintain that awareness. And that collective sound is *dīrgha* (long), without any successive movement. It is continuous, without breakage, although it is *krama saṁsthiteḥ*, successively [sounded], because the player puts that finger successively on those strings. The one who is one-pointed on that one collective sound, after contemplating on that collective sound, *pratyante,* in the end, *para vyoma vapur bhavet*, he becomes one with *cidākāśa*, one with the supreme ether of consciousness. This is *śāktopāya* touching *śāmbhavopāya*. As long as he is seeking that collective sound in those differentiated sounds, that is *śāktopāya*. When he has found that collective sound, he is in *śāmbhavopāya*. [This] *śāmbhavopāya* practice, it is *nimīlanā*. Afterwards, that *krama mudrā* will take place and then he will enter in *unmīlanā samādhi*." *Vijñāna Bhairava*, additional audio (USF archives). See Appendix for an explanation of *krama mudrā* and *nimīlanā* and *unmīlanā samādhi*.

Dhāraṇā 19

Now, next will be *āṇavopāya* rising to *śāmbhavopāya*. Forty-second [verse]:

पिण्डमन्त्रस्य सर्वस्य
स्थूलवर्णक्रमेण तु ।
अर्धेन्दुबिन्दुनादान्तः
शून्योच्चाराद्भवेच्छिवः ॥४२॥

piṇḍamantrasya sarvasya
sthūlavarṇakrameṇa tu /
ardhendubindunādāntaḥ
śūnyoccārādbhavecchivaḥ / / 42 / /

[Swamiji also gives the following alternative reading for the second half of the verse:]

बिन्द्वर्धचन्द्रनादान्तः
शून्योच्चाराद्भवेच्छिवः ॥

bindvardhacandranādāntaḥ
śūnyoccārādbhavecchivaḥ / /

This process is *āṇavopāya* rising to *śāmbhavopāya*. First *āṇavopāya* and [then] he rises to the *śāmbhava* state.

Piṇḍa mantras are those *mantras* where vowels are found only in the end. [Where] the vowel is found only in the end, that is *piṇḍa mantra*, e.g., '*klīṁ*'. '*Sauḥ*' is also a *piṇḍa mantra* because '*sa*'[162] is a consonant and '*auḥ*' is in the end, '*auḥ*' is actually in the end ('*au*' and *visarga* is in the end). That is . . .

GEORGE: Vowel.

SWAMIJI: . . . that is a vowel, where the vowel is in the end.

162 Here, '*s*' is pronounced without an '*a*'.

The vowel must not be in the center or in the beginning.

JAGDISH: Consonant must not come after these?

SWAMIJI: No, the consonant is first. Those are *piṇḍa mantras.*[163] You'll see everywhere *piṇḍa mantras* like this. There must not be a vowel in any case between one consonant and another consonant. For instance, there is "*namaḥ śivāya.*" There is '*n*' (that is a consonant), after '*n*' there is an '*a*'.

JAGDISH: That is vowel.

SWAMIJI: That is a vowel [in between the consonants], so it cannot be a *piṇḍa mantra.*

JAGDISH: And then again a consonant.

SWAMIJI: And then again a consonant. When there are [only] consonants in the beginning and ending in a vowel, that is a *piṇḍa mantra*. This is the difference between a *piṇḍa mantra* and ordinary *mantras*.

By utterance, *śūnya uccārāt*, *piṇḍa mantrasya sarvasya sthūla varṇa krameṇa*, by uttering them from their grossness (first utter them in their gross state), then carry that grossness in its subtle state, and then in [its] subtlest state.

For instance, utter '*auṁ*'-*kāra*. When you utter '*auṁ*', this is also actually a *piṇḍa mantra*, although it is not a *piṇḍa mantra*. '*Auṁ*' is not a *piṇḍa mantra* because it has got vowels also in-[between] consonants, and *piṇḍa mantras* are those *mantras* without vowels [except at the end]: '*h*', '*r*', '*kṣ*', '*m*', '*l*', these are *piṇḍa mantras.*[164] '*Auṁ*' is not a *piṇḍa mantra*, but here, Shaivism has recognized this as a *piṇḍa mantra*. When you recite '*auṁ*', this is *sthūla varṇa krama*: "*a-u-ṁ*", this is the recitation of '*auṁ*'-*kāra* in its grossness. Then *ardhendu bindu nādāntaḥ*, . . .

In place of "*ardhendu bindu nādāntaḥ*", put this reading also, at the same time: "*bindvardha candra nādāntaḥ*". Add this reading also of this *śloka*: "*bindvardha candra nādāntaḥ śūnyoccārād bhavet śivaḥ.*"

163 *Piṇḍa* literally means, compact, dense or solid. In relation to this verse, *piṇḍa mantras* are a collection of consonants with only one vowel in the end.

164 The *Navātma mantra*, "*h-r-kṣ-m-l-v-y-ṇūṁ*" and the *Piṇḍanātha mantra* "*r-kṣ-kh-e-ṁ*" are *piṇḍa mantras* because they both have consonants without vowels in-between but they end in a vowel.

When you recite '*auṁ*', '*auṁ*'-*kāra*, you recite '*auṁ*'-*kāra* in its grossness, and that grossness ends in '*ma*'-*kāra* ("*a-u-ma*"). That grossness is over. Then comes its subtleness–*bindu ardhacandra*. This is its subtleness–*bindu* and *ardhacandra*. *Bindu* is–I will show you–*bindu* is this and *ardhacandra* is this [Swamiji illustrates]. This is the subtle formation of ['*auṁ*'-*kāra*]. Then up to *nādānta* (*nādānta* means, *nāda*, *śakti*, *vyāpinī*, *samanā*, and *unmanā*, too), that is its most subtle formation.

'*A*'-*kāra*, '*u*'-*kāra*, '*ma*'-*kāra* are the gross formation of '*auṁ*'-*kāra*. *Bindu ardhacandra* is the subtle formation of '*auṁ*'-*kāra*. *Nirodhinī*, *nāda*, *nādānta*, *śakti*, *vyāpinī*, *samanā*, and *unmanā* are the subtlest formation of '*auṁ*'-*kāra*.[165]

And, when you recite '*auṁ*'-*kāra*, and while reciting '*auṁ*'-*kāra*, you enter in the *unmanā* state (the *unmanā* state is that state of '*auṁ*'-*kāra* where the mind is over, the functioning of the mind stops altogether–that is *unmanā*), when you reach [*unmanā*], reciting this '*auṁ*'-*kāra,* if you reach to the topmost point of *unmanā*, . . .*

DEVOTEE: Simply, this is just *śāmbhavopāya*?

SWAMIJI: It is *āṇavopāya* rising to *śāmbhavopāya*. Because first he has to recite '*auṁ*'-*kāra*, and after recitation of '*auṁ*'-*kāra*, he has to rise more and more and more and more to its subtle formation, and from that subtle formation, he has to rise to its most subtle formation.[166]

---

165 "First, you have to recite [the *piṇḍa mantra*]. It is *sthūla varṇa krameṇa tu*, this is the flux of gross words in *vaikarī*. Then *ardhendu, bindu, nādāntaḥ*, up to *bindu* it will go to *madhyāma*. *Nādānta*, it will go to *pāśyanti*. And then *śūnya*, it will go to *parā*. That is how we have to recite it. It is not the recitation of *mantras* to be recited for centuries and centuries and nothing will happen." *Vijñāna Bhairava*, additional audio (USF archives). See also *Kashmir Shaivism–The Secret Supreme*, 6.41-46.

166 After producing these four sounds [*a-u-m* and *bindu*] there are other sounds which are not spoken, which are not uttered. After *oṁ* you have to go in *ardhacandra*, then you have to get entry in *nirodhikā,* then *nāda,* then *nādānta,* then *śakti,* then *vyāpinī,* then *samanā* and then *unmanā*. Where *unmanā* is situated, there you find the actual position of God consciousness. So there are twelve

*. . . and by *śūnyoccārāt*, by the utterance of voidness, or by the trance of voidness, . . .*

"Utterance" means, trance. You have not to utter this voidness. Voidness is to be felt. That is, the feeling of voidness is "to utter" voidness. You have not to utter voidness, you can't utter voidness. You can utter words (letters you can utter), but you can't utter voidness. You have to feel voidness. That is *śūnya uccāra*, to "utter *śūnya*". So, *uccāra*[167] is here a feeling, not an uttering.[168]

. . . bhavet-śivaḥ, he becomes one with Śiva.

---

letters in the cycle of the reciting of *prāṇava*." *Parātriśikā Vivaraṇa*, (USF archive).

167 Swamiji explained that *uccāra* here is equated directly with *samāveśa* (the trance of one's own nature), but not in its highest form as found in the *Parātriṁśikā*, because here the aspirant is treading on a path, the path of *śāmbhavopāya*. That *uccāra* explained in the *Parātriṁśikā* is not a path. Swamiji says, "*Śūnyoccārat*, by the utterance of *unmanā*, by the feeling of *unmanā*, you enter in the state of Lord Śiva, you become one with Lord Śiva, and when you become one with Lord Śiva, that is the real *uccāra* found in *Parātriṁśikā*." *Vijñāna Bhairava*, additional audio (USF archives).

168 *Uccāra* is held by feeling that *śūnya*, voidness. However, this feeling is not of the senses, it is felt internally. That is called *ṛtaṁbharā prajñā*. It is the feeling of *prajñā* (wisdom), it is not the feeling of the senses. This *ṛtaṁbharā prajñā* is not my word of Shaivism, it is the word of Patañjali. He says there in his *Yoga darśana* that this *prajñā* is full of actuality, full of truth, filled with *ṛt* (*satyam*)–*ṛtaṁbharā tatra prajñā*. (Paraphrase taken from *Vijñāna Bhairava*, additional audio, USF archives). See *Yoga Sūtras* of Patañjali, 1.48.

Dhāraṇā 20

Now, next will come *āṇavopāya* sentenced to *śāmbhavopāya*. This is another process.

निजदेहे सर्वदिक्कं
युगपद्भावयेद्वियत् ।
निर्विकल्पमनास्तस्य
वियत्सर्वं प्रवर्तते ॥ ४३ ॥

nijadehe sarvadikkaṁ
yugapadbhāvayedviyat /
nirvikalpamanāstasya,
viyatsarvaṁ pravartate / / 43 / /

Just sit in some posture, just like this [Swamiji demonstrates]. Sit in some posture and close your eyes, and feel that, "From my right side, from the left side, from the front, from the back, there is nothing". It is just to imagine that, "Around my body, there is nothing. It is all voidness–right, left, front, and back."

Nija dehe sarva dikkam, all-round, *yugapat*, you must simultaneously, *bhāvayet*, concentrate on, *viyat*, voidness. *Nirvikalpamana*–how you must concentrate on that voidness?–by remaining *nirvikalpamana*, by remaining deprived of all thoughts, deprived from all impressions in your mind. Don't put any impression or any thought in your mind. Don't let any thought come in your mind and see that from all your sides of your body, there is only a vacuum, nothing. This thought of voidness, in the beginning, you have to maintain this thought of voidness.

DEVOTEE: So this is *āṇavopāya* in the beginning?

SWAMIJI: It is why I told you it is *āṇavopāya* sentenced to *śāmbhavopāya*.

DEVOTEE: What about the body?

SWAMIJI: Because it is *āṇavopāya*, in the beginning it is *āṇavopāya*. You have to feel that you have got a body, and afterwards, you have to feel that you have got, . . .

DEVOTEE: No body.

SWAMIJI: No.

. . . you have got sides of your body (right, left, front and back, bottom and top). So it is *āṇavopāya*. Up to that point, it is *āṇavopāya*. This is the boundary of *āṇavopāya*, first, in the beginning. And then, by maintaining that thought-lessness, *nirvikalpamana*, afterwards, contemplating on that voidness, that voidness dissolves all that grossness everywhere, all around. His body is over, his body is finished, sides are finished, only voidness remains–*viyat sarvaṁ pravartate.* To him, everything is a vacuum, only a vacuum. And whatever is a vacuum, that is Lord Śiva. Nothingness is Lord Śiva, because Lord Śiva is not this thing, not this thing. What is Lord Śiva? No-thing. No-thing is something, something which is not thinkable, [not] expressible, which is not felt, which can't be felt, which can't be imagined, which can't be known, which can't be sought. That is "nothing".[169] So, it is *āṇavopāya* sentenced to *śāmbhavopāya*.

169 This "nothing" is *mahā-gūhyam* or *śūnyātiśūnya*, that void which is perceived in the end by holding *śūnya*. (Paraphrase taken from *Vijñāna Bhairava*, additional audio, USF archives)

Dhāraṇā 21

Another process:

पृष्ठशून्यं मूलशून्यं
युगपद्भावयेच्च यः ।
शरीरनिरपेक्षिण्या
शक्त्या शून्यमना भवेत् ॥४४॥

pṛṣṭhaśūnyaṁ mūlaśūnyaṁ
yugapadbhāvayecca yaḥ /
śarīranirapekṣiṇyā
śaktyā śūnyamanā bhavet / / 44 / /[170]

This is *śāmbhavopāya* with the slightest touches of *āṇavopāya.*

Pṛṣṭha śūnyaṁ mūla śūnyaṁ, now you have to imagine first that, "Above me there is voidness, below me there is voidness (below my body)", and afterwards just try to find out your body. This is another process. But when you are trying to find out your body, where your body is existing, there is no body, the body is missing. When the body is missing, then this *dhāraṇā*, this process, will be completed. The body must be missing. You must feel that your body is missing afterwards.

This is just the intensity of maintaining awareness on voidness. When you maintain awareness on voidness intensively above and below, your body will be missing. Just try, just try for half an hour and you will see your body is missing, because, when there is no support for your body, [when] there is a vacuum, where your body will remain? And above, there is a vacuum, there is voidness, so your body will be missing. You must be missing. If it is not missing, then this process is not complete.

---

170 Swamiji corrected the original text which reads: "*pṛṣṭhaśūnyaṁ mūlaśūnyaṁ hṛcchūnyaṁbhāvayetsthiram, yugapan-nirvikalpatvānnirvikalpodayastataḥ*" (*KSTS* vol. 8, p40, v45).

So this is *śāmbhavopāya*. This is the process of *śāmbhavopāya* with the slightest touches of *āṇavopāya*.[171]

And you have to concentrate on these two [voids], top and bottom, simultaneously (*yugapad bhāvayet ca yaḥ*), *śarīra nirapekṣiṇyā śaktyā*, by that energy, which energy is forcing your body to get missed. He is missing; when you try to find out somebody, he is missing. So your body is missing like that (that is "*śarīra nirapekṣiṇyā śaktyā*"). Then he enters in that voidness[172] of Lord Śiva.[173]

---

171 "It is *āṇavopāya* at first because you must meditate on the two voids defined by your body." *Vijñāna Bhairava*, additional audio (USF archives).

172 *Vikalpa śūnya.*

173 "Now it is just a *dhāraṇā* for that voidness. You have to think that your body is nothing, behind this body is nothing, in front of the body is nothing, on the right side of the body is nothing, on the left side of the body is nothing, on the bottom side of the body is nothing, and on the top side of the body is nothing. That is what He says. It is just like you have to imagine that there is nothing outside this body, and this body, inside it, there is nothing–*pṛṣṭha śūnyaṁ mūlaśūnyaṁ*. *Yugapad bhāvayet ca yaḥ*, you have to concentrate on that voidness simultaneously from all sides–right, left, front, back, up, and below. And then *śarīra nirapekṣiṇyāśaktyā*, then you have to put that kind of energy in your mind that this body must also get diluted in that voidness. There will be nothing left. *Śūnya manā bhavet*, he will enter in that great voidness (that is Lord Śiva)." *Vijñāna Bhairava*, additional audio (USF archives).

Dhāraṇā 22

पृष्ठशून्यं मूलशून्यं
हृच्छून्यं भावयेत्स्थिरम् ।
युगपन्निर्विकल्पत्वा-
न्निर्विकल्पोदयस्ततः ॥४५॥

pṛṣṭhaśūnyaṁ mūlaśūnyaṁ
hṛcchūnyaṁ bhāvayetsthiram /
yugapannirvikalpatvān-
nirvikalpodayastataḥ // *45* //

Simultaneously (*yugapat*, simultaneously), one should *bhāvayet*, one should imagine with firmness (*sthiram bhāvayet*), simultaneously one should imagine that on the upper side of [their] body, where subjective consciousness is existing, it is a void, [and] *mūla śūnyaṁ*, on the lower side of the body, where the objective field is concerned, there also you should imagine a voidness. On the upper side of your body, where subjective consciousness is prevailing, and on the lower side of your body, where the objective field is existing, and, in the midst of the heart, where the cognitive state is existing, you must imagine that it is all a void. On the upper side, in subjective consciousness, there is nothing; in objective consciousness, there is nothing; and, in the center of the cognitive state, in the heart, there is nothing. And this you should imagine simultaneously, all-round in your body. Then the state of thought-lessness is revealed (*nirvikalpa udayas tataḥ*). *Tataḥ*, then, *nirvikalpa udayaḥ*, the state of thought-lessness is revealed.

This is *śāktopāya*.

Dhāraṇā 23

तनूदेशे शून्यतैव
क्षणमात्रं विभावयेत् ।
निर्विकल्पं निर्विकल्पो
निर्विकल्पस्वरूपभाक् ॥४६॥

tanūdeśe śūnyataiva
kṣaṇamātraṁ vibhāvayet /
nirvikalpaṁ nirvikalpo
nirvikalpasvarūpabhāk // 46 //

Actually, *samādhi* is where there is no mind, when mind does not work. The functioning of mind is just to think of things, which are not concerned with anything. Things which are not concerned with anything, it is mind. This is the actual formation of the mind. The formation of mind is–you don't need it–e.g., "This is paper", "This is [a pair of spectacles]", etc. You don't need [spectacles] but it comes in your mind. "This is [spectacles]", [but] you have nothing to do with those [spectacles]. "This is paper", you have nothing to do with paper, you have no concern with that paper, but it . . .

DENISE: Comes in your mind.

SWAMIJI: . . . comes in [and you consider that] it is your paper. That is the functioning of the mind. Actually, the mind is nothing. If the mind is one-pointed, it is God.

So, this is what He says: *tanu deśe śūnyataiva kṣaṇa-mātraṁ vibha*, just for one moment, you concentrate on voidness. Because the mind is actually nothing. It thinks without any [real] concern. "This is a book", "This is a pot", "This is a hand", [but] I have nothing to do with the hand, I have not to utilize anything.

DENISE: It collects useless information.

SWAMIJI: Yes, useless impressions. It creates useless impressions which are not connected, which he has nothing to do with. This is the formation of the mind. And when this [mind] takes [its] end, this [mind] is put to an end, . . .

What?

JOHN: This mind.

SWAMIJI: This functioning of this useless [thoughts]. *Śūnyata*, in your body, you should just for one moment concentrate on that voidness. The mind is actually void of everything. The mind is very great, the highest, and this is one with Lord Śiva.

. . . *nirvikalpaṁ nirvikalpo nirvikalpa svarūpa bhāk*, he becomes *nirvikalpa* (thought-less) and he takes the formation of thought-lessness, and he gets entry in the thought-less state. That is Śiva.

This is *śāktopāya* sentenced to *śāmbhavopāya*.[174]

174 "*Tanū deśe*, at the place where your body is seated, just imagine that your seat is nowhere (*kṣaṇamātraṁ vibhāva*). You have to just imagine, "My body is seated nowhere." With your thought-less state, you have to imagine that, although you are seated, just see that, "I am seated nowhere, my body is seated nowhere", and discard all your thoughts in your mind. [Then], the state of thought-lessness rises, the *nirālambana* state of *samādhi* is obtained." *Vijñāna Bhairava*, additional audio (USF archives).

Dhāraṇā 24

सर्वं देहगतं द्रव्यं
वियद्व्याप्तं मृगेक्षणे ।
विभावयेत्ततस्तस्य
भावना सा स्थिरा भवेत् ॥४७॥

sarvaṁ dehagataṁ dravyaṁ
viyadvyāptaṁ mṛgekṣaṇe /
vibhāvayettatastasya
bhāvanā sā sthirā bhavet // 47 //

This is also *śāktopāya*.

Just imagine that *dravyam*, the material, *deha gatam,* that is existing in your body (flesh, bones, and marrow, those are existing in your body), just imagine there is nothing inside.

DENISE: It's hollow?

SWAMIJI: It is hollow there. Then that awareness on the void becomes established. *Tatas tasya bhāvanā sā*, *sā bhāvanā sthirā bhavet*, that awareness, that state of awareness on the void, becomes established (*sthirā bhavet*). It becomes firm and so enters in the *nirvikalpa* state of *samādhi*.

This is *śāktopāya*, pure *śāktopāya*.

Dhāraṇā 25

देहान्तरे त्वग्विभागं
भित्तिभूतं विचिन्तयेत् ।
न किञ्चिदन्तरे तस्य
ध्यायन्नध्येयभाग्भवेत् ॥४८॥

dehāntare tvagvibhāgaṁ-
bhittibhūtaṁ vicintayet /
na kiñcidantare tasya
dhyāyannadhyeyabhāgbhavet // 48 //

Or, consider this way.

This is one *dhāraṇā* in the forty-seventh and forty-eighth [verses]. This is only one technique of process.

Dehāntare tvag vibhāgaṁ bhitti bhūtaṁ vicintayet. You have to imagine that your body is enclosed, supported, by your skin, by the skin, *na kiñcid antare tasya*, and inside there is nothing, it is hollow. You try to concentrate this way. Or, that [previous] way, that all this flesh, bones, and marrow, are nothing but void. Or, concentrate that in your body there is nothing existing. There are only walls, outside walls of skin to make your body, and inside there is nothing existing. [The *yogi*] who is contemplating this way perceives Lord Śivā (*adhyeya bhāk bhavet*; *adhyeya* means the one who is the knower and never the known). He perceives that Lord Śiva.

This is *śāktopāya* sentenced to *śāmbhavopāya*.

Dhāraṇā 26

हृद्याकाशे निलीनाक्षः
पद्मसंपुटमध्यगः ।
अनन्यचेताः सुभगे
परं सौभाग्यमाप्नुयात् ॥ ४९ ॥

hṛdyākāśe nilīnākṣaḥ
padmasaṁpuṭamadhyagaḥ /
ananyacetāḥ subhage
paraṁ saubhāgyamāpnuyāt / / 49 / /

Subhage, O Pārvatī, the one whose thought is focused in the ether of the heart (*hṛdyākāśe nilīnākṣaḥ*, whose thought is focused, centralized, in the ether of the heart, in the voidness of the heart), that heart which is situated between two lotuses therein (up and down; one lotus is facing upwards and the other lotus is facing downwards [and] in-between there is the ether of the heart), and there, [he] whose thought is focused (*akṣaḥ* means "thought"; *akṣaḥ* does not mean only "the eyes"), *nilīnākṣa*, whose thought is melted, focused, without the interruption of thought-fulness, *ananya cetāḥ*, when he becomes one-pointed in this process, he attains the glory of entering in the kingdom of God consciousness; *paraṁ saubhāgyam āpnuyāt*, he attains the glory of entering in the kingdom of God consciousness.

This is *śāktopāya*.

JOHN: What is the point of these lotuses, one up and one down? Is that just a simile or a way of speaking?

SWAMIJI: No, they are existing, these lotuses are existing there. One who perceives that in *samādhi*, he perceives these two lotuses: one in the upper side and the other in the lower side.[175]

---

175 In his translation of this verse in the *Śiva Sūtra Vimarśinī*, Swamiji refers to the two lotuses as representing "this-ness" and "I-ness." See *Shiva Sutras–The Supreme Awakening*, 1.15.53.

Dhāraṇā 27

सर्वतः स्वशरीरस्य
द्वादशान्ते मनो लयात् ।
दृढबुद्धेर्दृढीभूतं-
तत्त्वलक्ष्यं प्रवर्तते ॥५०॥

sarvataḥ svaśarīrasya
dvādaśānte mano layāt /
dṛḍhabuddherdṛiḍhībhūtaṁ-
tattvalakṣyaṁ pravartate / / 50 / /

Sarvataḥ, from all sides, *svaśarīrasya dvādaśānte mano*, [focus your mind on] one *dvādaśānta* in your body. It may be between the two eyebrows, it may be in the heart, it may be the throat-pit–anywhere.[176] Just dissolve your mind in one *dvādaśānta* with strong alertness (that is *dṛḍha buddher*). *Dṛḍha buddher*, to [that *yogi*], *dṛḍhī bhūtaṁ tattva lakṣyaṁ pravartate*, that *tattva lakṣyaṁ* appears, that appearance of the reality of God consciousness appears, which is *dṛḍhī bhūtaṁ*, which does not get subsided at all.

JAGDISH: *Dṛḍha buddhe* is . . .

SWAMIJI: *Dṛḍha buddhe* is *sādhakāsya*, the one who is doing this, the one who is practicing like this.

JAGDISH: Yes, sir.

---

176 "Imagine the vacuum that is perceived by you in-between the two eyebrows. That voidness is found in each and every pore of your body. You have to imagine that for a while, and let your mind melt in that one-pointedness–in each and every point of your body. Actually, those pores in the body are also *dvādaśānta*. *Dvādaśānta* is not only in between the two eyebrows, in the throat pit, and in [the heart]. Everywhere there is *dvādaśānta*! [Take] any point and, *bas*, be just firm-minded, one-pointed. But you should think that this is the formation of the body, [that] *dvādaśānta* is only the formation of the body. If you think that the body is separate from *dvādaśānta*, you are lost!" *Vijñāna Bhairava*, additional audio (USF archives).

SWAMIJI: *Dṛḍhī bhūtaṁ* is the qualification of Śiva–*tattva lakṣyaṁ dṛiḍhī bhūtaṁ*–because the *tattva lakṣyaṁ*, the appearance of the real nature of his God consciousness, appears in such a way that it does not get vanished, it does not get away from his consciousness. It is *dṛḍhī bhūtaṁ*, it is firm, that is firm.

JOHN: That is Lord Śiva?

SWAMIJI: That is Lord Śiva.

JOHN: And *dṛḍha buddher* is the person who has that firm intellect?

SWAMIJI: *Dṛḍha buddher* is [he] who has got a firm strength of awareness (*dṛḍha buddher*). For the *sādhaka*, *dṛḍha buddher sādhakāsya*, *dṛḍhī bhūtaṁ*.

You have to put the mind in *dvādaśānta*, any *dvādaśānta* (it may be between the two eyebrows, it may be the throat pit, the heart, or the navel, whatever it is). *Bas*, there must be one-pointedness just like a flame, the candle flame, without the disturbance of air.

yathā dipo nivātastho neṅgate sopamā smṛtā /[177]

Like that, like that, the position of mind must remain like that. Otherwise, there is no possibility, [the *yogi*] won't get hold of that. And you have to put yourself, your awareness, in that voidness firmly in such a way [that] *dṛḍha buddher*, your intellect must be firm [and] you must not get moved from that [awareness]. It must be just one-pointed, just like that flame without air, unflickering. Just like this.

And then, *dṛḍhī bhūtaṁ tattva lakṣyaṁ*, then *tattva lakṣya*, the appearance of Lord Śiva will also be just like straight; It will not go, It will not move, from [the *yogi's*] consciousness.

This is *śāktopāya*, pure *śāktopāya*.

---

177 "Just as *nivātastho dīpo*, when there is a flame and when there is no wind passing, and that flame of that candle, *neṅgate*, it does not show its trembling movement . . . *sopamā smṛtā*, you should [understand that] this is an example of how your God consciousness is established in one point." *Bhagavad Gita–In the Light of Kashmir Shaivism,* 6.20.

Dhāraṇā 28

यथा तथा यत्र तत्र
द्वादशान्ते मनः क्षिपेत् ।
प्रतिक्षणं क्षीणवृत्ते-
र्वैलक्षण्यं दिनैर्भवेत् ॥५१॥

yathā tathā yatra tatra
dvādaśānte manaḥ kṣipet /
pratikṣaṇaṁ kṣīṇavṛtter-
vailakṣaṇyaṁ dinairbhavet // 51 //

Next, fifty-one.

Or, in each and every action, focus your mind in *dvādaśānta*. *Yathā tathā yatra tatra dvādaśānte manaḥ kṣipet*, when you are walking or talking, or doing some household work, or doing any other nonsense act, just concentrate your mind on [any] *dvādaśānta*. Your mind must hold the state of *dvādaśānta* in each and every act of your daily routine of life. But this must be held in continuity (*pratikṣaṇa*). Then, one is born anew. One is born anew in days, not in months. *Vailakṣaṇyaṁ dinair bhavet*, some days will take place and he will be born anew, he will become new, all-round new.

This is *āṇavopāya* towards *śāmbhavopāya*.

JOHN: Both fifty and fifty-one are *āṇavopāya*?

SWAMIJI: Fifty is *śāktopāya*. Fifty-one is *āṇavopāya* to *śāmbhavopāya*.

DEVOTEE: How is the area of *dvādaśānta* found?

SWAMIJI: For instance, I have put the [spectacles] in my case and I am taking it [out]. Just do all these [mundane] actions in that, in that awareness of *dvādaśānta*. That state must be held in each and every act, in continuity. If [your awareness] remains in continuity, then you will be born anew in days, not in months. Some days will be . . .

DEVOTEE: . . . enough.

SWAMIJI: Um, yes.

For this *śloka, "kṣanair bhavet"* is another reading. *Vailakṣaṇ-yaṁ, vailakṣaṇātha*, something new will happen to him, not in days, [but] in moments–*vailakṣaṇyaṁ kṣanair bhavet.*

JOHN: And the other reading is, "after some time."

SWAMIJI: In days, in days, not in months. It won't take a month. In a few days, you will get that bliss.

JAGDISH: "*Kṣīṇa vṛtter*" is the *sādhaka*?

SWAMIJI: *Kṣīṇa vṛtter sādhakasya*, the *sādhaka* who is *kṣīṇa vṛtter*, whose mind is just one-pointed, who has become one-pointed, [this happens] to him, not to that *sādhaka* whose mind is not one-pointed.

GEORGE: Is *dvādaśānta* a state or *dvādaśānta* is the heart?

SWAMIJI: No, *dvādaśānta* is the center, any center. Wherever you go, if you are talking, put your mind in the center. If you are laughing, put there also your mind in the center. That is to be done. It is not to just only laugh. While laughing, you have to put your mind in the center. While making jokes, put your mind in the center without a break. Because the center, once you have realized [it]–you just breathe in and breathe out and be acquainted with the center–and that center you have to visualize in each and every movement of your livelihood. It must come into your vision. That is . . .

JOHN: State of *dvādaśānta*.

SWAMIJI: . . . *dvādaśānta*.

Yathā tathā yatra tatra, it is not only in the *pūjā* room, the meditation room. While walking, while doing any absurd things, *dvādaśānte manaḥ kṣipet*, the mind must be centered in *dvādaśānta*. Any movement, in any movement, not once, not twice, not thrice, [but] *pratikṣaṇa*, in continuity you have to put that mind in *dvādaśānta*. Then *kṣīṇa vṛtter*, his mind will cease to function. His mind will cease to function altogether and he will become a new man in some moments, or in a few days, not months. Then nothing is to be done afterwards. Then his everything is there.

The state of *dvādaśānta* is not only between the two eyebrows, [or] only [in the throat pit], [or] only in the heart.

GEORGE: That center, any center.

SWAMIJI: Any center![178]

GEORGE: Yes.

SWAMIJI: *Bas*, you must visualize it. You must keep it in vision and then put your mind breaklessly [there], without a break, then you will become new within days, or within moments.

178 "One *dvādaśānta* [at a time], not every *dvādaśānta* [together]." *Vijñāna Bhairava*, additional audio (USF archives).

Dhāraṇā 29

Now, fifty-two:

कालाग्निना कालपदा-
दुत्थितेन स्वकं पुरम् ।
प्लुष्टं विचिन्तयेदन्ते
शान्ताभासस्तदा भवेत् ॥५२॥

kālāgninā kālapadād-
utthitena svakaṁ puram /
pluṣṭaṁ vicintayedante-
śāntābhāsastadā bhavet / / 52 / /

When *kālāgninā* (*kālāgninā* is the state of *kālāgni-rudra*[179]) . . .

The place of *kālāgnirudra* is the left toe of your foot–the left toe [of your] left foot.

JOHN: Left foot.

SWAMIJI: Toe of your left foot.

JOHN: Big toe?

SWAMIJI: Big toe.

Just imagine that *kālāgni*, the fire of God consciousness, has risen from that point, the fire of God consciousness has risen–you have to imagine that from that point–and you have to imagine that your whole body has been put to ashes, [that] it is burnt. *Svakaṁ puraṁ*, your body, *pluṣṭaṁ vicintayet*, you have to imagine that it is *pluṣṭam*, fired to ashes. *Ante*, in the end, *śāntābhāsas tadā bhavet*, the peaceful state of Lord Śiva is revealed; *śāntābhāsas* takes place, the peaceful state of Lord Śiva takes place. Or, the peaceful state of Lord Śiva is revealed, is attained.

This *dhāraṇā* is *śāktopāya* sentenced to *śāmbhavopāya*.

---

179 See *Shiva Sutras–The Supreme Awakening*, 1.6, 33-34.

Dhāraṇā 30

एवमेव जगत्सर्वं
दग्धं ध्यात्वा विकल्पतः ।
अनन्यचेतसः पुंसः
पुंभावः परमो भवेत् ॥५३॥

evameva jagatsarvaṁ
dagdhaṁ dhyātvā vikalpataḥ /
ananyacetasaḥ puṁsaḥ
puṁbhāvaḥ paramo bhavet / / 53 / /

In the same way, just imagine (*vikalpataḥ*, you have to imagine; it is a *dhāraṇā* [based] on imagination) that this whole universe is burnt to ashes. And this imagination should take place in one-pointedness (*ananya cetasaḥ puṁsaḥ*). This imagination must be just like in a chain formation. It should not be stuck. It should not be cut down into pieces. This imagination must go like a chain.

DEVOTEE: "*Vikalpataḥ*", what does that mean, sir?

SWAMIJI: By imagination. You have to imagine, and that imagination will [come true]. Sometimes you say, "Let this dream come true", [and] this imagination will come into existence afterwards. This imagination won't remain imagination, it will be true.

JOHN: Only in meditation or in activity like walking, etc.?

SWAMIJI: No, it is just to meditate when you are seated and see that the whole universe is burnt to ashes.

Then, to him, supreme God consciousness (*paramaḥ puṁbhāvaḥ*)–*paramaḥ* means "supreme", *puṁbhāvaḥ* (God consciousness), *bhavet* (takes place)–to him, supreme *ahaṁ*[180], *puṁbhāvaḥ*, supreme God consciousness, is revealed.

This whole universe, you [must] think that it is all put to fire and it is nothing, only ashes are left. *Evam eva jagat sarvaṁ dagdhaṁ dhyātvā vikalpataḥ*, just imagine (*vikalpataḥ* means, just imagine) that this whole universe is burnt to

180 I-consciousness.

ashes.

Ananya cetasaḥ puṁsaḥ puṁbhāvaḥ paramo bhavet, and he will become the real possessor of *puṁbhāvaḥ* (*puruṣa bhāva*; *puṁbhāva* means *puruṣa bhāva*), the state of being a real man. He'll become just like a man, a real man–that is God. A real man is God.

JOHN: *Ananya cetasaḥ puṁsa.*

SWAMIJI: *Ananya cetasaḥ puṁsaḥ.*

JOHN: That means?

SWAMIJI: *Ananya cetasaḥ*, by concentrating on those ashes without any break, without any pause, that it is only ashes now left, nothing else. It is just imagination.

JOHN: "Breaklessly", you mean.

SWAMIJI: Breaklessly, yes.

JOHN: So, the thought doesn't start itself.

SWAMIJI: The thought doesn't start that, "It is still existing". That should not come.

JOHN: That it is still existing.

SWAMIJI: No [affirmative].

JOHN: It should be confirmed that it is only ashes.

SWAMIJI: Yes.

JOHN: You had mentioned that it's a chain formation in the beginning. It shouldn't be cut. It should be just . . .

SWAMIJI: No, the process must be like a chain, without a break.

JOHN: Without break, this imagination.

SWAMIJI: Concentration.

JAGDISH: So "chain" doesn't mean "succession"?

SWAMIJI: Not succession. "Chain" means "continuity". When there is succession, there is the possibility [that a] foreign agency will step in the gap. When there is succession, one after another, there will be a gap, [and] it will be filled with foreign matter (foreign matter, i.e., *vikalpa*[181]). No, only it is just a chain of *nirvikalpa*[182], one-pointed. That is what He says.

This is *śāktopāya*.

---

181 Thoughts.

182 Thought-lessness.

Dhāraṇā 31

स्वदेहे जगतो वापि
सूक्ष्मसूक्ष्मतराणि च ।
तत्त्वानि यान्ति निलयं
ध्यात्वान्ते व्यज्यते परा ॥५४॥

svadehe jagato vāpi
sūkṣmasūkṣmatarāṇi ca /
tattvāni yānti[183] *nilayaṁ*
dhyātvānte vyajyate parā / / 54 / /

Actually, your world is your body,[184] and it is attached with your own world. Or, *jagataḥ*; *jagataḥ* means, you can concentrate on the world of others, not your world. *Svadehe jagato vāpi sūkṣma sūkṣmatarāṇi ca tattvāni yānti nilayaṁ*, those elements which are existing in your body or in the body of the universe, *sūkṣma sūkṣmatarāṇi ca*, you have to think in your body, . . .

Because the body consists, your own body consists, of thirty-six elements, and this whole universe also consists of thirty-six elements. So you can do, you can concentrate, on the world or in your body (*svadehe*). That is the indication of *vāpi*. *Vāpi* means, either you concentrate in your body or you concentrate in the outside *jagat*[185] (*jagato vāpi, sūkṣma sūkṣmatarāṇi tattvāni*).

. . . *yānti nilayaṁ*, you have to . . .

For instance, there is earth, the element of earth. The element of earth should be concentrated [upon, and one should inquire] wherefrom this earth has come. There must be some subtle formation of earth. And that too, there must

---

183 Here Swamiji preferred *yānti* instead of *yāni,* and commented that the word "*yānti* makes it very clear." *Vijñāna Bhairava*, additional audio (USF archives).

184 *Svadehe.*

185 World.

be a subtle formation of *jala*[186], because the subtle formation of earth is *jala*, and the subtle formation of *jala* is fire, and the subtle formation of fire is *vāyu*[187], and the subtle formation of *vāyu* is *ākāśa*[188]. In the same way, then the *tanmātras* and *karmendriyas*, *jñānendriyas*, *manas*, *buddhi*, and *ahaṁkāra*, and *prakṛti* and *puruṣa*, and then the *ṣaṭ kañcukas,* then *māyā*, then *śuddhavidyā*, *īśvara*, *sadāśiva*, and *śakti* and *śiva* in the end. The subtlest is Śiva, the grossest is earth.[189]

. . . and, in this body, you must find out that the grossest element existing in your body has to touch its original state of its manifestation, wherefrom it has manifested.

[For example, earth] manifests from *jala*, and, in the same way, you must find out *jala*, you must find out *agni*, you must find out *vāyu*, [and] *ākāśa*. And, in the same way, you must find out where is *śakti*, wherefrom *śakti* has risen. In the end, you will find Śiva.

Yānti nilayam, by this process, [the elements] become dissolved in one another.

JAGDISH: Is this *śāktopāya*, sir?

SWAMIJI: It will be *śāktopāya* and *āṇavopāya* also, because there is so much, so much botheration. As long as botheration is concerned, it is *śāktopāya* and *āṇavopāya*. It can't be *śāmbhavopāya*. Wherever there is botheration, it is either *śāktopāya* or *āṇavopāya*. Without botheration is *śāmbhavopāya*. And total negation of botheration is *anupāya*[190]. That is found in the second *āhnika* of the *Tantrāloka*.

JAGDISH: So, "*tattvāni*" here are the thirty-six elements?

SWAMIJI: *Tattvāni*, thirty-six elements.

JAGDISH: Not the five states of the individual?

SWAMIJI: No, no, no, that is incorrect. I saw that written in

---

186 Water.

187 Wind or air.

188 Ether or space.

189 The elements are listed in ascending order from the grossest to the subtlest, from the effect to its cause. See Appendix for a list of the 36 elements.

190 Lit., "no means".

that[191]. It is [written that] the five states of the individual, i.e., *jāgrat*, *svapna*, *suṣupti*, etc.? No, that is not [correct].

191 This is in reference to an earlier draft of this commentary, which Swamiji later amended.

Dhāraṇā 32

Now, next. It is *āṇavopāya* sentenced to *śāmbhavopāya*.

पीनां च दुर्बलां शक्तिं
ध्यात्वा द्वादशगोचरे ।
प्रविश्य हृदये ध्यायन्-
सुप्तः स्वातन्त्र्यमाप्नुयात् ॥५५॥

pīnāṁ ca durbalāṁ śaktiṁ
dhyātvā dvādaśagocare /
praviśya hṛdaye dhyāyan-
suptaḥ svātantryamāpnuyāt[192] */ / 55 / /*

"*Svapna svātantryam*"[193] is the real reading of Lord Śiva in the *Vijñāna Bhairava*.

This is the Kingdom in the dreaming state, how you attain the Kingdom in the dreaming state. The dreaming state is the cause of our being involved in repeated births and deaths. If our dreaming state is living, then the repeated births are there, movement in repeated births are living. Movements in repeated births are due to our dreaming state.[194]

If you, in your dreaming state, only dream that you are

---

192 Three different readings can be found for the last line of this verse: "*suptaḥ svācchandyam*" (*Tantrāloka*, 15.480-481), "*svapna svātantryam*" (*Spanda Nirṇaya*, *KSTS* vol. 42, p56); and "*muktaḥ svātantryam*" (*Vijñāna Bhairava*, *KSTS* vol. 8, p45). Swamiji said the readings "*suptaḥ svācchandyam*" and "*svapna svātantryam*" convey the same meaning.

193 He attains absolute independent power (*svātantrya*) in the dreaming state (*svapna*).

194 Viz., *puryaṣṭaka* ("the city of eight": mind, intellect, ego, and the five *tanmātras*). "The subtle body causes rebirth, because the subtle body will carry you here, there, and everywhere; from heaven to hell, and from hell to the body of a bird, worm, bug, cow, beast, dog, human, and a rock also. In the subtle body, impressions are stored." *Tantrāloka* 16.149, (USF archives).

doing *abhyāsa*[195], there is liberation, there is no rebirth, you won't be born again. This is the certificate of your being liberated.[196]

What is the certificate?

JOHN: That you dream that you are doing *abhyāsa*.

SWAMIJI: Yes.

Pīnāṁ ca durbalāṁ śaktiṁ dhyātvā dvādaśa gocare. You have to do this practice first. *Pīnāṁ* means "with sound". You have to breathe with sound, *durbalāṁ*, very slowly (*durbalāṁ* means "very slowly"). Produce this breath very slowly, move your breathing very slowly, and put sound in it (that is *pīnāṁ*). It must be gross, i.e., your ear must hear the sound of your breath, the movement of your breath. That is *pīnāṁ ca durbalāṁ*. *Śaktiṁ* means *prāṇa śakti*, the energy of breath.[197]

Dhyātvā dvādaśa gocare, and you must not [ignore] the center also (*dvādaśa gocare* means, this center, this center, or the heart, any, any), the energy of breath should be focused in a *dvādaśānta*. *Dvādaśānta* prevails in three places: either in the heart, or in the throat, or between the two eyebrows. [Choose] one out of these three. Put your concentration of

---

195 Meditation.

196 "Because when your meditation is strengthened totally, just when you enter the dreaming state (that is the subtle body), you'll enter in *samādhi*. It is sure!" *Tantrāloka* 16.149, (USF archives).

197 "In the practice of *cakrodaya*, the breath is to occupy a minimum of space. At the time of practice, you must be able to hear the sound of the inhaling and exhaling breath. The sound of your breathing should be loud enough so that even those sitting near you can hear it. There are two various understandings (*vidhi*) of how *cakrodaya* is to be practiced. Some say that the breath is to be inhaled and exhaled by the throat. Others say that the breath is to be inhaled and exhaled by the heart. Those that say that the breath should be inhaled and exhaled by the heart are wrong. It is a very dangerous and deadly procedure to adopt. To practice in this manner will produce such a powerful and intense heat that the heart is adversely effected and severely damaged. You will die in as short a time as a few weeks. The practice of *cakrodaya*, therefore, must be practiced by inhaling and exhaling by the throat, not by the heart." *Self Realization in Kashmir Shaivism – Talks on Practice*, 2.47-48.

breath on any of these, either between the two eyebrows, or this throat pit, or the heart.

And the remaining thing to tell you [is that] you must be postured in some posture (*āsana*) first, and then lie straight flat, flat straight[198], and go on doing this practice.

This energy of breath should be functioned in such a way that it produces sound and it is lengthened more and more and more and more, so that your consciousness is held permanently.

JOHN: You say you sit in a posture first and then lay down?

SWAMIJI: Yes, go on doing this practice for a while, and when you find that you are giddy, giddiness has come for taking a rest, go on doing this practice and lie flat. But that giddiness has to come, it must come, and it will come.

GANJOO: And if it is started while lying flat?

SWAMIJI: While lying in the beginning? Then you will go only into the dreaming state. You won't find this [*svapna svātantrya*]. It must be developed in a posture first for some time, some particular time. It must be developed in a [sitting] posture (*āsana*) without leaning, and then, when you find giddiness, then [you may lie down flat] with this practice.

JOHN: What is this giddiness? It's a kind of drowsiness?

SWAMIJI: Drowsiness, drowsiness. But you must not stop this functioning of practice while laying down.

Then what will happen? *Ananya cetasaḥ*, by doing this thought-lessly[199], *ananya cetasaḥ*, with one-pointedness, *dhyāyan*, just when he concentrates like this, *hṛdaye praviśya*, when he is situated in *hṛdaya*, in the real heart (either in the throat-pit, or between the two eyebrows, or the heart–all these three places are called "the heart"), and in that heart, *dhyāyan*, the one who practices this in continuity and *praviśya,* while entering in the dreaming state (*praviśya* means, "entering" in the dreaming state), *svapna svātantryam āpnuyāt*, he attains the power to rule in *svapna* also, in the dreaming state. As soon as he enters in that dreaming state, he knows that he has entered in the dreaming state, he is not unconscious of that. And when he enters in the dreaming state, it is for him to decide what

198 Viz., *śavāsana* or corpse pose.

199 That is, without allowing fluctuations of various thoughts.

dream he will see. If he wants to see Lord Śiva in the dream, Lord Śiva will appear before him. If he wants to see something, worldly things also, he will dream that. Anything, whatever he wants to dream, he will dream.[200] He becomes the holder of the power in the dreaming state also, not only in wakefulness.

JOHN: So, this isn't a way to enter into that gap?

SWAMIJI: Yes.

JOHN: This is the way.

SWAMIJI: Yes, because he enters in *turya*, and finds the dreaming state in *turya*, and is conscious of that dreaming state, and he can dream whatever he likes.

DEVOTEE: If he falls asleep when he lays down?

SWAMIJI: He has to.

DEVOTEE: Then why . . . there will be no sound [of his breath] then when he falls asleep?

SWAMIJI: No, there will be sound in the dreaming state also.

DENISE: It will continue.

SWAMIJI: It will continue because he has practiced that. You will see. You try for two hours. You sit in one posture doing this practice and then lie down, and you will do the same practice unconsciously in the dreaming state also. Although you won't enter in that *svapna svātantrya* in the beginning, but you will be practicing in the dreaming state also. You will see that you are practicing in the dreaming state. You will see that dream, too. In the dreaming state, you will see in dreaming that you are practicing, [that] you are breathing deeply.

Praviśya hṛdaye, when he enters in *hṛdaye* (*hṛdaye* means *purī tattva*), . . .

---

200 "Perfect *svapna svātantrya* is when you see Lord Śiva existing before you." *Spanda Kārikā* of Vasugupta, with the *Nirṇaya* (commentary) of Kṣemarāja, translation and commentary by Swami Lakshmanjoo (original audio recording, USF archives, Los Angeles, 1975), 3.2.

Purī tattva is a place where we go first.[201] We touch that and are thrown in the dreaming state. We touch that and are thrown in the dreamless state. We touch that and are thrown in wakefulness.

JAGDISH: *Purī*?

SWAMIJI: *Purī tattva.* There is that point, there is that point between sleep and waking, between waking and sleeping, between waking and dreamless state. There is that point [called] *purī tattva*. When you touch it [and maintain awareness of it], then you can change your position of your being. If you are wakeful, you'll get entry in the dreaming state [and remain wakeful]. If you are in the dreaming state, you will get wakeful in the dreamless state. If you are in the dreamless state, you will get wakeful in wakefulness, you'll be awake in *jāgrat*[202].

. . . that is *purī tattva*, that is *hṛdaye*, *hṛdaye praviśya*[203]. "*Hṛdaye*" means there that *hṛdaye*[204].

JOHN: That's the real heart.

SWAMIJI: And when you are doing this practice, *pīnāṁ ca durbalāṁ*, [when] you are doing this *cakrodaya*[205], you are

---

201 "Between in the three states of the individual subjective body, waking, dreaming, and deep sleep, there is a gap. This gap is a junction between the waking state and the dreaming state. There is also a junction between the dreaming state and dreamless sound sleep and there is a junction between sound sleep and the waking state. These transitions take place automatically within every human being.
"This junction is only a gate, the entrance to *turya*. . . . This junction is known to be the start of *turya*. In entering this junction, the aspirant enters into another world. It is not wakefulness, nor is it the dreaming state, nor is it sound sleep, but a fourth world." *Kashmir Shaivism–The Secret Supreme*, 16.107-109.

202 Wakefulness.

203 Entry into the heart.

204 That is, *purī tattva*.

205 "Through practice, this gross movement of breath is refined, and, with the passage of time, becomes more and more subtle. This can only be accomplished through one's own will and concentration.

doing this *cakrodaya* and you touch that [*purī tattva*], then you will enter in that vastness of God consciousness. Although it is not yet quite clear (in the beginning it is not quite clear), but it is vastness.

Even the guru's grace (*guru kṛpā*) will not help a seeker unless [the seeker] is determined and fully devoted to maintaining awareness and concentration." *Self Realization in Kashmir Shaivism*, 2.44.

Dhāraṇā 33

भुवनाध्वादिरूपेण
चिन्तयेत्क्रमशोऽखिलम् ।
स्थूलसूक्ष्मपरस्थित्या
यावदन्ते मनोलयः ॥५६॥

bhuvanādhvādirūpeṇa
cintayetkramaśo'khilam /
sthūlasūkṣmaparasthityā
yāvadante manolayaḥ / / 56 / /

This *dhāraṇā* is also *śāktopāya* towards *śāmbhavopāya*.

The gross formation of the world is *bhuvanādhva*, the subtle formation of the world is *tattvādhva*, and the subtlest formation of the world is *kalādhva*.[206]

Just take the gross formation of the world and make it enter in its subtle formation of the world through imagination. Take the gross formation of the objective world in its subtle formation and take that subtle formation of the objective world in its most subtle formation. *Sthūla sūkṣma para sthityā*, by making the journey successively from gross to subtle, and from subtle to subtlest, *ante*, in the end, *manolayaḥ*, [the *yogi*] transcends the state of the mind, he becomes un-minded. That is his *samādhi*.

Sthūla is *bhuvanādhva*, *sūkṣma* is *tattvādhva*, and *para* is *kalādhva*. Take these successively one in another, one in another, and, in the end, you will find that the mind transcends its state, the mind becomes un-minded.

---

206 "In Shaivism, this objective universe is said to be threefold because it is composed of three paths (*adhvans*). These *adhvans* are gross (*sthūla*), subtle (*sūkṣma*), and subtlest (*parā*). The gross path is called *bhuvanādhva* (118 worlds), the subtle path *tattvādhva* (36 elements), and the subtlest path *kalādhva* (5 circles)." *Kashmir Shaivism–The Secret Supreme*, 2.11.

Dhāraṇā 34

अस्य सर्वस्य विश्वस्य
पर्यन्तेषु समन्ततः ।
अध्वप्रक्रियया तत्त्वं
शैवं ध्यात्वा महोदयः ॥५७॥

asya sarvasya viśvasya
paryanteṣu samantataḥ /
adhvaprakriyayā tattvaṁ
śaivaṁ dhyātvā mahodayaḥ / / 57 / /

This is also another way of *dhāraṇā*, a supreme *dhāraṇā*. Just you have to put some addition to it.

Just sit or stand outside in your garden and imagine that around you this whole universe is existing, and there you see *adhva prakriyā* (*adhva prakriyā*, according to the *Tantrāloka's* eighth *āhnika*[207]), that how great is this universe, how wide and vast is this universe. And below, also what is there? And above, what is there? All these one hundred and eighteen worlds, just imagine these one hundred and eighteen worlds around you, above you and below you (below your body). And you have to imagine that, "This whole universe is my own God consciousness." Just imagine that, "I am pervading in each and every part of this universe of one hundred and eighteen worlds."

This is *adhva prakriyā*. This is a technical term–*adhva prakriyā*. *Prakriyā* means "path of *adhvan*"–*adhva prakriyā*. *Prakriyā* means "journey", the journey of *adhva*, the universal path.

JOHN: This is *śāktopāya*?

SWAMIJI: Yes, this is *śāktopāya*, supreme *śāktopāya*.

Just imagine the vastness of the universe and think that,

207 The eighth *āhnika* (chapter) of Abhinavagupta's *Tantrāloka* describes the measurement of the one hundred and eighteen worlds (*bhuvanās*), the beings (*rūdras*) who rule these worlds, and how these worlds relate to each of the thirty-six elements (*tattvas*).

"This whole is only the kingdom of God consciousness there, the kingdom of My-consciousness, Self-consciousness, I-consciousness." And that *mahodayaḥ* (*mahodayaḥ* means, God consciousness) is revealed in the end.

This is *adhva prakriyā*. At many places you have read, "*na prakriyā paraṁ jñānam*", there is no other supreme knowledge than *prakriyā* knowledge.[208] This is *prakriyā* knowledge.

When *prakriyā* knowledge takes place, . . .*

Prakriyā knowledge means this knowledge that, "This whole universe is my own Self, the expansion of my Self." This is pure *śāktopāya*.

JOHN: This is the state of *sadāśiva*?

SWAMIJI: Yes, "*ahaṁ sarvam*[209]".

*. . . *śaivaṁ tattvaṁ adhva prakriyayā dhyātvā mahodayaḥ*, God consciousness is revealed, supreme God consciousness is revealed to him.

208 *Tantrāloka* 8.11, (USF archives).

209 "I (*ahaṁ*) am everything (*sarvam*)", viz., "*aham idam*".

Dhāraṇā 35

Now another one:

विश्वमेतन्महादेवि
शून्यभूतं विचिन्तयेत् ।
तत्रैव च मनो लीनं
ततस्तल्लयभाजनम् ॥५८॥

viśvametanmahādevi
śūnyabhūtaṁ vicintayet /
tatraiva ca mano līnaṁ
tatastallayabhājanam / / 58 / /

O Pārvatī, just imagine, just think, that this universe is with no substance and is only a vacuum. *Viśvam etat mahādevi śūnya bhūtaṁ vicintaye*, it is only a vacuum, there is nothing (e.g., you perceive this, that this is a key, [but you imagine that] this is not a key, this is nothing, this is only a vacuum). And in that vacuum, establish Your mind firmly.

Tatraiva ca mano līnaṁ, let Your mind melt in that vacuum, in that great and vast vacuum. *Tataḥ*, then [the *yogi*] is befitted in entering in that vacuum, in that supreme vacuum. When he establishes, or makes his mind melt, in that vacuum, then he becomes worthy of entering in that supreme vacuum of God consciousness.

This is *śāmbhavopāya* with some slight touches of *śāktopāya*.

JOHN: This is more *śāmbhavopāya*?

SWAMIJI: This is more *śāmbhavopāya*. The next is pure *śāmbhavopāya*.

Dhāraṇā 36

घटादिभाजने दृष्टिं
भित्तीस्त्यक्त्वा विनिक्षिपेत् ।
तल्लयं तत्क्षणाद्गत्वा
तल्लयात्तन्मयो भवेत् ॥५९॥

ghaṭādibhājane dṛṣṭiṁ
bhittistyaktvā vinikṣipet /
tallayaṁ tatkṣaṇādgatvā
tallayāttanmayo bhavet / / 59 / /

SWAMIJI: Just keep one pot before you.

JOHN: Pot?

SWAMIJI: Some pot, jug, or tumbler, or anything.[210] Focus your sight on it for a while. Focus your sight on it with one-pointedness and imagine that it is only a pot without the substance of its outside, [that it is without] that circle, or mud, or that copper, or glassware. There is nothing. It is only a pot to hold, and outside, there is nothing to make it in its shape (*bhittis tyaktvā*).

GANJOO: Without material or shape.

SWAMIJI: Without material or shape.

DEVOTEE: An idea only?

SWAMIJI: Not an idea. Just look on that pot [and] imagine it is only a vacuum, [that] there is nothing, no covering of that mud or earth.

DEVOTEE: You just imagine the shape.

SWAMIJI: Only shape, only shape without this substance. This is *śāmbhavopāya*.

Ghaṭādi bhājane dṛṣṭim, or just imagine [that] someone sitting before you, just imagine that this [person] is a shape but there is no substance of the body, it is only a vacuum. *Ghaṭādi bhājane dṛṣṭi bhittis tyaktvā*, you must discard all these *bhittis* (*bhittis* means, the supports of that shape).

---

210 *Ghaṭa* (a pot) refers to any object.

DENISE: Yes, the characteristics.

SWAMIJI: Yes, characteristics and shape.

Tat layaṁ tat kṣaṇād gatvā tat layāt tanmayo bhavet, and at that very moment when he enters[211] in that vacuum of that pot, he enters in the vacuum of God consciousness, just there and then.

This is *śāmbhavopāya*.

JOHN: This is done with the eyes closed?

SWAMIJI: No, eyes open, eyes open, wide open.

DEVOTEE: There is no *śāktopāya*.

SWAMIJI: This is not *śāktopāya* here. It is only *śāmbhavopāya* because you have to see nothing, you have to look and see nothing, just only go on seeing. What is seen? Only a vacuum–there is nothing.

JOHN: That's like seeing the reflection and understanding that the reflection has no substance.

SWAMIJI: There is no substance, yes.

DEVOTEE: Can we say that it is a creation of my thought?

SWAMIJI: Huh?

DEVOTEE: It is creation of my thought.

SWAMIJI: Whose?

DEVOTEE: Of my thought?

SWAMIJI: Whose thought?

DEVOTEE: My thought.

SWAMIJI: Who are you?

DEVOTEE: I am seeing the pot, but if there is no pot . . .

SWAMIJI: This is the creation of the thought of God consciousness. Don't put "I", because as soon as you put "I", the body will make you limited. Your body will make your "I" limited. Think it is only the God consciousness of "I", I-God consciousness. It is not "I" in "my" consciousness, it is not in "my" consciousness, it is in God consciousness. That "I" is in God consciousness. That is universal.

---

211 *Laya*, melts or is absorbed.

Dhāraṇā 37

निर्वृक्षगिरिभित्त्यादि-
देशे दृष्टिं विनिक्षिपेत् ।
विलीने मानसे भावे
वृत्तिक्षीणः प्रजायते ॥६०॥

nirvṛkṣagiribhittyādi-
deśe dṛṣṭiṁ vinikṣipet /
vilīne mānase bhāve
vṛttikṣīṇaḥ prajāyate // 60 //

Or, just go out in some field where there are no trees, no mountains, or nothing; no houses, no roads, no shade, no waterfalls, nothing; only barren, a desert, just like a desert; *nirvṛkṣa giri bhittyādi deśe*, where there are no trees, there are no mountains, there are no walls. At that place, come and sit or stand and *dṛṣṭiṁ vinikṣipet*, put your sight wide open on that field, on that desert, and see [that] there is nothing.

Vilīne mānase bhāve, when you put your sight on the land without trees, mountains, etc., then thought-fulness is ended in thought-lessness. *Vilīne mānase bhāve*, *mānase bhāve vilīne*, when *mānase bhāve* (this thought-fulness) is *vilīne*, established, resting, when that thought-fulness of that [barrenness] is resting, it takes place and is established well, *vṛtti kṣīṇaḥ prajāyate*, thought-lessness appears–at once thought-lessness appears. *Mānase bhāve vilīne*, when that thought-fulness on that [barren] state is established, then *vṛtti kṣīṇaḥ prajāyate*, thought-lessness arises.

This is *śāmbhavopāya,* pure *śāmbhavopāya*.

Dhāraṇā 38

Another one, sixty-first:

उभयोर्भावयोर्ज्ञाने
ध्यात्वा मध्यं समाश्रयेत् ।
युगपच्च द्वयं त्यक्त्वा
मध्ये तत्त्वं प्रकाशते ॥ ६१ ॥

ubhayorbhāvayorjñāne
dhyātvā madhyaṁ samāśrayet /
yugapacca dvayaṁ tyaktvā
madhye tattvaṁ prakāśate // 61 //

Just take any two pots or [any] two things. Meditate on any two objects (*ubhayorbhāvayoḥ*), e.g., this case of [spectacles] and this paper. Concentrate on these two objects and reside and rest in-between the two objects. When you perceive [these spectacles], after perceiving this object, [then] you perceive this paper; when you perceive [these spectacles], and [when] this perceiving of this object is over and this perceiving of this paper has not yet come, that is *madhyam*, that is "in-between". Put your consciousness there. *Madhyam dhyātvā*, concentrate on that center. And while concentrating on that center, be established in that center. And when you are established in that center, simultaneously leave the impression of these objects altogether. Leave the impression of all these two objects altogether, and in making yourself established in that center, the reality of God consciousness is revealed.

JOHN: This is *śāktopāya*?

SWAMIJI: This is *śāktopāya*. In *Tantrāloka* also you will find that this [practice] is *śāktopāya*.[212]

While entering in the center of these two objects, you have to take the support, every now and then, of these two objects. For instance, while you concentrate on that center, this center

212 *Tantrāloka* 1.240, (USF archives).

will disappear, and you have to take the support of these two objects again; and then again and again, see this and see this, see this and see this, and see what is in-between, and focus your mind in the center, and when that center is established well, then you have to discard the impression of both these objects and be established in the center, and then the Universal center will be revealed.

[Or], take the support of breathing in and breathing out for establishing your center. When the center of these two breaths is established well, then leave the breath aside and enter in that center, and that Universal center will be revealed. There you will enter in the *śāktopāya* state. That is not *śāmbhavopāya*.

Dhāraṇā 39

भावे त्यक्ते निरुद्धा चित्
नैव भावान्तरं व्रजेत् ।
तदा तन्मध्यभावेन
विकसत्यति भावना ॥ ६२ ॥

bhāve tyakte niruddhā cit
naiva bhāvāntaraṁ vrajet /
tadā tanmadhyabhāvena
vikasatyati bhāvanā / / 62 / /[213]

There are two readings in this *dhāraṇā.*

One *dhāraṇā* is, just look at one pot (*bhāve atyakte*).[214] When you look on that one pot, go on looking at [that] one pot, don't think of any other thing. Go on thinking of this pot, don't think of this paper, or cardamom, or any flower, or anything [else]. Go on concentrating on that pot, and *niruddhā cit*, establish your thought (*cit* is there, "thought"[215]), your thought must be established in that one object (objective consciousness). *Naiva bhāvāntaraṁ vrajet*, don't go to [the thought of] any other object. Don't go at all to any other object. Keep your consciousness alive there. [Your awareness] must not be dead.

When you are fed up with seeing [an object] again and again, [then] your consciousness [of that object becomes] dead and your consciousness wants to see another object because you want to see something new. But don't do that. It must not be dead. Keep it alive. This one objective consciousness should remain alive. If it is not [kept] alive, it [will become] dead [and then] the *dhāraṇā* is over, [then] there is no *dhāraṇā*. You have to keep it alive for the time being. *Naiva*

---

213 Swamiji corrected "*nyakte*" to read "*tyakte*" in the first half of the verse, and "*tanmayabhāvena*" to read "*tanmadhyabhāvena*" in the second half of the verse.

214 Or any object.

215 *Cit* is generally translated as "consciousness".

bhāvāntaraṁ vrajet, [at] no cost . . . you must not go to [the thought of] any other object.

Then the reading is there: *tanmaya bhāvena*, then you become one with that object. When you become one with that object, [when] objective consciousness melts in your subjective consciousness, [then] that subjective consciousness [with] the mixture of objective consciousness (that particular objective consciousness and your subjective particular consciousness of that object only) enters in that Universal consciousness.

JOHN: This "keeping alive" means having that as your sole object of attention.

SWAMIJI: Attention only on that object.

JOHN: Any time that slips and [another] thought comes, or anything comes, . . .

SWAMIJI: [If] any other thought slips in, finished, the *dhāraṇā* is over, the *dhāraṇā* is not complete. So this consciousness must be kept alive.[216]

Now, another reading of this [verse from the] *Vijñāna Bhairava*.

Or (there is another explanation of this *śloka*), *bhāve tyakte*, look at this object[217], go on looking at this object full of your life-full awareness, go on looking at this object, and when you are aware of that and when you perceive it well, leave it. [Then] try to find another object, [but] don't look at another object. Leave this object [with the intent of] perceiving another object, [but] don't go to [the perception of] another object at all. When you leave this [previous] object and you don't [yet] reach [the perception of] another object, . . .

You travel only up to [the intent of perceiving] another object [but you] don't enter in the kingdom of another object. Leave the kingdom of this object, the previous object, [but] don't enter in the kingdom of another object.

---

216 Swamiji also said that this practice is to be done with the eyes open, without moving the body. *Vijñāna Bhairava*, additional audio (USF archives).

217 Any object.

. . . [then] roam in the center.[218] Leave [the previous object] for good [but] don't enter [the perception of] another objective kingdom. And *tanmadhya bhāvena*, so, [when] you roam in that center, the center of *tanmadhya bhāvena*, *vikasati*, [then] blooms forth *ati bhāvanā*, the supreme state of God consciousness.

JOHN: So, one practice is *āṇavopāya* and the other is *śāktopāya*?

SWAMIJI: No, one practice is *śāktopāya* and another practice is *śāktopāya*.

JOHN: Both?

SWAMIJI: These are both *śāktopāya*.

JOHN: But why? That one when you have the support of one object, why would that be *śāktopāya*?

SWAMIJI: When there is the support of the [perception or knowledge of the] objective world, it can't be *āṇavopāya*. *Āṇavopāya* is when you take the support of *mantra*, when you take the support of breath, when you take the support of *dhāraṇā*, place, all these things. When [these activities] are united, that is *āṇavopāya*.[219] When [there is] only [the knowledge or perception of an] objective support, and that God consciousness is meditated on, that is *śāktopāya*, that can't be *āṇavopāya*.[220]

---

218 "So you can post your mind there, in-between [the perception of] two objects." *Vijñāna Bhairava*, additional audio (USF archives).

219 "United" in the sense of when you combine *mantra*, breathing, contemplation, and awareness on some particular point in the body, it is practice in *āṇavopaya*.

220 "The means which exists in *jñāna śakti* is *śāktopāya* and is called *jñānopāya*. *Āṇavopāya* is called *kriyopāya* because it is the means which is found in *kriyā śakti*." *Kashmir Shaivism–The Secret Supreme*, 5.39.

Dhāraṇā 40

सर्वं देहं चिन्मयं हि
जगद्वा परिभावयेत् ।
युगपन्निर्विकल्पेन
मनसा परमोदयः ॥ ६३ ॥

sarvaṁ dehaṁ cinmayaṁ hi
jagadvā paribhāvayet /
yugapannirvikalpena
manasā paramodayaḥ / / 63 / /

You have to just imagine that your body is–although it is individual and it seems to be limited–[that] this, your individual body, is actually your universal body (it is why He has put, *sarvaṁ dehaṁ jagat vā*). You have to imagine that this whole body of yours, from toe to head[221], or this whole universe, [that] this is full of God consciousness. *Sarvaṁ dehaṁ jagat vā, cinmayaṁ paribhāvayet*, just imagine that this whole universe is filled with God consciousness [and that] your body is filled with God consciousness from toe to head (*sarvaṁ dehaṁ jagat vā*). And you have to imagine and think this simultaneously (*yugapat*).

JOHN: Think what simultaneously? That my body and this universe . . .

SWAMIJI: This universe.

JOHN: . . . are the same?

SWAMIJI: Yes, the same. Simultaneously, you should think that this body of yours, from toe to head, and this whole universe are one, filled with God consciousness.[222] *Nirvikalpena manasā*, you have to adopt this consciousness with thought-lessness, . . .

JOHN: It has to be *śāmbhavopāya*?

221 "*Sarvaṁ*" means, from toe to head, i.e., your entire body.

222 Swamiji said that "*vā*", which is often translated as "or", here means "and".

SWAMIJI: No, this is *śāktopāya*.[223]

JOHN: Higher state.

SWAMIJI: Highest state of *śāktopāya*.

. . . [and think that], "*sarvo mamāyaṁ vibhavaḥ*[224]", and the supreme state of God consciousness will arise.

---

223 "If it was *śāmbhavopāya*, then there would be no question of thinking even." *Vijñāna Bhairava*, additional audio (USF archives).

224 "'I am Śiva, this whole universe is My own glory'. . . . That *vikalpa* is *śuddha* (pure) *vikalpa*" *Tantrāloka* 4.170, Jayaratha's commentary, (USF archives).

Dhāraṇā 41

वायुद्वयस्य संघट्टा-
दन्तर्वा बहिरन्ततः ।
योगी समत्वविज्ञान-
समुद्गमनभाजनम् ॥ ६४ ॥

vāyudvayasya saṁghaṭṭād-
antarvā bahirantataḥ /
yogī samatvavijñāna-
samudgamanabhājanam // 64 //

Vāyu dvayasya saṁghaṭṭāt, when these two breaths meet, . . .

They meet at one place. The beginning of ingress is the ending point of egress; the beginning of *prāṇa* is the ending point of *apāna*. That is *saṁghaṭṭa*, the meeting of these two.

. . . *antar vā bahir*, *antar bahir vā*, it may take place inside or it may take place outside (inside between the two eyebrows or the heart, or outside in [*bāhya*] *dvādaśānta*), but *antataḥ,* in the end, when both the breaths stop (*antataḥ* means "in the end"), when both breaths stop, the *yogi* becomes capable of *samatva vijñāna samudgamana bhājanam*, the *yogi* becomes capable of knowing the rise of the oneness of the Self; *samudgamana bhājanam* (*bhājanam* means "capable"), he becomes capable, fit, to know the rise of the oneness of the Self.

This is *āṇavopāya*.

Dhāraṇā 42

सर्वं जगत्स्वदेहं वा
स्वानन्दभरितं स्मरेत् ।
युगपन्स्वामृतेनैव
परानन्दमयो भवेत् ॥६५॥

sarvaṁ jagatsvadehaṁ vā
svānandabharitaṁ smaret /
yugapansvāmṛitenaiva
parānandamayo bhavet / / 65 / /

Take the whole universe or your own body (either this whole universe or your own body). You must think that it is filled with one's own bliss of the Self. Either you imagine that this whole universe is filled with your own bliss or [that] your body is filled with bliss. But you must not fill it in succession. You [must] think that it is already filled *yugapat* (simultaneously). You must think that it is filled with that blissful Kingdom of Lord Śiva. And by that bliss, one becomes melted in supreme bliss.

In the sixty-third *śloka*, you must know that it is that the whole universe is filled with *prakāśa*, and here [it is] that the whole universe is filled with bliss (*vimarśa*). [The universe] is the coagulation of one's own consciousness, the coagulated form of one's own consciousness.

This is *śāktopāya*.

Dhāraṇā 43

कुहनेन प्रयोगेन
सद्य एव मृगेक्षणे ।
समुदेति महानन्दो
येन तत्त्वं प्रकाशते ॥ ६६ ॥

kuhanena prayogena
sadya eva mṛgekṣaṇe /
samudeti mahānando
yena tattvaṁ prakāśate / / 66 / /

Kuhana prayoga is one kind of trick. This is a trick:

By tickling in the armpits, when somebody tickles you in the armpits, both armpits, and you laugh, you laugh wildly without any limit, and there you have to see where this laughing comes [from].

If actually this laughing was blissful, why [would] you hate it? So there is something unknown to you that makes you laugh. Otherwise, you are worried by that. Are you not worried? Why do you laugh? You ought to have wept. [But] you don't weep, you laugh.

So You must find out the source of that laughing, and [when You do], there and then, *mṛgekṣaṇe*[225], O Devī, the supreme bliss shines forth, by which bliss Your own Self is revealed (*yena tattvaṁ prakāśate*)–[by remaining] aware of the tickling act.

DEVOTEE: At the moment of tickling.

DEVOTEE: Swamiji, then it takes two people to do that *sādhanā*?

DEVOTEE: Can't you tickle yourself?

SWAMIJI: Then [you] won't laugh. Tickling must be done by somebody else.

DEVOTEE: [Is this] *āṇavopāya* still?

SWAMIJI: No, this is *śāktopāya*. This is *śāktopāya* [because] here is no *mantra*, there is no recitation of *mantra*, no breath,

225 Here, Bhairava addresses Devī as "O Fawn-eyed one."

no breath procession, only observation of that source of that laughing.

Dhāraṇā 44

सर्वस्रोतोनिबन्धेन
प्राणशक्त्योर्ध्वया शनैः ।
पिपीलस्पर्शवेलायां
प्रथते परमं सुखम् ॥ ६७ ॥

sarvasrotonibandhena
prāṇaśaktyordhvayā śanaiḥ /
pipīlasparśavelāyāṁ
prathate paramaṁ sukham / / 67 / /

Sarva sroto nibandhena, by checking slowly all the flows of the cognitive senses, *sarva sroto nibandhena* ([*sarva*] *sroto* means, all the flows of the cognitive senses), by checking them *śanaiḥ*, slowly, . . .*

But how can this checking be done? He puts that, *prāṇa śakti ūrdhvayā*, by the elevated energy of *prāṇa*. Because, if the elevated energy of *prāṇa* is not functioning, these flows of the cognitive senses can't be checked. These flows of the cognitive senses will be checked only by adjusting the elevated energy of *prāṇa śakti*, not the individual energy of *prāṇa śakti*. The elevated energy of *prāṇa śakti* means one-pointed *prāṇa śakti*, when the *prāṇa śakti* is without the movement of thought.

DEVOTEE: Is it in *madhyā dhāma*?

SWAMIJI: It is not in *madhyā dhāma*. It is *madhyā dhāma* in the outside world,[226] not in *suṣumnā*, not in the central vein.

DEVOTEE: Where is this *madhyā dhāma* in the outside world?

SWAMIJI: *Madhyā dhāma* is everywhere, if you are aware.

DEVOTEE: So, when it says, "with *prāṇa śakti* elevated", it simply means, the time of centering?

---

226 The universal center.

SWAMIJI: Yes.

DEVOTEE: Then why does that mean that *prāṇa śakti* is elevated? Because She is brought to one-pointedness?

SWAMIJI: When there is one-pointedness in *prāṇa śakti*, that *prāṇa śakti* is elevated. And then that *prāṇa śakti* is already existing in *suṣumnā*, in *madhyā dhāma*.

DEVOTEE: Already existing in *madhyā dhāma*?

SWAMIJI: Yes, functioning in *madhyā dhāma*. It is not functioning in the individual field of life. When one-pointedness is prevailing in *prāṇa śakti*, that *prāṇa śakti* is not simple *prāṇa śakti*, it is elevated *prāṇa śakti*.

DEVOTEE: How is the flow of the cognitive senses . . . how is it checked?

SWAMIJI: By the elevated energy of *prāṇa*, the checking is done of the cognitive senses.[227]

GANJOO: Is this *prāṇa śakti* the *prāṇa* of the movement of breath?

SWAMIJI: Breath, yes, yes, yes. Breath, ordinary breath. That breath without any movement of thoughts.

DEVOTEE: Breath is still going in and out? It is real breath?

SWAMIJI: Yes, yes, real breath.

DEVOTEE: Is it not *prāṇa kuṇḍalinī*?

SWAMIJI: No, it is not *prāṇa kuṇḍalinī*. It is *prāṇa śakti*, energy of *prāṇa*. When there is one-pointedness in that *prāṇa śakti*, that *prāṇa śakti*, that is not *suṣumnā*.

DEVOTEE: That point is *madhyā dhāma*.

SWAMIJI: That point is *madhyā dhāma*.

DEVOTEE: But that's not *suṣumnā*? I thought *madhyā dhāma* meant *suṣumnā*?

SWAMIJI: The outside field.

DEVOTEE: Outside field *madhyā dhāma*–anywhere.

SWAMIJI: Everywhere, everywhere!

---

227 "Checking slowly all the flows of cognitive senses, all the five flows, all at once–*śabda*, *sparśa*, *rūpa*, *rasa*, and *gandha*. When one-pointedness prevails, then all the cognitive senses are already merged in that one point. That is "checking", when they merge in oneness." *Vijñāna Bhairava*, additional audio (USF archives).

*. . . then *kuṇḍalinī* rises (*pipīla sparśa velāyāṁ*). Time comes when *pipīla sparśa* takes place, [when] you feel the sensation of the movement of an ant moving from the bottom to the top in your body. And there, *paramaṁ sukhaṁ prathate*, supreme bliss is revealed, supreme bliss takes place.

DEVOTEE: What is the difference between this rise of *kuṇḍalinī* and the rise of *prāṇa kuṇḍalinī*, which you describe at other times?

SWAMIJI: Here, this breath does not enter in *madhyā dhāma*.

DEVOTEE: It doesn't enter in *madhyā dhāma*?

SWAMIJI: No, because it resides in *madhyā dhāma*, [so] where shall it enter? It is already residing in *madhyā dhāma*, in the external world.

DEVOTEE: Swamiji, we are not clear on that at all. Why, if *prāṇa* is centered outside, should it not also lead to entering *suṣumnā*?

SWAMIJI: If it has already entered, if it is already in *suṣumnā*, why to make it enter in somewhere else?

DEVOTEE: Because this is external *madhyā dhāma*?

SWAMIJI: *Bas*, external and internal *madhyā dhāma* are one.

DEVOTEE: That means it does enter *suṣumnā*?

SWAMIJI: It has entered, it has entered already. It has entered universal *suṣumnā*.

DEVOTEE: Your body and your mind and everything is just . . . This point, this *madhya dhāma* in the outside world, means that you are in complete harmony with everything . . .

SWAMIJI: Yes.

DEVOTEE: . . . and once you achieve this complete harmony of everything . . .

SWAMIJI: You are in *madhyā dhāma*.

DEVOTEE: . . . you are there.

SWAMIJI: Yes.

DEVOTEE: But from the point of view of realization, what is happening to *prāṇa*? What is happening to *prāṇa* that moment of centering?

SWAMIJI: *Kuṇḍalinī* takes place; just *kuṇḍalinī* rises at once.

DEVOTEE: There is no stopping of breath?

SWAMIJI: No.

DEVOTEE: What *upāya* is this?

SWAMIJI: This is also *āṇavopāya* but sentenced to *śāmbhavopāya*.

JOHN: So this centering, this is that centering between two steps, that kind of centering in terms of that *madhyā dharma*?

SWAMIJI: No, not two steps. There are no two steps. It is checked simultaneously, all the flow of senses, by *prāṇa śakti*.

JOHN: By centering, by having that higher *prāṇa śakti*.

SWAMIJI: Yes, higher *prāṇa śakti*, by maintaining that higher *prāṇa śakti*.

JOHN: But that higher *prāṇa śakti* comes about through centering, external centering, *madhyā dhāma*?

SWAMIJI: No, by thought-lessness, by one-pointedness. For instance, when you breathe, or breathe in and out, you breathe in and out without any thought, without any impressions of outward movements. That is the energy of *prāṇa śakti*. *Prāṇa śakti* becomes *śakti*.

DEVOTEE: From *citta vṛtti*[228] to *śakti*, from *vṛtti* to *śakti*?

SWAMIJI: Yes, now you have come to the point.

DEVOTEE: But why does that not lead to the sucking down of the breath?

SWAMIJI: It is already sucked.

DEVOTEE: But it is moving. You said it is moving?

SWAMIJI: It is moving, but the basis is *madhyā dhāma*.

DEVOTEE: This is with open eyes?

SWAMIJI: Yes, open eyes.

JOHN: So then if your attention is on breath so much that it becomes one-pointed . . .

SWAMIJI: There is no attention.

JOHN: But one-pointedness is gained.

---

228 Fluctuations (*vṛtti*) of thoughts (*citta*).

SWAMIJI: One-pointedness is gained while breathing.

DEVOTEE: That leads to the rise of *kuṇḍalinī*?

SWAMIJI: That leads to the rise of *kuṇḍalinī*. That is *pipīla sparśa*. And that *kuṇḍalinī* rises very minutely there.

DEVOTEE: Very?

SWAMIJI: Minutely, not in an abrupt [way], not in a flash.

DEVOTEE: Is this *prāṇa kuṇḍalinī* or *cit kuṇḍalinī*?

SWAMIJI: No, this is *cit kuṇḍalinī*. It is *cit kuṇḍalinī*, but the rise of *cit kuṇḍalinī* takes place very slowly here, not in a flash. It is why He has put, *pipīla sparśa velā*, the movement of an ant.

DEVOTEE: If there is succession, what does he experience on the way between. What is this successive form of *cit kuṇḍalinī*? This goes through the *cakras*?

SWAMIJI: No, no *cakras*.

DEVOTEE: Then how is *cit kuṇḍalinī* realized gradually? I don't see how *cit* can be realized gradually. Surely *cit* can only manifest Itself.

SWAMIJI: You will see when it flows like that. You will see by yourself.

DEVOTEE: But that movement is the movement of *nimīlanā*?

SWAMIJI: It is not in a flash.

DEVOTEE: It is movement of *nimīlanā*?

SWAMIJI: It is movement of *nimīlanā*, but firm movement of *nimīlanā*.

DEVOTEE: What is weak movement of *nimīlanā*?

SWAMIJI: In a flash. When it rises in a flash, then it is the weak movement of *kuṇḍalinī*. Yes, you scratch your head [laughs]!

DEVOTEE: You always told us that instantaneous revelation of *cit* was the highest.

SWAMIJI: That was the highest, yes.

DEVOTEE: So how are you saying this is lower?

SWAMIJI: But it is lower than this.

DEVOTEE: But this is in *āṇavopāya*.

SWAMIJI: Yes, *āṇavopāya* also will take you there, will carry you there.

JOHN: Why is it in *āṇavopāya*?

SWAMIJI: Because breath has to be recited, breath has to be taken in and out. In *śāktopāya*, there is no breath, there is no breathing exercise. In *āṇavopāya*, there is a breathing exercise. There is a breathing exercise here.

DEVOTEE: But this moves quickly to *śāmbhavopāya*.

SWAMIJI: *Śāmbhavopāya* quickly, without touching *śāktopāya*.

It starts in *āṇavopāya* and ends in *śāmbhavopāya*.

JOHN: So this one-pointedness is gained through breathing?

SWAMIJI: This one-pointedness is meant for those who are elevated *sādhakas*, elevated *yogis*. It is not done by everybody. It can't be done by everybody. This *āṇavopāya* is superior *āṇavopāya*. It is thought-less. It is why it carries you from *āṇavopāya* to *śāmbhavopāya*–straight.

DEVOTEE: Swamiji, the concentration, is it on just *prāṇa* itself, not just *prāṇa* inside but *prāṇa* in everything? Like *prāṇa* in a leaf or prāṇa . . . ?

SWAMIJI: No, it is not that. It is just breathing, ordinary breathing.

JOHN: So you just breathe and center yourself?

SWAMIJI: No, just center yourself and then breathe.

JOHN: First you center yourself . . .

SWAMIJI: . . . and then breathe, in that center. That is the elevated energy of *prāṇa śakti*.

JOHN: That seems a very high state to center yourself.

SWAMIJI: Yes, exactly.

Dhāraṇā 45

वह्नेर्विषस्य मध्ये तु
चित्तं सुखमयं क्षिपेत् ।
केवलं वायुपूर्णं वा
स्मरानन्देन युज्यते ॥६८॥

vahnerviṣasya madhye tu
cittaṁ sukhamayaṁ kṣipet /
kevalaṁ vāyupūrṇaṁ vā
smarānandena yujyate // 68 //

Now He puts another process. It is *śāktopāya*.

Make your mind rest between the energy of will and knowledge. Give your mind rest between the energy of will and knowledge (*icchā* and *jñāna*; *vahni* is will, *viṣa* is knowledge).

Or, between the rise of sex excitement and the appeased state of that act; when the rise of sex excitement takes place and when that excitement is appeased. When the rise of sex excitement takes place, that is *vahni*, that is the state of *vahni*. And when the sex excitement is appeased, that is *viṣa*.

JOHN: "Appeased" means "fulfilled" or just "taken away"?

SWAMIJI: No, when it is *śāntā*.[229]

DEVOTEE: This is *vyāpti kale*?

SWAMIJI: *Vyāpti kale*.[230]

DEVOTEE: This is *kāma* in *viṣa tattva*?

SWAMIJI: *Viṣa tattva*, yes.[231]

---

229 Appeased, pacified, tranquil, calm, free from passions, undisturbed.

230 The moment of pervasion.

231 "*Kāma kalā* is the technique of grasping the moment of union (*saṁghaṭṭa*) of the senses and their objects. *Viṣa tattva* is the state of being where you are either given to expansion or to the state of contraction. In Shaivism, the word "*viṣa*" is explained in two ways. The word "*viṣa*" means, literally, "poison." When you are in the

Make your mind rest between these two states: between the energy of will and knowledge, or between the rise of sex excitement and its appeased state.

Smarānandena yujyate, [the *yogi*] is united in *smarānanda* (*smarānanda* means the *saṁghaṭṭa*[232] of Śiva and Śakti) and attains the state of supreme *ānanda*. That is *smarānanda*.

Smarānanda here does not mean the *ānanda* of the sexual act. *Smarānanda* [literally] means, it is *kāmānanda*, it is the bliss of, the joy of, the sexual act. But, in fact, here you must not take it that way. You must see "*smarānanda*" is the *ānanda* risen in the union of Śiva and Śakti.

DEVOTEE: *Rudrayāmala*?

SWAMIJI: [Yes], *Rudrayāmala*.[233] This is *śāktopāya* also.

DEVOTEE: But this *ānanda* is the highest *ānanda*. It leads eventually to *jagadānanda* through *krama mudrā*.

SWAMIJI: It is not *jagadānanda*. It is *cidānanda*.[234]

DEVOTEE: *Cidānanda–nimīlanā*.

SWAMIJI: Yes, it is *nimīlanā*.[235]

---

sexual act (*viṣa tattva*) and you are elevated and situated in the expansion of your nature, then at the very moment of union, you will gain entry in *kuṇḍalinī*. If, however, you are given to the sexual act, then this sexual act will cause you to fall. This is also *viṣa tattva*, but in this case you are carried away from your nature. So, in *viṣa tattva*, when, in that act, you do not get entry into your nature, that act is poison for you. For those who are elevated, this same poison is actually ecstasy (*amṛta*)." *Self Realization in Kashmir Shaivism*, 5.102, footnotes 13, 14.

232 Union.

233 "*Rudrayāmala* means, the copulation of Rūdra and Rudrāṇī. This is the transcendental language of love of Śiva with Pārvatī. This is the real language of love." *Parātriśikā Laghuvṛtti,* with the commentary of Abhinavagupta, translation and commentary by Swami Lakshmanjoo (original audio recording, USF archives, Los Angeles, 1982).

234 See Appendix for an explanation of the seven states of *ānanda*.

235 "All of the states of *turya* from *nijānanda* to *cidānanda* comprise the various phases of *nimīlanā samādhi*. With the occurrence of *krama mudrā*, *nimīlanā samādhi* is transformed into *unmīlanā samādhi*, which then becomes predominant. And when

When you are not married, you [can] put your mind rested between will and knowledge. When you are married, you can put your mind in [between] the beginning of sex excitement and in the end when it is appeased.

DEVOTEE: Only if you are married?

SWAMIJI: Yes.

Kevalaṁ vāyupūrṇaṁ vā, and don't let your breath move out. There, you must not let your breath move out. If you let your breath move out–after this act or after this state–if you leave your breath out and in, you are gone, you have not achieved anything. You have to maintain the breath inside. You won't die. There, you won't die.

DEVOTEE: But this is not *kumbhakā*?

SWAMIJI: This is not *kumbhakā*[236]. It is automatic *kumbhakā*–automatic.

DEVOTEE: *Nimīlanā.*

SWAMIJI: *Nimīlanā.*

DEVOTEE: Then how will it work in will and knowledge?

SWAMIJI: Will means *icchā*, knowledge means *jñāna*. For instance, this is a handkerchief [Swamiji demonstrates]. "What is this?"–this is will. "This is a handkerchief"–this is *jñāna*. Between these two movements, you must make your mind rest. Your mind must remain there.

DEVOTEE: That is, soon after will, it must stop.

SWAMIJI: Soon after will, it must stop; and, before knowledge, it must stop.

DEVOTEE: So it should not move to knowledge, rather?

SWAMIJI: Yes, it should not move to knowledge [but] it should come out from will. This is between.

DEVOTEE: The point between *nirvikalpa* and *savikalpa*[237]?

SWAMIJI: Yes.

DEVOTEE: When we see firstly and say, "What is this?" this

---

unmīlanā samādhi becomes fixed and permanent, this is the state of *jagadānanda*. See Appendix for an explanation of *krama mudrā*, *nimīlanā* and *unmīlanā samādhi*.

236 Retention of breath.

237 The point between thought-lessness (*nirvikalpa*) and thoughtfulness (*savikalpa*).

is will.

SWAMIJI: This is will. When you see, "This is a handkerchief", that is knowledge, that is *jñāna*. Don't come to that. Move out from that, "What is this?" Move out from that state. You have to move out from that. Which? That perceiving state that, "What is it?" You have to come out from that state [of will] and not to reach that state [of knowledge]. There you have to put your mind [to] rest.[238]

DEVOTEE: It means, almost the first impression?

SWAMIJI: First *ālocana*, *prathamābhāsa*.[239] It is just *prathamābhāsa*. But it is not actually *prathamābhāsa*. If it were actually *prathamābhāsa* . . . when actual *prathamābhāsa* takes place, it is without support. [Here], you have to take support also. So I have put this [*dhāraṇā*] as *śāktopāya*. You have to take support of these two first. Before resting your mind in *śāmbhavopāya*, you have to take support of these two movements first–the support of will and the support of knowledge, where you see the gap in-between for resting. That is *śāmbhava*; where you rest, that is the *śāmbhava* state. As [long as] that resting place takes place by these two supports, it is *śāktopāya*, it won't be *śāmbhava*.

DEVOTEE: So, simply seeing the handkerchief, because the cognition goes out, that is will?

SWAMIJI: You have not to see the handkerchief. "What is it?"–that is the movement of will. "This is a handkerchief"–this is the movement of knowledge. So, you have to find out the movement in-between. Come down from that will, [but] don't reach that knowledge. Look at this movement also [Swamiji demonstrates]. There are two movements. I want to join these two fingers. They are not yet joined. When I am about to move for joining, that is will. When it is joined, it is knowledge. But this movement must not take place. You have to come down from this movement, the first movement, [but]

---

238 It is *nirvikalpa*, thought-lessness.

239 *Ālocana* and *prathamābhāsa* refer to the initial flow of objective perception or sensation. "*Prathamābhāsa* means the appearance of God consciousness in universal objectivity." *Festival of Devotion and Praise–Śhivastotrāvalī, Hymns to Shiva* by Utpaladeva, Swami Lakshmanjoo, ed. John Huges, (Universal Shaiva Fellowship, Los Angeles, 2014). Chapter 9, verse 5.

you have not to reach this [second] movement. That is "*ālocana*[240]". That is *śāktopāya* because it is through these two supports of movements.

JOHN: So then, in any perception, the first moment of perception is *nirvikalpa*, and then automatically that *savikalpa* comes. And so that moment between, . . . ?

SWAMIJI: . . . that is *nirvikalpa*.

DEVOTEE: That is *nirvikalpa*, but when you go straight into that *nirvikalpa* moment, into that *ālocana*, . . .

SWAMIJI: That is *śāmbhavopāya*.

DEVOTEE: . . . that is *śāmbhavopāya*. Here you are trying to find the moment between these two points?

SWAMIJI: By support. [With] support, that is *śāktopāya*.

---

240 Lit., seeing, perceiving.

Now, these two *ślokas*–from my point of view–these two are not *dhāraṇās* (from my point of view). Some saints say that these two *ślokas* are also two processes, separate processes of *sādhanā*–these two ways. These are sexual.

JOHN: Sixty-nine and seventy.

SWAMIJI: Sixty-nine and seventy.

शक्तिसंगमसंक्षुब्ध-
शक्त्यावेशावसानिकम् ।
यत्सुखं ब्रह्मतत्त्वस्य
तत्सुखं स्वाक्यमुच्यते ॥ ६९ ॥

लेहनामन्थनाकोटैः
स्त्रीसुखस्य भरात्स्मृतेः ।
शक्त्यभावेऽपि देवेशि
भवेदानन्दसंप्लवः ॥ ७० ॥

śaktisaṁgamasaṁkṣubdha-
śaktyāveśāvasānikam /
yatsukhaṁ brahmatattvasya
tatsukhaṁ svākyamucyate / / 69 / /

lehanāmanthanākoṭaiḥ
strīsukhasya bharātsmṛteḥ /
śaktyabhāve'pi deveśi
bhavedānandasaṁplavaḥ / / 70 / /

The direct way of the sex act is first (sixty-ninth) and the indirect way of the sex act is the seventieth *śloka*.

JOHN: Direct way is sixty-nine.

SWAMIJI: Sixty-nine is the direct way of the sex act.

When you are united with each other (*śakti saṁgama*) and when *saṁkṣubdha śakti*, when your other female partner is agitated, *āveśa āvasānikam*, at the end of that agitation[241], whatever joy is experienced by these partners, that joy has got a similarity to that supreme realization of Lord Śiva.

It is just like that joy. It is not processed, it is not to do.[242] It is just a simile–what kind of joy you perceive in *samādhi*. You perceive that kind of joy.

Or, you perceive that kind of joy [of] *samādhi* when you think of this sex act (by *lehana*; *lehana* means, thinking of kissing or embracing, or all these acts). But this thinking is to be done not by-the-way, *bharāt smṛteḥ*, it is to be done in an intensive way, because if you don't think of this act in an intensive way, you won't get that joy. Although there is not your other partner, *śakti abhāve'pi*, [even] if the other partner is not there, by only thinking in an intensive way, that *ānanda* rises, that *ānanda* (that bliss) of that sexual bliss takes place, which is just like the *ānanda* of your state of *samādhi*.

This is not a process. These two are not *dhāraṇās* from my point of view, but some professors of these books say that this is also a *dhāraṇā*, [that] this must also be functioned like this. Here, from my point of view, this is not a *dhāraṇā*.

[Bhairava] puts the similarity of *brahma sukha*[243], how *brahma sukha* can be taken. What sort of bliss you get in *samādhi*? You get the blissful state of *samādhi*, just like this bliss.

DEVOTEE: But other *ācāryas* including Abhinavagupta[244] have taken it as a *dhāraṇā* here.

SWAMIJI: If you ask me, I won't agree, I have got a disagreement with that, in this point. [These two verses are] only just to show you what kind of bliss and joy you perceive in *samādhi*. And the *Vijñāna Bhairava* will tell you that this is not a process. The *Vijñāna Bhairava*, this book itself, will tell you in the seventy-first *śloka* that this was not a process, [that] this was only a similarity.

---

241 That is, the climax or orgasm.

242 Nothing is to be done apart from simply acknowledging the intensity and divinity of sexual joy.

243 The joy (*sukha*) of Brahman.

244 Abhinavagupta quotes this verse as a *dhāraṇā* in his *Īśvara Pratyabhijñā Vivṛti Vimarśinī*.

Dhāraṇā 46

आनन्दे महति प्राप्ते
    दृष्टे वा बान्धवे चिरात् ।
आनन्दमुद्गतं ध्यात्वा
    तल्लयस्तन्मना भवेत् ॥७१॥

ānande mahati prāpte
    dṛṣṭe vā bāndhave cirāt /
ānandamudgataṁ dhyātvā
    tallayastanmanā bhavet / / 71 / /

Now, this is a process. Now, the process of the sex act He will explain to you.

Here, [in the previous two verses], there was no process at all. There was only to enjoy the sexual act. The enjoyment of the sexual act was to be enjoyed–finished! There was no process. Is there a process written? Now He will tell you what we have to do there in the sexual act.

Ānande mahati prāpte[245], when that supreme bliss takes place in the sexual act, or *dṛṣṭe vā bāndhave cirāt*, or [when] your own dear, dearest one, is seen after a long interval of period (when you see your dearest one, who has been out of sight for so many years, and you have seen him), when you see him, at the very first moment, you are filled with that joy. This is like that [sexual] joy–*dṛṣṭe vā bāndhave cirāt*.

What you have to do there in these two states–in the sexual act (in the enjoyment, in the joy, the rise of joy, in the sexual act; when the rise of joy takes place in the sexual act) or when the rise of joy takes place when you see your dearest one after a long interval of period?

There you have to do *ānandam udgataṁ dhyātvā*, you have to find out wherefrom this joy has appeared. Just find out from which point this joy has appeared. Situate your mind there with full awareness, and then you will attain that

245 *Prāpte* is *saptamī* (locative case). *Ānande mahati prāpte* means the supreme *ānanda* when it has been *prāpte*, realized.

nirvikalpa state of *samādhi*.

This is the process of the above two *ślokas*.[246]

Or, *dṛṣṭe vā bandhave cirāt*.

Tat layaḥ tanmanā bhavet. Tat layaḥ, the one who has melted in that, the one who has absorbed himself in that, he becomes one with that, his thought becomes one with that (*tanmanā bhavet*). [His thought becomes one with] *udgacchantam*, where it rises.

DEVOTEE: At the moment of rising?

SWAMIJI: At the very moment of rising.

JOHN: So he maintains his awareness and puts all his attention on that, . . .

SWAMIJI: Yes.

JOHN: . . . on that bliss.[247]

SWAMIJI: And when he recognizes that *udgama sthāna*, recognizes the place of the source, *tat layaḥ*, he must melt his energy in that, he must melt his awareness in that, [and] he becomes one with that; then he will become one with that (*tanmanā bhavet*).

DEVOTEE: Which *upāya* is this?

SWAMIJI: Which *upāya*? This can be *śāktopāya* or *śāmbhavopāya* even.

---

246 In the previous two *ślokas* (69-70), there was no process (*upāya*), but if one is to apply a process (*upāya*), then this verse (71) teaches the process which is to be applied for both the direct sexual act (verse 69) and indirect sexual act (verse 70), i.e., "to find out wherefrom this joy has appeared."

247 He maintains awareness, not on the bliss itself, but on the source of the bliss.

Dhāraṇā 47

Now, next:

जग्धिपानकृतोल्लास-
रसानन्दविजृम्भणात् ।
भावयेद्भरितावस्थां
महानन्दस्ततो भवेत् ॥७२॥

jagdhipānakṛtollāsa
rasānandavijṛmbhaṇāt /
bhāvayedbharitāvasthāṁ
mahānandastato bhavet / / 72 / /

Or, take some sweet dish, put some sweet dish before you, or a sweet drink.

Jagdhi means, a sweet edible thing. *Pāna* means, a sweet drink. It will be *kṣīra pāna*[248] or it will be *vīrapāna*[249], anything you like. What[ever] is delicious to the drinker or eater. Whatever you like most [to eat], eat that. Whatever you like most to drink, drink that.

And, at that moment, what is to be done is told here: *jagdhi pāna kṛtollāsa rasānanda vijṛimbhaṇāt*, when you are full of that blissful taste while eating or while drinking [and] you [have] merged yourself in that blissful taste, *bhāvayed bharitāvasthām*, don't think [of] yourself as an individual being; consider yourself, or imagine that you are, all-full, all-round full (*bhāvayet bharitāvasthām*). *Pūrṇā avasthāṁ bhāvayet*, you must imagine that you are situated in the supreme and full state of Lord Śiva (*mahānanda*[250]).

It is *śāktopāya*.[251]

---

248 A sweet milk drink.

249 Lit., "heroic-water", viz., a spirit.

250 Supreme bliss.

251 "Because, with support, whatever *nirvikalpa* (thought-lessness) takes place, wherever it takes place, [it] is *śāktopāya*, it can't be *śāmbhavopāya*. When it takes place without support, that is *śāmbhavopāya*." *Vijñāna Bhairava*, additional audio (USF archives).

Dhāraṇā 48

गीतादिविषयास्वादा-
समसौख्यैकतात्मनः ।
योगिनस्तन्मयत्वेन
मनोरूढेस्तदात्मता ॥७३॥

gītādiviṣayāsvādā-
samasaukhyaikatātmanaḥ /
yoginastanmayatvena
manorūḍhestadātmatā / / 73 / /

Gītādi viṣaya āsvāda. Now take musical instruments, a music performance (*gītādi viṣaya*; that is also *viṣaya*, that is also our diet, our diet through the ears, an aural diet).[252] *Gītādi viṣaya āsvāda*, the *yogi* whose mind is focused in the unparalleled ecstasy while experiencing these songs (*gītādi viṣaya āsvādā*), *asama saukhyaikatātmanaḥ* (*asama saukhya* means "unparalleled [bliss]"; *asama* means "unparalleled", *sukha* means "bliss"), when he is united, has become one, with that unparalleled bliss there, . . .

I think this way you should understand it: when the *yogi tanmayatvena manorūḍheḥ*, becomes one with that sound of a song, and when his mind is absorbed in the one collective sound of a song (not different [sounds], and you have to put your mind on that collective sound there), . . .*

DEVOTEE: That *nāda*.[253]

SWAMIJI: The *nāda* that prevails in all the seven *svaras* (*pañchamam*, *gandhāram*, . . . what is that? There are

---

252 Swamiji said that "*gītādi*" (songs, etc.) includes poetry.

253 "And the embodiment of that sound is *nāda*; *nāda* means, internal sound. And that sound is not particular sound. It is that sound which resides in each and every sound. *Tantrāloka* 6.218, (USF archive.)

seven[254]).

. . . when he concentrates on that collective sound, there in that string instrument, . . .

He touches all the seven strings; simultaneously he touches all the seven strings, and one collective sound is produced from seven sounds, and you have to put your mind on that collective sound, only one collective sound, where seven sounds are produced. Don't put your mind in a successive way on each and every sound of these seven *svaras*.

DEVOTEE: But Swamiji, when music is being played, it is not often that you hear a collective sound. In any *rāga*, you hear one note after another. Sometimes they will be collective notes.

SWAMIJI: But still then you hear.

*. . . when that collective way is being functioned, there you have scope to enter in *samādhi*.

DEVOTEE: But elsewhere here it said that the *yogi* can enter in *samādhi* through perceiving that sound, which is not a sound in any sound.

SWAMIJI: Elevated ones are capable of doing that.

DEVOTEE: Even this is in *śāmbhavopāya*, isn't it? When you listen to that collective sound?

SWAMIJI: Then it goes to the *śāmbhava* state, but [the practice itself] is *śāktopāya* because there is support.

yeṣāṁ na tanmayībhūtiste dehādinimajjanam //
avidanto magnasaṁvit mānāstvahṛdayā iti /[255]

These are the sayings of Abhinavagupta himself in the *Tantrāloka*.

Yeṣāṁ na tanmayībhūtiḥ, those who have no capacity to find that collective sound there in that music, *te dehādi*

---

254 These refer to the names of the seven notes in classical Indian music: *shadjam* for '*sa*', *rishabham* for '*ri*', *gandhāram* for '*ga*', *madhyamam* for '*ma*', *pañchamam* for '*pa*', *dhaivatam* for '*dha*', and *nishādham* for '*ni*'.

255 *Tantrāloka*, 3.240.

nimajjanaṁ avidanto, they have no technique, they have no way in hand, [of] how to absorb their individuality in universality. They have no capacity of that. *Tva hṛdaya iti*, so they are without heart, they are *jaḍa*[256].

DEVOTEE: Abhinavagupta says you can rise very high with that collective meaning that is suggested in poetry.

SWAMIJI: For elevated souls.

DEVOTEE: *Sahṛdayā*, only for *vīras*.[257]

SWAMIJI: It is for elevated souls. They can rise in the ordinary talk of life, this rough talk. In rough talk also they can rise–those elevated souls.

DEVOTEE: But the words in poetry are not the same as the words in real life.

SWAMIJI: Not only poetry, even in ordinary talk also there is scope of rising, but [only] for those who are elevated.

DEVOTEE: But in poetry there is a special power for rising.

SWAMIJI: Yes, rising for those who are a bit elevated. For those who are fully elevated souls, they can rise in ordinary talk also (e.g., in hearing bad names) *adivāda*[258], for them, for those elevated souls, not for everybody.

This is *śāktopāya*.

---

256 Inert, senseless, duffers.

257 Heroes.

258 Offensive words.

Dhāraṇā 49

यत्र यत्र मनस्तुष्टि-
मनस्तत्रैव धारयेत् ।
तत्र तत्र परानन्द-
स्वरूपं संप्रवर्तते ॥७४॥

yatra yatra manastuṣṭir-
manastatraiva dhārayet /
tatra tatra parānanda-
svarūpaṁ sampravartate // 74 //
[not recited in full]

Wherever your mind becomes peaceful, wherever your mind is situated peacefully, put your mind there.

If your mind is situated peacefully in working in the garden, put your mind there; don't go in the prayer room for prayer. Going in the prayer room at that moment is a sin for you, and working in the garden is the right way for you.

Wherever your mind is fixed, attracted, put your mind there; *yatra yatra manas tuṣṭiḥ*, *manas tatraiva dhārayet*, there you must fix your mind. Don't go anywhere else. Don't think that this is an impure act.[259] That is a pure act for you [whereas] the "pure" act is an impure act for you.

Tatra tatra parānanda svarūpaṁ sampravartate, there and then, at that very place, the supreme *ānanda* state will take place. Wherever your mind is appeased in peace, there and then the supreme kingdom of *ānanda* will appear to you.[260]

259 Whatever activity it is that pleases you.

260 Swamiji did not indicate the *upāya* for this *dhāraṇā*.

Dhāraṇā 50

अनागतायां निद्रायां
    प्रणष्टे बाह्यगोचरे ।
सावस्था मनसा गम्या
    परा देवी प्रकाशते ॥७५॥

anāgatāyāṁ nidrāyāṁ
  praṇaṣṭe bāhyagocare /
sāvasthā manasā gamyā
  parā devī prakāśate / / 75 / /

When sleep has not yet come (*anāgatāyāṁ nidrāyāṁ*, when sleep has not yet taken place), *prāṇaṣṭe bāhya gocare*, and when wakefulness is over–wakefulness is over and sleep has not yet come–there, if, by your mind, you realize that state in-between, the supreme energy of God consciousness will appear to you.

This is *śāmbhavopāya*. This is the *śāmbhava* state because there is no support.

DEVOTEE: This is not that emerging of awareness into that moment of sleep that takes place in *cakrodaya*, which you describe in the seven *ānandas*[261]? Not that moment–same moment, but here it is in *śāmbhavopāya*.

SWAMIJI: Yes, it is *śāmbhavopāya*.

DEVOTEE: But here he experiences no drowsiness?

SWAMIJI: No, no drowsiness.

DEVOTEE: No drowsiness at all?

SWAMIJI: No, it is not drowsiness here, it is just awareness. It is only when awareness is developed in such a way that you are aware of that entering in the dreaming state.[262]

---

261 See Appendix for an explanation of the seven states of *ānanda*.

262 With reference to *āṇavopāya* and gaining the fitness for this *śāmbhavopāya* practice, Swamiji said: "The only way to experience this junction is to concentrate on any center of the heart while breathing, while talking, or while moving about. You must

If you maintain that awareness when you are to be operated on in a surgical theater and you are given that chloroform, you can't be affected by that chloroform–if you maintain that awareness. Those people cannot be prey of this chloroform because they are always aware. How can they forget their Being?

DEVOTEE: He is aware even in sleep.

SWAMIJI: Aware in sleep, in-between sleep. He knows where this wakefulness has ended and the dreaming state has started.

DEVOTEE: But he goes into the dreaming state?

SWAMIJI: He doesn't go into the dreaming state.

DEVOTEE: He never sleeps?

SWAMIJI: He never sleeps.

DEVOTEE: Because he is always aware at that point?

SWAMIJI: Yes. It is that point which gives you rest, and that relaxation of going to sleep is because of entering through that channel.

DEVOTEE: But he doesn't go to sleep, he doesn't lie down . . .

SWAMIJI: But he enters in that channel.

DEVOTEE: But he comes out? Or he stays there but he does not enter sleep?

SWAMIJI: No, he doesn't enter sleep.

DEVOTEE: He can then, he may walk, he may . . . ?

SWAMIJI: No, he can't walk; at that moment, he can't walk.

DEVOTEE: At that moment. But then does he enter sleep or not?

SWAMIJI: No, he doesn't enter sleep.

DEVOTEE: So he is still awake and aware?

---

concentrate on the center. You should watch the center of any two movements, any two breaths. Concentrate on that junction. After some time, when that concentration is established, then, whenever you go to bed to rest, you will enter the dreaming state through that junction. In this case, though, you will not enter into the dreaming state. Instead, you will be aware at that point, at that junction. This junction is only a gate, the entrance to *turya*." *Kashmir Shaivism–The Secret Supreme*, 16.108.

SWAMIJI: He is not aware of the body.

DEVOTEE: Is the body asleep?

SWAMIJI: Yes. The body is not there. He doesn't see his body, he doesn't see his body, he doesn't see dreams, but he is aware of his Being.

DEVOTEE: But, from a medical point of view, the body is asleep.

SWAMIJI: The body is not there–for him.

DEVOTEE: For him it is not, but from the point of view from others?

SWAMIJI: For others, the body is there.

DEVOTEE: The body is sleeping?

SWAMIJI: The body is not sleeping.

JOHN: No, the body is not sleeping. This is *nimīlanā samādhi*. The body doesn't sleep.

SWAMIJI: Actually, the body is not sleeping. Every other person will observe that he is in *samādhi*, that he is in *samādhi*, [that] he is looking like this.

DEVOTEE: But the . . . is missing, body is missing at that time?

SWAMIJI: He does not see his body.

DEVOTEE: He is not body-conscious.

SWAMIJI: He is not body-conscious. He is conscious of the Self.

DEVOTEE: His body will require rest?

SWAMIJI: But this is the real rest. The *turya* [state] is the real rest. That center is the real rest. It is the *turya* state.

This is *śāmbhavopāya*.

Dhāraṇā 51

तेजसा सूर्यदीपादे-
राकाशे शबलीकृते ।
दृष्टिर्निवेश्या तत्रैव
स्वात्मरूपं प्रकाशते ॥७६॥

tejasā sūryadipāder-
ākāśe śabalīkṛte /
dṛṣṭirniveśyā tatraiva
svātmarūpaṁ prakāśate / / 76 / /

Just imagine that the whole *ākāśa*[263] is filled with the effulgent light of the sun.

It is outside, it is a *dhāraṇā* done outside, and [also] a *dhāraṇā* done in your room at night. Put the bulb on, the light on, and go on concentrating and putting your eyesight on that light of the bulb, and don't think of any other thing in-between, [and] you will enter in *samādhi*. Only see the light of the bulb without that glass [encasement]. The enclosure of glass you must ignore, [and see] only the light in the room. Or, [see] only the light of the sun in the whole ether, atmosphere.

JOHN: That doesn't means you should look at the sun like you are looking at the bulb?

SWAMIJI: No, you have to look at the light. It is just imagination.

DEVOTEE: Also flame here–*dīpa*.

SWAMIJI: A flame in the room, *dīpa* is in the room. The sun is outside in the garden. In the garden there is an exercise [and] in the room also there is an exercise.

DEVOTEE: So by *ādi*[264], He means "the light bulb"?

SWAMIJI: Yes, bulb also. The light [of the sun] is there, just have some acquaintance with that light and *bas*, think that–

263 Ether, space.

264 *Ādi* can mean, "beginning with" or "etcetera".

[by] internal *dṛṣṭi*[265]–the whole atmosphere is filled with light. Or, look at the light of the bulb in the room, and just have acquaintance with that light for some time, and close your eyes, and see that the whole room is effulgent, filled with that light.

DEVOTEE: Swamiji, can we do it in moonlight?

SWAMIJI: Moonlight is not said here.

DEVOTEE: You look at the light and then close the eyes. You don't just continue looking at the light.

SWAMIJI: No. Continue not. It is not [looking at it] in continuity. It is just imagination. Just look at it, have acquaintance with it, know it, remember it, and get lost in it.

DEVOTEE: This is *śāktopāya*?

SWAMIJI: Yes, this is *śāktopāya*.

DEVOTEE: But not very . . . not the highest *śāktopāya*, because it is very much with support.

SWAMIJI: Yes, it is [with] support.

DEVOTEE: Highest *śāktopāya* is that one described in that *śūnya pañcakam*?

SWAMIJI: *Śūnya pañcakam* or "this whole universe is my own Self."[266]

---

265 Sight.

266 Here, Swamji is referring to the highest practices in *śāktopāya*: *śūnya pañcakam* (verse 32) and *adhva prakriyā* (verse 57).

Dhāraṇā 52

करङ्किण्या क्रोधनया
भैरव्या लेलिहानया ।
खेचर्या दृष्टिकाले च
परावाप्तिः प्रकाशते ॥७७॥

karaṅkiṇyā krodhanayā
bhairavyā lelihānayā /
khecaryā dṛṣṭikāle ca
parāvāptiḥ prakāśate // 77 //

These are the five states of the five saints, five ancient saints, five states of schools, schools of five, . . .

DEVOTEE: Schools of thought.

SWAMIJI: . . . schools of thought of five ancient [types of] saints. The five ancient [types of] saints are: *jñāna siddhas* (saints risen from knowledge), saints risen from *mantras*[267], saints risen from *melāpa* (*yoginī melāpa*)[268], and saints risen from enjoyment[269], and saints risen by thought-lessness (*nirvikalpa*)[270].

DEVOTEE: Isn't thought-lessness in all those?

SWAMIJI: Yes, in the end.

DEVOTEE: So why is it made a special category?

SWAMIJI: Thoughtlessness: to begin and end in thought-lessness. The process begins in thought-lessness and ends in thought-lessness. *Śāmbhava siddha* is the highest. *Śāmbhava siddhas* are the highest producers [among the five] schools.

DEVOTEE: This, the *śāmbhava siddhas*.

SWAMIJI: *Śāmbhava siddhas*. [The five *siddhas* are]: *jñāna siddhas*, *mantra siddhas*, *melāpa siddhas*, *śākta siddhas*, and *śāmbhava siddhas*.

---

267 *Mantra siddhas.*

268 *Melāpa siddhas.*

269 *Śākta siddhas.*

270 *Śāmbhava siddhas.*

Jñāna Siddhas

Now for *jñāna siddhas*, those who have become elevated by knowledge of books. They have got the final position of the *mudrā* that is called *karaṅkiṇī*. *Karaṅkiṇī* is that position of your body when your body is flat on the ground, . . .

DEVOTEE: Like a corpse.

SWAMIJI: . . . just like a corpse, a dead body, without any movement. They lie down and have no movement in the end. That is *karaṅkiṇī mudrā*. This *karaṅkiṇī mudrā* was from ancient times, innumerable ancient times, functioned by *jñāna siddhas*, for those saints who were *siddhas* from knowledge.

DEVOTEE: They maintain enlightenment–does this mean only from *śāstras*?

SWAMIJI: Only from *śāstras*.

DEVOTEE: Without a guru?

SWAMIJI: With a guru. With a guru everywhere, without a guru nowhere. Without a guru nowhere, with a guru everywhere.

DEVOTEE: But isn't it explained in the *Tantrāloka* that there are enlightened people without gurus–*samsiddhika*? *Svasamvid devībhiḥ dīkṣitaḥ*[271].

SWAMIJI: *Sva saṁvid devī* is the guru there–*svasaṁvitti devībhirdīkṣitaḥ*[272]. So there is the guru.

Mantra Siddhas

The *krodhanī* posture is [the *mudrā*] of those who have become *siddhas* by *mantra yoga*, by the recitation of *mantras*; those ancient saints who have attained *siddhi* powers by the recitation of *mantras*. Those are called *mantra siddhas*. For them, the ending posture of the body is *krodhana*. *Krodhana* is that posture of your body when you are posed in the furious position of the body.

DEVOTEE: What is that position?

---

271 Initiated by *devīs* (goddesses).

272 "*Abhiṣiktaḥ svasaṁvitti devībhirdīkṣitaśca saḥ*. How he achieves without masters and without *śāstras*? For that, [Abhinavagupta] says, his own internal energies of Lord Śiva (*śakti-cakra*) have initiated him." *Tantrāloka* 4.42, (USF archives).

SWAMIJI: Anger. You make your face furious, without movement, wide-open eyes, wide-open mouth, wide-open teeth. And they lie down and rest in that oneness of awareness. That is *krodhana*, the posture of *krodhana*.

DEVOTEE: This is a *dhāraṇā*?

SWAMIJI: This is the ending *dhāraṇā* of *mantra siddhas*. They end in that.

DEVOTEE: And *karaṅkiṇī* is the ending *dhāraṇā* of *jñāna siddhas*.

SWAMIJI: *Jñāna siddhas*.

DEVOTEE: And what do they attain through this *mudrā*?

SWAMIJI: Oneness of Lord Śiva.

DEVOTEE: They experience *kuṇḍalinī*, *cit kuṇḍalinī*?

SWAMIJI: Yes, *cit kuṇḍalinī*.

DEVOTEE: And *krama mudrā*[273] and everything?

SWAMIJI: Everything.

DEVOTEE: *Jagadānanda*[274] . . . in that position?

SWAMIJI: *Ūrdhva kuṇḍalinī*.[275]

DEVOTEE: Why is there *niyama* of position here when it is this high? Why is there restriction of position here when it is so high?

SWAMIJI: This is what they do in the end and rise.

DEVOTEE: But they can rise without doing that?

SWAMIJI: Not those [*siddhas,* because] they have risen like this. By *mantras* you have to put that [*krodhanī mudrā*] because, by the recitation of *mantras*, your body has become more attached to you, to your soul. So you have to shatter it out by *krodha*, by wrath, by the posture of wrath.[276]

Melāpa Siddhas

And there is *bhairavī*. *Bhairavī* is another posture [*mudrā*] for those who have become saints by *melāpa*, by the union of

---

273 See Appendix for an explanation of *krama mudrā*.

274 See Appendix for an explanation of the seven states of *ānanda*.

275 See Appendix for an explanation of *kuṇḍalinī*.

276 "The word '*krodha*' does not denote wrathfulness in the present context. Here, it simply has reference to *krodha mudrā*, a kind of posture in *yoga*, and has nothing to do with your anger." *Vijñāna Bhairava*, additional audio (USF archives).

yoginīs, in a dream or in *samādhi*.

Nidrā jagaryor madhye adhirūhya daśāṁ parām, that is a dream, that is the dreaming state, when sleep has not yet come and the wakefulness is over. There, a *yoginī* appeared to him.[277] That is *melāpa*. *Yoginī melāpa* takes place there.

Yoginī melāpa does not take place just [while] we are sitting here. A *yoginī* will come during the night [in a dream] and embrace me, or kiss me, or give me some filthy thing to eat, or . . . because whatever they give is divine. You must consider everything divine, whatever they give.

DEVOTEE: Nothing can bring you down?

SWAMIJI: Nothing can bring you down. If they give you filth to eat, you must eat it. While eating, you will find the nectar in it, but it will appear to you as filth. *Yoginī melāpa* takes place there.[278] That is *bhairavī*. *Bhairavī mudrā* is meant for those [*melāpa siddhas*] in the end.

JOHN: What is *bhairavī mudrā*?

SWAMIJI: *Bhairavī mudrā* is to keep your eyes wide-open without twinkling, and your mouth also wide-open. *Bhairavī mudrā* is actually a combination of *bhairavī* and *cakita mudrā*. *Bhairavī mudrā* is a combination of *bhairavī* and *cakita mudrā*. *Antar lakṣyo bahir dṛṣṭiḥ*[279]–that is *bhairavī mudrā*: just keep your eyes wide-open, and [keep] your breath in a fix ("should I move it out or should I take it in?"), not going out, not coming in. This state of the *mudrā* you will come to know in *cakita mudrā*. *Cakita mudrā* is the pose of astonishment.

This is *bhairavī mudra*. Actually this is *bhairavī mudrā* because you do not breathe in and out. This is *bhairavī mudrā* [Swamiji demonstrates]: your eyes are wide-open, your mouth is open, and you don't breathe.

Understand?

DEVOTEE: This is not occurring only at the time of *yoginī melāpa*?

SWAMIJI: No, it is not. *Bhairavī mudrā* is the ending point

---

277 Swamiji is referring to the *yoginī* who appeared to Maheśvarānanda, the author of the *Mahārthamañjarī*.

278 In the dreaming state.

279 *Tantrāloka* 5.80, (USF archives).

of *yoginī melāpa*. When the *melāpa* is over, then you enter in *bhairavī mudrā*.

DEVOTEE: But, by this *melāpa*, one is sealed in *anupāya*.

SWAMIJI: Yes, it is *anupāya*.

DEVOTEE: This is the highest?

SWAMIJI: All are divine. All *upāyas* are divine.

DEVOTEE: All?

SWAMIJI: All are divine. This is *melāpa siddha*.

Śākta Siddhas

Now is *lelihāna*.[280]

Lelihāna is just to taste the grape of Kabul. That is a delicious grape of Kabul that used to come in those sealed plates in ancient times, when we were young. Just taste those. At the moment of doing this movement of the lips [Swamiji demonstrates, making a sound with his lips], *bas*. Now you go to the *śloka*: that is *lelihāna*, that is *lelihāna mudrā*. This *mudrā* is *lelihāna*.

What is *lelihāna mudrā*, the posture of *lelihāna*?

[Swamiji demonstrates]–this is a *mudrā*. This *mudrā* is *lelihāna mudrā*, when you are filled with the taste of some sweet thing.

DEVOTEE: Licking, licking (*lelihāna*).

SWAMIJI: This is functioned by saints who are *śākta siddhas*.

Śāmbhava Siddhas

And in the end is *khecarī mudrā*. *Khecarī mudrā* is another *mudrā* for those who are *siddhas* in the *śāmbhava* state, *śāmbhava siddhas*. *Khecarī* is meant for *śāmbhava siddhas*, in the end.

Khecarī mudrā is actually no *mudrā*. *Khecarī mudrā* is functioned in each and every act of daily life. For instance, I talk to you. When I talk to you [and say], "How do you do? Are you well?" actually I don't mean what I tell you. At that very moment, I am elevated, I am residing in the elevated state.

---

280 Lit., frequently licking or darting out the tongue, *lelihāna* denotes the enjoyment of tasting.

When I talk to you [and say], "How do you do?" I don't mean "How do you do?" at that time. I am above, I am in *ākāśa*, I am in a vacuum. I am talking in a vacuum, I am putting words in a vacuum, I am smelling in a vacuum, I am embracing in a vacuum, I am doing the sex act in a vacuum, I am doing every degraded thing in a vacuum. This is some elevated state. You are not where you are looked at. When you talk, you are talking in the elevation of the talking world, but actually you are not existing there, you are above it. When you are eating, you are not actually eating, you are above it. That is *khecarī*.

Khecarī mudrā is functioned by those who are *śāmbhavas*, who have practiced *śāmbhavopāya* for their whole life and who have established their thought in the *śāmbhava* state every now and then.

JOHN: So, this is the fullness of '*sauḥ*' *bīja*?

SWAMIJI: This is the fullness of '*sauḥ*'.[281]

DEVOTEE: In this, whatever he perceives, yet he is still aware.

SWAMIJI: It is a bit lower because [Kṛṣṇa] says, *indriyāṇī nidriyārtheṣu vartanta iti dhārayan.*[282]

DEVOTEE: There is no registration?

SWAMIJI: There is no registration of that (*indriyāṇī nidriyārtheṣu vartante*). He is above that. It is the state of all the acts of Lord Kṛṣṇa, what He did in His life. He did all these acts in the *śāmbhava* state. He was actually situated in the *śāmbhava* state of life–*khecarī*. [Likewise], we should elevate ourselves from what we say, we should be above it. That is *khecarī*. You don't mean what you mean.

DEVOTEE: You mean you are separate from that?

SWAMIJI: Not separate–above. You are that and above, above it also, above it, too.

DEVOTEE: Residing in both places.

DEVOTEE: You are in and out (*sarvottīrṇā*, *sarvamāyā*).

SWAMIJI: *Sarvamāyā*.

---

281 See Appendix for an explanation of *sauḥ*.

282 *Bhagavad Gita – In the Light of Kashmir Shaivism*, 5.9.

DEVOTEE: This is that '*sauḥ*' *bīja uccaranaṁ* . . .

SWAMIJI: Yes.

DEVOTEE: . . . in which you register everything but you are still your Self.

SWAMIJI: Yes. That is *khecarī*.

DEVOTEE: That is registering everything as *khecarī sāmya*.

SWAMIJI: Yes, *khecarī sāmya*[283]. That is *khecarī*.

DEVOTEE: But you don't go into individual things.

SWAMIJI: No, [into] the individual thing he goes, [but] while going in individual things, he is above that, . . .

DEVOTEE: *Pradeśo'pi brahmaṇa sarvam*.

SWAMIJI: . . . in each and every movement.

JOHN: He is always universal?

SWAMIJI: Yes.

DEVOTEE: Swamiji, when he perceives one individual thing, he perceives everything. Is that right?

SWAMIJI: Yes.

DEVOTEE: *Pradeśo'pi brahmaṇaḥ* . . .

SWAMIJI: . . . *sārvarūpyam anatikrāntaśca avikalpyaśca*.[284]

Khecarī is done while sitting, *lelihāna* is done while sitting, *bhairavī* is done while sitting, *krodhanī* is done while sitting, and *karaṅkiṇī* is done while lying flat, just like a dead body.

Dṛṣṭi kāle ca (*dṛṣṭi kāle ca* does not mean here, "when you experience these states of *mudrās*"; *dṛṣṭi kāle* means, "at the time when you practice these states"), *dṛṣṭikāle*, while practicing these *mudrās*, *parā vyāptiḥ prakāśate*, the pervading-ness of supreme God consciousness or universal God consciousness takes place.

This is *śāmbhavopāya*.

---

283 *Sāmya* means samenes or oneness with *khecarī*.

284 *Paramarthasāra* of Abhinavagupta, *KSTS* vol. 7, p15.

Dhāraṇā 53

मृद्वासने स्फिजैकेन
हस्तपादौ निराश्रयम् ।
निधाय तत्प्रसङ्गेन
परा पूर्णा मतिर्भवेत् ॥७८॥

mṛdvāsane sphijaikena
hastapādau nirāśrayam /
nidhāya tatprasaṅgena
parā pūrṇā matirbhavet / / 78 / /

This is *āṇavopāya-cum-śāktopāya*.[285]

Mṛdvāsane, sit on your soft seat (for instance, just a Dunlop cushion, a Dunlop pillow), sit on that soft seat, and then *hasta pādau nirāśrayaṁ nidhāya sphijaikena*, sit on the soft seat only on [one of] your buttocks. *Hasta pādau nirāśrayam nidhāya*, put your hands and feet *nirāśrayam*, without any support. Only sit on [one of] the buttocks, but on a soft seat. *Mṛdu āsane* (*mṛdu* means "soft"; *āsana*, "seat"), on the soft seat, *sphijaikena*, while sitting only on [one of] the buttocks, *hasta pādau*, put your hands and feet *nirāśrayam*, without any support (*nirāya,* "put"). *Tat prasaṅgena*, by doing this act, his individual consciousness rises to the supreme full state of universal consciousness.

DEVOTEE: There is no *mantra*? Nothing?

SWAMIJI: No *mantra*. Because, as you have to sit on the buttocks, it is *āṇavopāya*. As there is no *mantra*, nothing to be done, it will take you to *śāmbhavopāya*. From *āṇavopāya* you will rise to *śāmbhavopāya*. So I have put it as *āṇavopāya-cum-śāmbhavopāya*.

---

285 Later, Swamiji will explain that this practice is actually *āṇavopāya-cum-śāmbhavopāya*.

Dhāraṇā 54

उपविश्यासने सम्यक्
बाहू कृत्वार्धकुञ्चितौ ।
कक्षव्योम्नि मनः कुर्वन्
शममायाति तल्लयात् ॥७९॥

upaviśyāsane samyak
bāhū kṛtvārdhakuñcitau /
kakṣavyomni manaḥ kurvan
śamamāyāti tallayāḥ / / 79 / /

Upaviśyāsane samyak, be seated on some seat (it may be hard or it may be soft–it is not written there), *upaviśyāsane*, be seated on some seat, *bāhū kṛtvārdha kuñcitau*, and keep your arms half-curved, not fully curved.

For instance, when you sit on [some] *āsana*, put your arms half-curved, not fully curved, not like this [Swamiji demonstrates[286]]–half-curved. Fully curved is this, or fully curved is this. [Your arms must be] half-curved, only half-curved.

DEVOTEE: Half-bent.

SWAMIJI: Half-bent (*ārdha kuñcita*; *kuñcita* means "curved, bent").

And then what do you have to do?

Kakṣa vyomni manaḥ kurvan, find out your armpits, find out the place of your armpits, and see what is there, what vacuum is there. Put your mind and awareness in that vacuum of the armpit, both vacuums of the armpits, and you will enter in *samādhi*.

[This is] *āṇavopāya* and *śāktopāya*.

Find out the vacuum of the armpits and concentrate on that vacuum. You will enter in your own nature (*tat layāt*)

---

286 Arms crossed over the chest, the fingers of each hand tucked under the opposite armpits, with the thumbs free, pointing upwards.

when the concentration on the armpits has taken the appeased state, [when] it is over.

Kakṣa vyomni means "[the vacuum of the] armpits".

DEVOTEE: You say it is a touch of *āṇava* because of *āsana*?

SWAMIJI: *Āsana*, yes.

DEVOTEE: Would it be possible to interpret "*āsana*" just as any seat, not as a particular posture?

SWAMIJI: You see that only a seat won't do [for it to be] *āṇavopāya*. In *śāmbhavopāya* also we sit like that. It is not for that [*āsana* that] it is *āṇavopāya*. It is for this position of the arms [that] it is *āṇavopāya*, because, while maintaining the position of the arms, you have to keep your attention there for some time in order to find out the vacuum, the two vacuums of the armpits.

And when that concentration on the armpits is over, the revealing state of Lord Śiva takes place. Lord Śiva is revealed because that vacuum will carry you there, that uninterrupted concentration on that vacuum. That [concentration on the] vacuum is *śāktopāya*.[287]

287 Leading to the *śāmbhava* state and *unmīlanā samādhi* in the end. (Paraphrase taken from *Vijñāna Bhairava*, additional audio, USF archives).

Dhāraṇā 55

स्थूलरूपस्य भावस्य
स्तब्धां दृष्टिं निपात्य च ।
अचिरेण निराधारं
मनः कृत्वा शिवं व्रजेत् ॥८०॥

sthūlarūpasya bhāvasya
stabdhām dṛṣṭiṁ nipātya ca /
acireṇa nirādhāraṁ
manaḥ kṛtvā śivaṁ vrajet / / 80 / /

Just put before yourself some most well-ornamented, beautiful-shaped lady, or a beautiful-shaped flower vase, or anything [beautiful]. Put some very attractive thing before yourself, and then, . . .*

Bhāvasya means there, *strī ādi vastunaḥ*.

DEVOTEE: Something like a woman?

SWAMIJI: Something like . . . not every woman–that attractive [woman]! Or–it is not only a woman–an attractive girl, just an attractive girl of seven years old.

DEVOTEE: Something beautiful.

SWAMIJI: Something beautiful, attractive.

DEVOTEE: A painting?

SWAMIJI: Not a painting.

DEVOTEE: Why not?

SWAMIJI: It must be something substantial, full of substance. A painting is only imagination.

DEVOTEE: A flower vase?

SWAMIJI: Flower vase, yes.

DENISE: Some beautiful scenery, like a sunset?

SWAMIJI: No. It must be very near to you, very close, because *stabdhāṁ dṛṣṭiṁ nipātya ca*; *stabdhāṁ dṛṣṭiṁ*, [you have to] put your eyes on it without any movement of the eyelids.

*. . . *stabdhāṁ driṣṭiṁ nipātya ca*, and while doing so,

acireṇa nirādhāraṁ manaḥ kṛitvā, at the same time, simultaneously, don't let any thought appear in your mind. [Then] *śivaṁ vrajet*, he becomes one with Śiva at once, in no time. This is a five-minute course–five minutes from individuality to universality.

This is *śāmbhava*.

DEVOTEE: But there is the object?

SWAMIJI: There is not an object, because in the beginning, there is not an object at all.

DEVOTEE: But then why must it be beautiful? Why has it to be beautiful?

SWAMIJI: Only beauty is the object, not the object; the object is not the object, beauty is the object. But beauty is a subtle thing, so it won't catch *śāktopāya*.

DEVOTEE: But surely, for the man in *śāmbhava*, everything is beautiful anyway. Why does he need one thing more than another? If he needs that extra support, isn't that bringing it down to *śākta*?

SWAMIJI: No. Excitement for *śāmbhavopāya* must be maintained first, then real *śāmbhavopāya* will take place.

DEVOTEE: Excitement?

SWAMIJI: Excitement. Excitement must take place.

DEVOTEE: The mind must be caught.

SWAMIJI: Caught. How can you catch that mind abruptly? It is done in one instant.

DEVOTEE: So the object of beauty is not important. It is the beauty.

SWAMIJI: It is beauty only that will carry you there.

DEVOTEE: But the beauty is not something in the object?

SWAMIJI: It is only appearing, appearing.

DEVOTEE: It is a way of looking at it.

SWAMIJI: Yes, looking–that *prathamābhāsa*[288]. Because he has not to look at the girl, he has not to look at her features. Only beauty, beauty is counted there. You have not to touch it, you have not to talk to it, you have not to do anything with

288 The initial flow of objective perception or sensation. "*Prathamābhāsa* means the appearance of God consciousness in universal objectivity." *Festival of Devotion and Praise–Śhivastotrāvalī*, 9.5.

it. It is just, look at it and you will enter.

> My Swamiji [Swami Mahatābakāk] went to some invitation. There was a marriage function, and tea was served in the room, and Swamiji was seated, and I was also seated. By chance, there was a small beautiful girl with the best ornaments sitting in front of my master, and he went inside[289]. He was only looking at her and he went inside. And tea was served, and he was nowhere. Who could take tea? He was there, inside. Then afterwards, he came out and he told me that he had held this *dhāraṇā* there.

289 He experienced the mystical trance of *nirvikalpa samādhi*. See appendix for an explanation of *nirvikalpa samādhi*.

Dhāraṇā 56

मध्यजिह्वे स्फारितास्ये
मध्ये निक्षिप्य चेतनाम् ।
होच्चारं मनसा कुर्वं-
स्ततः शान्ते प्रलीयते ॥८१॥

madhyajihve sphāritāsye
madhye nikṣipya cetanām /
hoccāraṁ manasā kurvaṁ-
stataḥ śānte pralīyate / / 81 / /

Put your tongue in the middle of your mouth, inside, and *sphāritāsye*, the space of your mouth must become widened, internally, not outwardly, like this [Swamiji demonstrates]. Put your tongue in the center of your mouth and *sphāritāsye*, internally open your mouth (don't open your lips), *madhye nikṣipya cetanām*, and concentrate in the center of your tongue. *Hoccāraṁ manasā kurvan*, and while breathing in and out, you must recite '*sa*' and '*ha*'–'*so'haṁ*'. '*So'haṁ*' is the *mantra* for this practice, but internally.[290] *Tataḥ śānte pralīyate*, then [the *yogi*] enters in that supreme peace of God consciousness.

DEVOTEE: What is "*hoccāram*"?

SWAMIJI: *Hoccāram* means, *sahoccāraṁ–sa-kārasya, ha-kārasya ca uccāram–'so'ham'*.

DEVOTEE: You put *bindu* (*ṁ*) and *visarga* (*ḥ*) there as well?

SWAMIJI: '*So'haṁ*', yes.[291]

DEVOTEE: Like in the first *dhāraṇā*.[292]

SWAMIJI: Yes, but it is in the mouth, it is not by the nostrils.

DEVOTEE: So this is *āṇavopāya* leading to *śāmbhava* . . .

---

290 In Kashmir Shaivism, '*sa*' is recited with the outward breath and '*ha*' with the inward breath.

291 That is, '*saḥ*' and '*haṁ*'.

292 Verse 24.

SWAMIJI: No, this is *āṇavopāya*, simple *āṇavopāya* (inferior one), and it will carry you to the *śāmbhava* state.

Dhāraṇā 57

आसने शयने स्थित्वा
निराधारं विभावयन् ।
स्वदेहं मनसि क्षीणे,
क्षणात् क्षीणाशयो भवेत् ॥८२॥

āsane śayane sthitvā
nirādhāraṁ vibhāvayan /
svadehaṁ, manasi kṣīṇe
kṣaṇāt kṣīṇāśayo bhavet / / 82 / /

Either be seated on some *āsana* or on your bed (*śayane*). *Āsane śayane vā sthitvā*, either be seated on an *āsana* or on a bed. *Svadehaṁ nirādhāraṁ vibhāvayan* (put a comma after "*svadehaṁ*"), *svadehaṁ nirādhāraṁ vibhāvayan*, the one who thinks of his own body without any support, the body resting on nothing (*svadehaṁ nirādhāraṁ vibhāvayan*), and then by continuity of this contemplation, *manasi kṣīṇe*, when thought-lessness arises, instantly he enters in the thought-less state of God consciousness.

This is *śāktopāya* to *śāmbhavopāya*.

DEVOTEE: To *śāmbhava* state or *śāmbhavo* . . . ?

SWAMIJI: *Śāmbhavopāya* and then its state also.

DEVOTEE: And then its state also.

SWAMIJI: Yes. When thought-lessness arises, he enters in the thought-less state of God consciousness. *Nirādhāraṁ vibhāvayan svadeham*, you have to throw your body as if it is thrown on nothing. There is no support for the body. It is just [resting on nothing]. You have to imagine it like that. And then, when thought-lessness arises, he enters, in an instant, in the thought-less state of God consciousness.

This is *śāktopāya* leading to *śāmbhavopāya* and its state.

Dhāraṇā 58

चलासने स्थितस्याथ
शनैर्वा देहचालनात् ।
प्रशान्ते मानसे भावे
देवि दिव्यौघमाप्नुयात् ॥८३ ॥

calāsane sthitasyātha
śanairvā dehacālanāt /
praśānte mānase bhāve
devi divyaughamāpnuyāt / / 83 / /

Calāsane sthitasya, the one who is seated on *calāsana*, that seat which is moving, . . .*

It can be on horseback, or a *tonga*[293] (but not a motorcar), or an inferior motorcar (not a well-tuned motorcar).

DEVOTEE: Or on a bumpy road?

SWAMIJI: Yes.

JOHN: Scooter?

SWAMIJI: Scooter, yes. Scooter is *calāsana*. Horseback is the best *calāsana*, riding on horseback. Like this [Swamiji demonstrates], because your body moves like this.

*. . . *calāsane sthitasya*, he who is seated on that *calāsana*, on horseback or a *tonga* or a scooter, [but] not the best motorcar, . . .

DEVOTEE: Not a smooth ride.

SWAMIJI: No [affirmative]. The body must be moving.

. . . *śanair vā deha cālanāt*, or if that is not available, if horseback or a *tonga* is not available at that moment, *śanair vā deha cālanāt*, let your body be moving (move your body slowly on one side and the other side, one side and the other side–like this [Swamiji demonstrates]), . . .

DAN: Swaying.

SWAMIJI: Sway.

. . . and then, *praśānte mānase bhāve*, when the state of the

293 A horse-drawn two-wheeled vehicle.

mind is appeased, O Devī, *divyaugham āpnupyāt*, the state of *cidākāśa* is attained (*divyaugham* means, the state of *cidākāśa*, the state of *ākāśa*[294] of consciousness–*cidākāśa*).

This is *śāktopāya*, pure *śāktopāya*. [There is] no *āṇavopāya* here because there is no *mantra*, nothing. You have to concentrate between the two movements. On horseback, if your body is moving up and down, you have to ignore the up and down [and] put your mind in-between the up and down. Or, if you move your body like swaying, then you have to ignore the right-side movement and the left-side movement and centralize your mind in-between. There you can find your mind in the appeased state.

By that, O Devī, *divyaugham āpnuyāt*, the state of *cidākāśa* is attained.

This is *śāktopāya*.

294 The vacuum or supreme voidness of God consciousness.

Dhāraṇā 59

आकाशं विमलं पश्यन्
कृत्वा दृष्टिं निरन्तराम् ।
स्तब्धात्मा तत्क्षणाद्देवि
भैरवं वपुराप्नुयात् ॥८४॥

ākāśaṁ vimalaṁ paśyan
kṛtvā dṛṣṭiṁ nirantarām /
stabdhātmā tatkṣaṇāddevi
bhairavaṁ vapurāpnuyāt / / 84 / /

When you see sometimes this *ākāśa* (sky) *vimalam*, absolutely pure, without any clouds, only blueish, all blueish, *kṛtvā dṛṣṭiṁ nirantarām*, then you must put your sight on that *ākāśa* without any pause, *nirantarām*, without any gap–*nirantarām dṛṣṭiṁ kṛtvā*–and *stabdhātmā*, the sun[295]. . .

Ātma here means, the body. *Ātma* does not mean the mind or ego or individual soul. *Ātma* means the body here.

. . . *stabdhātmā*, without movement of your body (don't move your body in any way; be *stabdhātmā*, absolutely just like a rock), *stabdhātmā tat kṣaṇāt devi*, at that very moment, O Goddess, *bhairavaṁ vapur āpnuyāt*, [the *yogi*] attains the *svarūpa* of Bhairava.

This is *śāmbhava*, absolutely *śāmbhavopāya*, pure *śāmbhavopāya*. There is no *śāktopāya* in this *dhāraṇā*.

DEVOTEE: Because there is no two?

SWAMIJI: There is no two. It is only *ākāśa* (*śūnya*).

295 One of the translations of "*Ātman*" is "the sun".

Dhāraṇā 60

लीनं मूर्ध्नि वियत्सर्वं
भैरवत्वेन भावयेत् ।
तत्सर्वं भैरवाकार-
तेजस्तत्त्वं समाविशेत् ॥ ८५ ॥

līnaṁ mūrdhni viyatsarvaṁ
bhairavatvena bhāvayet /
tatsarvaṁ bhairavākāra-
tejastattvaṁ samāviśet / / 85 / /

Just imagine that the whole *ākāśa* is situated in your *brahmasthāna* (in the skull)–this whole *ākāśa* is situated in the skull. Imagine that your skull is so wide and broad just like the *ākāśa*, just like the sky, without sides, absolutely wide, broad. You have to imagine that your skull is as broad as the *ākāśa* and [that] the *ākāśa* is situated in your skull (it is just imagination), and *bhairavatvena bhāvayet*, you should consider that this *ākāśa* in your skull is full of the Bhairava state (*bhairavatvena bhāvayet*). And *tat sarvaṁ*, then [the *yogi*] enters the *svarūpa* of *prakāśa* (*tejas tattvam*; *bhairav-ākāra tejas tattvam*), [that] *prakāśa* which is the embodiment of Bhairava. He enters in that *prakāśa*, which is the embodiment of the Bhairava state. He enters in that.

It is *śāktopāya*. It is not *śāmbhavopāya* because there are two. There is the outside *ākāśa* and the *ākāśa* in the space of your skull. And the space of your skull is expanded to such an extent that it becomes one with that outside sky. So it is *śāktopāya*, it can't be *śāmbhavopāya*.

Dhāraṇā 61

किंचिज्ज्ञातं द्वैतदायि
बाह्यालोकस्तमः पुनः ।
विश्वादि भैरवं रूपं
ज्ञात्वानन्तप्रकाशभृत् ॥८६॥

kiñcijjñātaṁ dvaitadāyī
bāhyālokastamaḥ[296] *punaḥ /*
viśvādi bhairavaṁ rūpaṁ
jñātvānantaprakāśabhṛt / / 86 / /

Kiñcit jñātaṁ dvaitadāyī, that which is full of duality, *dvaitadāyī*, that gives the cognition of dualism, after knowing that state which gives you the cognition of duality (i.e., the state of wakefulness), *bāhyālokaḥ*, . . .*

Bāhyāloka means *svarūpa āloka*. *Bāhyāloka* does not mean all the *prakāśa* from outside. *Bāhyāloka* means *svarūpa āloka*.

DEVOTEE: Internal *tejas*[297]?

SWAMIJI: Internal *deha*[298].

DEVOTEE: Why does he use the word "external"?

SWAMIJI: *Bāhya*? Because it is *bāhya*, because the impression is *bāhya*. In the dreaming state, the impression comes from *bāhya*. It is *āloka*. *Āloka* is the important factor here. *Āloka* means, when that appears to you, when *bāhya* appears in the dreaming state. Because you experience that *bāhya* in your *āloka*, in your own *prakāśa*, in your own thought–that is a dream. *Bāhya* means, the outside world,

296 In his commentary, Swamiji included an alternative reading of "*brahmālokastataḥ*" in place of "*bāhyālokastamaḥ*", which appears in the original text.

297 Light.

298 Body.

the *āloka* of the outside world.[299] Where is the *āloka* of the outside world?

DEVOTEE: In *svapna*.

SWAMIJI: In *svapna*. In the dreaming state. You dream only those dreams which you have already seen in wakefulness.

*. . . *tamaḥ punaḥ*, and then absolute darkness (*punaḥ*, and then, in the end–*punaḥ tamaḥ*), . . .*

Tamaḥ means, absolute darkness. That is dreamless [sleep]. When you don't dream at all, that is dreamless *suṣupti*.

Kiñcit jñātvā dvaitadāyī, this state of *jāgrat avasthā*[300], and *bāhyāloka* means the state of *svapna* (the dreaming state), *tamaḥ punaḥ,* and, in the end, the darkness of the dreamless state. *Viśvādi bhairavaṁ rūpam*, and that will begin from *viśva–viśva*, *tejas*, and *prājña*. "*Viśva*" will go to wakefulness, "*taijas*" will go to the dreaming state, and "*prājña*" will go to *suṣupti* (the dreamless state).

*. . . in this way, after knowing *viśva*, *tejas*, and *prājña*, *viśvādi bhairavaṁ rupaṁ jñātvā*, you must think that *viśva* is not separate from Bhairava (the world of wakefulness is not separate from your God consciousness), the world of the dreaming state is not separate from your God consciousness (Self-consciousness), and, in the end, that dreamless state is not separated from the Self-consciousness. After knowing this way (*jñātva*), *ananta prakāśa bhṛt*, he enters in the infinite *prakāśa*, the infinite *prakāśa* of transcendental universal consciousness (*ananta prakāśa*). He enters in the *unmīlanā* state in an instant–*unmīlanā*.[301]

DEVOTEE: But first in *nimīlanā*.

SWAMIJI: First *nimīlanā*.

DEVOTEE: At what stage is *nimīlanā* here?

SWAMIJI: *Jñātvā*.[302] *Jñātvā* will go in *nimīlanā* and *ananta*

---

299 "*Bāhyāloka* means *svarūpāloka*: *svarūpa āloka*, *bāhya āloka*. It is not Pāṇini's grammar that can give a solution to this." *Vijñāna Bhairava*, additional audio (USF archives).

300 Wakefulness.

301 See Appendix for an explanation of *nimīlinā* and *unmīlanā*.

302 *Nimīlanā* is knowing (*jñātva*) that God consciousness (Bhairava) pervades the three states of waking, etc.

prakāśa bhṛt[303] is its fruit. [The *yogi*] enters in God consciousness in wakefulness, in dreaming, and in the dreamless state.

DEVOTEE: What is the nature of this knowing? How does he know that? What practice is there here? What sort of practice is this? How does he know that waking state, dreaming state, and dreamless state are one with Bhairava?

SWAMIJI: No, it is *śāktopāya*.

DEVOTEE: Since it is through *ahaṁ iti parāmarśaḥ*?

SWAMIJI: Yes, *ahaṁ iti parāmarśaṇaṁ*.

DEVOTEE: Self-awareness.

SWAMIJI: *Ahaṁ iti parāmarśaṇaṁ kāryam.*[304] And because it is *āṇava* [*upāya*]. In the beginning, it is *āṇava*, because there are three states, three different states. Where there are three different states concerned, it is *āṇava*, and it will go to *śāmbhava* in the end.

DEVOTEE: He thinks these in succession?

SWAMIJI: Yes.

DEVOTEE: But, how can he develop that awareness in the *prājña* state?

SWAMIJI: In *prājña*? The dreamless state?

DEVOTEE: How does he develop that awareness there?

SWAMIJI: When he enters in the center of the two.

DEVOTEE: Between sleep and . . . ?

SWAMIJI: Sleep and wakefulness, wakefulness and sleep, sleep and sound sleep.

DEVOTEE: He is aware of that point.

SWAMIJI: Yes, he must be aware.

This is *āṇava* sentenced to the *śāmbhava* state (*śāmbhavopāya* and its state–*unmīlanā*).

GURTOO: [In Kashmiri]: We need the next explanation. *Bāhyālokas* have already explained but *brahmālokas* you have not explained.

---

303 *Unmīlanā* is bearing or possessing (*bhṛt*) the eternal (*ananta*) light of God consciousness (*prakāśa*).

304 The application (*kāryam*) of Self-awareness (*ahaṁ iti parāmarśaṇaṁ*) in the three states of wakefulness, etc.

SWAMIJI:

kiñcitjñātaṁ dvaitadāyī brahmālokastataḥ punaḥ /

That is the internal state of God consciousness, the internal world of God consciousness. *Brahmāloka* is the internal world of God consciousness. Because, when you get entry in *samādhi*, you have to pass from the limited objective cycle of the world, then you have to pass through the *brahmāloka*.

ERNIE: Unlimited.

SWAMIJI: The unlimited cycle of the world, the internal world–by *yoga*, in *yoga*.

ERNIE: But you don't stay there?

SWAMIJI: If you stay there, you are stuck.

ERNIE: That is the liberation that's . . .

SWAMIJI: That is not liberation. You will be stuck there. That is *brahmāloka*.

ERNIE: But then, how can unlimited Brahman . . . how could you be stuck if you were in unlimited Brahman?

SWAMIJI: So you have to go further. [*Brahmāloka*] is the pathway.

ERNIE: What is further than unlimited?

SWAMIJI: *Viśvādi bhairavaṁ rūpam*: from *viśva*, *taijas*, and *prājña*,[305] this is the Bhairava state, this is all the Bhairava state. It is *kiñcit jñātaṁ dvaitadāyī*[306]: *viśva*, and then there is *prājña*, and then there is *taijas*. *Taijas* is *brahmāloka*. But you have to go further ahead.

ERNIE: No, but you are saying that you go through the limited world (internal), . . .

SWAMIJI: Internal.

ERNIE: . . . then you go through unlimited . . .

SWAMIJI: . . . state of God consciousness.

ERNIE: How could you get stuck in the unlimited state of God consciousness?

---

305 Waking, dreaming, and deep sleep, respectively.

306 Anything (*kiñcit*) known (*jñātam*) to give the cognition of dualism (*dvaitadāyī*).

SWAMIJI: No, I didn't say that. I said, you are stuck in the limited state of God consciousness–that is *brahmāloka.*[307]

ERNIE: And then you go to . . .

SWAMIJI: . . . that . . .

ERNIE: . . . unlimited . . .

SWAMIJI: . . . unlimited Bhairava state.

GURTOO: Bhairava state is beyond *brahmāloka.*

SWAMIJI: Beyond *brahmāloka.*

307 Viz., the dreaming state (*taijas*).

Dhāraṇā 62

एवमेव दुर्निशायां
कृष्णपक्षागमे चिरम् ।
तैमिरं भावयन् रूपं
भैरवं रूपमेष्यति ॥८७॥

evameva durniśāyāṁ
kṛṣṇapakṣāgame ciram /
taimiraṁ bhāvayan rūpaṁ
bhairavaṁ rūpameṣyati / / 87 / /

Sometimes you see there is *durniśā* (*durniśā* means, that night when it is raining tremendously). And that night must not be with the moon. *Kṛṣṇa pakṣāgame*, it must be a dark night without a moon, without moonlight, because there is some impression of moonlight also in those clouds when there is a moon on that rainy night. When there is no moon, then it is absolutely dark. *Evameva*, in this way, *durniśāyām*, on a rainy night, *kṛṣṇa pakṣāgame*, and in *kṛṣṇa pakṣa* (*kṛṣṇa pakṣa* means, the dark fortnight), *ciraṁ taimiraṁ bhāvayan rūpam*, and this rain must continue for hours, and–what you have to do?–you open your eyes in that darkness. Put off all your lights in the room, open the windows, and see outside with the eyes wide open. *Tamiraṁ bhāvayan rūpam*, then you must think that this whole atmosphere is full of the *taimira rūpa*[308] of Bhairava [and that] it is all Bhairava dancing outside. [Then] *bhairavaṁ vapur āpnuyāt*, one enters in the state of Bhairava, [the *yogi*] becomes one with Bhairava.

DEVOTEE: Is it necessary that there should be rain?

SWAMIJI: There should be rain[309] because the continuity of that sound of rain, rainfall, will carry you there swiftly. When there is no rainfall, then there will be other sounds also to

---

308 The dark (*tamira*) formation (*rūpa*).

309 "There must not be lightening or thunder; only rainfall, tremendous rainfall, and a dark night." *Vijñāna Bhairava*, additional audio (USF archives).

interfere with your meditation, your contemplation. Your meditation will be carried by the continuous sound of that rainfall.

This is *śāktopāya*. This is not *śāmbhavopāya*.

DEVOTEE: If a *yogi* was to meditate solely upon the absolute blackness in his room, if he were to go to Sonamarg[310], somewhere high . . . ?

SWAMIJI: That is also. That can be.

DEVOTEE: But if there is no impression, just darkness, is that of *śāmbhavopāya*? If there is just void, just darkness, and there is no sound, there is nothing, and he is just aware of that voidness?

SWAMIJI: Then you will be situated in *śāmbhavopāya*.

DEVOTEE: It's [*śāktopāya*] because of rain and that sound?

SWAMIJI: Yes, because you have to take the support of that sound. There you are taking the support of sound.[311] *Śāmbhavopāya* is soundless.

DEVOTEE: No support?

SWAMIJI: No, there is no support.

---

310 Sonamarg is a mountainous area in Kashmir.

311 "Because of the rainfall and because of seeing the outside." *Vijñāna Bhairava*, additional audio (USF archives).

Dhāraṇā 63

एवमेव निमील्यादौ
नेत्रे कृष्णाभमग्रतः ।
प्रसार्य भैरवं रूपं
भावयंस्तन्मयो भवेत् ॥८८॥

evameva nimīlyādau
netre, kṛṣṇābhamagrataḥ /
prasārya bhairavaṁ rūpaṁ
bhāvayaṁstanmayo bhavet / / 88 / /

Evameva, in this way, *nimīlyādau netre*, *ādau netre nimīlya*, first close your eyes. Don't close [them] by pressing your eyelids. Close [them] calmly without pressing your eyelids. *Agrataḥ kṛṣṇābham dhyātvā* (*dhyātvā* is to be [done]; it is [implied] there[312]), *agrataḥ*, at first you must think that *tamo rūpaṁ bhairavaṁ dhyātvā* (*kṛṣṇābham* means, *tamo rūpaṁ bhairavam*, *kṛṣṇābham bhairava*), [it is] full of darkness–dark Bhairava!

After closing your eyes, you see nothing but darkness. If you press your eyelids with pressure, then you will see some white spots also in that darkness–that you should avoid. Don't press your eyelids at that moment. Only close your eyelids peacefully, calmly. Then, for a considerable period, you have to meditate on that darkness and feel that this is the state of Bhairava, [that] this darkness is Bhairava, the vacuum of Bhairava.

Then *prasārya*, then you should abruptly open your eyes and, if you don't see anything before you, then your meditation is successful. If you see again these spots and things in that room or in front of you, then your meditation is not complete, then you have to close your eyes again and meditate on that Bhairava state of darkness. If that darkness persists after opening your eyes, then this meditation is

312 Thought or reflection (*dhyātvā*) of darkness upon closing one's eyes.

complete, otherwise it is not complete–you must [know] that this meditation has not proved successful.

Bhairavaṁ rūpaṁ bhāvayaṁ, and, after opening your eyes, when you see nothing in front of you, [then] you continue this meditation there also, that, "This is Bhairava." Outside also is Bhairava, not only inside when your eyes were closed. Outside also is Bhairava, the state of Bhairava.

DEVOTEE: But the *yogi* is not seeing a particular pot, or . . ?

SWAMIJI: If he sees particular pots, finished, this is an incomplete *dhāraṇā*; this process is incomplete [and] you have to repeat it again and again. You have to repeat it again and again so that that contemplation of that darkness prevails for some period.

DEVOTEE: But if he has the idea, "Now I shall open my eyes", surely that will break his meditation. Would that not break his meditation?

SWAMIJI: It won't break his meditation, but he must see, he has to perceive, that outside also there is nothing but darkness.

DEVOTEE: Nothing but darkness?

SWAMIJI: Darkness, dark vacuum, nothing. This is [from] the intensity of *bhāvana*[313] inside, when your eyes were closed. When it prevails for some period (i.e., that darkness), open your eyes at once and see [that] outside also there must be darkness. If darkness prevails outside also, then you are Bhairava, you have entered in the state of Bhairava.

DEVOTEE: This meditation should not be performed in darkness because otherwise . . .

SWAMIJI: No, not darkness.

DEVOTEE: But when there is light, when you close your eyes, you don't perceive . . .

SWAMIJI: Light must not be [too bright]. It must not be daylight. The light must be very dim, dim light, because you have to meditate in dim light [for] this practice, in your room.

Bhāvayaṁ stanmayo bhavet, [he] becomes one with that Bhairava state of darkness.

This is *śāktopāya*.

---

313 The state of mind or feeling.

Dhāraṇā 64

यस्य कस्येन्द्रियस्यापि
व्याघाताच्च निरोधतः ।
प्रविष्टस्याद्वये शून्ये
तत्रैवात्मा प्रकाशते ॥८९॥

yasya kasyendriyasyāpi
vyāghātācca nirodhataḥ /
praviṣṭasyādvaye śūnye
tatraivātmā prakāśate / / 89 / /

Yasya kasyendriyasyāpi vyāghātāt, any organ in your body, if it is struck against some object–when your eye, or your nose, or your ear, or your mouth, or your body[314] is struck against some other object–or *nirodhataḥ*, or give *vyāghāta* by your own self, strike it with some [object]–or if that strike happens incidentally or you make it happen by striking it with some object–*praviṣṭasyādvaye śūnye*, [the *yogi*] enters in that void of oneness where his reality of Self is revealed. Here you have to note that you have to meditate on the very starting sensation[315] of that strike. When you enter in that and contemplate on that, you enter in that supreme state of voidness.

This is *śāktopāya*.

314 Any limb or any external organ of your body.
315 *Ālocana / prathamābhāsa*.

Dhāraṇā 65

अबिन्दुमविसर्गं च
अकारं जपतो महान् ।
उदेति देवि सहसा
ज्ञानौघः परमेश्वरः ॥९०॥

abinduṁavisargaṁ ca
akāram japato mahān /
udeti devi sahasā
jñānaughaḥ parameśvaraḥ / / 90 / /

This is *śāktopāya* with *āṇava's* touch in the beginning.

Abinduṁ avisargaṁ ca akāraṁ japato mahān. Just take '*aḥ*', the letter '*aḥ*', or the letter '*ṁ*' in any *mantra* (in some *mantras*, the letter '*aḥ*' is recited; in some *mantras*, the letter '*ṁ*' is recited), [but] don't recite there the letter '*ṁ*' or the letter '*aḥ*'. Without *visarga*[316], recite this [*mantra*] without *visarga* [or] recite this [*mantra*] without '*ṁ*'.

So it will be the carrier to *cakita mudrā*, the carrier towards *cakita mudrā*.

DEVOTEE: *Bhairavī mudrā*?

SWAMIJI: It is not *Bhairavī mudrā* exactly. *Bhairavī mudrā* is when all your organs are wide open. [Here], it is only with the mouth, the recitation of '*a*'. You have to recite '*a*' without *visarga* [or] without '*ṁ*'-*kāra*.

DEVOTEE: Internal recitation?

SWAMIJI: No, outside [recitation]. It is not '*a-a-a*', it is not long '*ā*'. It is '*aṁ*' and '*aḥ*'.

So it is only *cakita mudrā*, the astonishing pose, the astonishing pose when you open your mouth. This is part of *cakita mudrā*.

DEVOTEE: This is how *cakita mudrā* is created?

SWAMIJI: Yes, *cakita mudrā* is created. If it does not happen, when there is nothing so much amusing to you,

316 The letter '*aḥ*'.

cakita mudrā won't take place. But you must give rise to *cakita mudrā* by this. When you open your mouth, just open your mouth, that is all–that is '*a*'. Open your mouth abruptly. Don't recite anything because it is only '*a*'. It can't be recited because it is without '*ṁ*' and without *visarga* (*abinduṁ avisargaṁ ca akāraṁ japataḥ*).

[Then] *sahasā*–O Devī!–*sahasā*, in an instant, *mahān jñānaughaḥ parameśvaraḥ udeti*, the supreme Parameśvara[317] rises, Who is flooded with knowledge (*jñānaughaḥ*; *jñānaughaḥ* means, who is flooded with knowledge of God consciousness).

Firstly, there is *āṇava's* touch, but in the end, it is *śāktopāya*, pure *śāktopāya*.

DEVOTEE: *Cakita mudrā* is normally in *śāktopāya*?

SWAMIJI: Yes, it is *śāktopāya*. And that *cakita mudrā*, one [other] *cakita mudrā*, is in *śāmbhavopāya*.

DEVOTEE: Which one is that?

SWAMIJI: Automatic, automatic *cakita mudrā*.

DEVOTEE: Same as *Bhairavī mudrā*?

SWAMIJI: Yes, the same as *Bhairavī mudrā*. When you are astonished, when you become astonished by seeing something new [and] you enter in *cakita mudrā*, that is *śāmbhavopāya*. When you give rise to *cakita mudrā*, you are in *śāktopāya*. [This] *cakita mudrā* belongs to *śāktopāya* and that automatic *cakita mudrā* belongs to *śāmbhavopāya*.[318]

DEVOTEE: And this is that . . . ?

SWAMIJI: This [*dhāraṇā*] is *śāktopāya*, with *āṇava's* touch in the beginning.

DEVOTEE: If the *yogi* beholds some beautiful thing, . . .

SWAMIJI: Yes.

DEVOTEE: . . . can he not go into the state of *cakita mudrā* in *śāktopāya* there?

SWAMIJI: Not beautiful. When it is hideous, when you see some hideous thing, then you will go to *cakita mudrā*.

DEVOTEE: Hideous?

SWAMIJI: Hideous, furious, terrifying thing. When you see

---

317 Lord Śiva, Bhairava.

318 See also commentary on verse 77.

some terrifying figure, then you will enter in *cakita mudrā*. [There], *cakita mudrā* will be produced in *śāmbhavopāya*.

DEVOTEE: It must not be real fear? If there is real fear, then he is finished. It must be just that flavor of surprise?

SWAMIJI: No, real fear.

DEVOTEE: But if he is really afraid, then he is in *vikalpa*?

SWAMIJI: No, real fear. For instance, when he sees a lion in front of him, he will go into *cakita mudrā*. When he goes into *cakita mudrā*, the lion will not touch him at all [because] he is Bhairava!

Dhāraṇā 66

वर्णस्य सविसर्गस्य
विसर्गान्तं चितिं कुरु ।
निराधारेण चित्तेन
स्पृशेद्ब्रह्म सनातनम् ॥९१॥

varṇasya savisargasya
visargāntaṁ cittiṁ kuru /
nirādhāreṇa cittena
spṛśedbrahma sanātanam / / 91 / /

Varṇasya savisargasya, [recite] any letter which has got a *visarga* in the end, e.g., *'kaḥ'*, *'khaḥ'*, *'paḥ'*, *'caḥ'*–it has got two *bindus* in the end.[319] Any letter, take any letter. Recite this, recite this only once. For instance, *'kaḥ'*: you have not to think of *'ka'*, you have to think of that ending *visarga*, *'aḥ'*. That *'aḥ'* is not real because *'aḥ'* is only when *'a'* is with this [*'ḥ'*].

You have to do *varṇasya savisargasya*. Take any *savisarga varṇa*, [any letter] which has got a *visarga* in the end, [and] *visargāntaṁ cittiṁ kuru*, just put consciousness in the *visarga*, not [in] that *varṇa*. *Nirādhāreṇa cittena*, the mind will become *nirādhāra*, the mind will have no place to sit. Because *'aḥ'* has got a place . . . as long as *'aḥ'* is concerned and as long as *'kaḥ'* is concerned, there is a place for the mind to get established, but where will that [mind get established in] *visarga*? The mind has no place to exist. So *nirādhāra*, the mind becomes *nirādhāra*, without any establishment. It is not established. The mind becomes without being established anywhere.[320]

---

319 In Sanskrit, the *visarga* (*'aḥ'*) is written as a colon.

320 Swamiji gives another example by knocking on the desk saying, "This sound will carry you to *śāmbhavopāya*, the end of this sound. You can't recite it. Can you recite it? Can you recite the sound of this string instrument? Can you recite the sound of the birds? No, no, you can't recite it. When that *varṇa* is recited, it can't carry you to the *śāmbhava* state. Only that sound will carry you to

JOHN: *Visarga* is like a soundless letter?

SWAMIJI: No, it is something, it is something. It can be found in consciousness. It cannot be recited. In consciousness, you can experience it, what is '*ḥ*' [without an] '*a*'. Just recite it! You cannot recite it! Can you recite it? You cannot recite *visarga* only; pure *visarga* you cannot recite. *Visarga* you can recite only when there is *upādhi*, when there is something attached with it: '*ka*' or '*a*' or '*ca*'–'*chaḥ*', '*khaḥ*'. Just [try and] recite *visarga*.

DENISE: '*Aḥ*' [laughter].

SWAMIJI: '*Aḥ*' not–not '*a*'.

JAGDISH: '*A*' is there.

SWAMIJI: It must be only ['*ḥ*']. It is supposed to be *kāma tattva*.[321]

GEORGE: Because you can't recite anything without '*a*'.

SWAMIJI: No [affirmative]. It comes out there at the time of sexual intercourse, that '*ḥ*' (*visarga*), only *visarga*, *śuddha visarga*, but nobody can catch it, nobody can catch it. All are duffers there.[322]

Nirādhāreṇa cittena, you should keep your mind *nirādhāra* (without support), then you will enter in the supreme

---

śāmbhavopāya which is not recite-able. When it is an automatic sound [Swamiji knocks on the desk], this sound will carry you to *śāmbhavopāya*. [On the other hand], '*oṁ*', this sound, the end of this sound, will carry you to *śāktopāya*. '*Oṁ namaḥ śivāya*', this sound too will carry you to *śāktopāya*. So, this '*oṁ namaḥ śivāya*' is inferior to this [Swamiji knocks on the table] from the Shaiva point of view." *Vijñāna Bhairava*, additional audio (USF archives).

321 "In the *Kulaguhvara Tantra*, this *visarga* is nominated as *kāma tattva*, the essence of *kāma*. *Kāma* means *icchā* (will); *tattva* means "the essence" of will. The essence of will is without producing it, when will is not produced. When will is produced, that is desire; when will rises, that is *kāma*." *Tantrāloka* 3.146, (USF archives).

322 Pure (*śuddha*) *visarga*. "And when you hear that sound [of *visarga*] from your beloved, at that moment, if you are a *yogi*, *tatra cittaṁ samādhāya*, when you put your mind fully aware on that sound, *vaśayet yugapat jagat* (Abhinavagupta has put only "*jagat*"), . . . the whole universe will be under your control if you produce and maintain that awareness on that sound at that moment." Ibid., 3.147.

Brahma.[323]

This is *śāmbhavopāya*.

323 "Brahma" refers to Brahman the Absolute, not Brahma the creator. "By keeping this support-less mind, one enters in that *sanātana brahma*, the *sanātana* state (the eternal state) of God consciousness." *Vijñāna Bhairava*, additional audio (USF archives).

Dhāraṇā 67

व्योमाकारं स्वमात्मानं
ध्यायेद्दिग्भिरनावृतम्।
निराश्रया चितिः शक्तिः
स्वरूपं दर्शयेत्तदा ॥९२॥

vyomākāraṁ svamātmānaṁ
dhyāyeddigbhiranāvṛtam /
nirāśrayā citiḥ śaktiḥ
svarūpaṁ darśayettadā / / 92 / /

Svamātmānam (here, "*ātmānam*" does not mean your individual soul; "*ātmānam*" means your body), just imagine that your body is only a vacuum, it is nothing (*vyomākāraṁ svamātmānam*). *Svamātmānam* (*svaṁ śarīram*) *vyomākāram* (*vyomākāram bhūtaṁ*, *vyomākāra rūpaṁ*), *dhyāyet*, you must think, you must imagine, that your body is *vyomākāra* (*vyomākāra* means, absolutely void); *digbhir anāvṛtam*, [that] there are no sides even (not east, west, north, and south).

Your body is absolutely void, without the sensation of sides. There are no sides at all. That is *digbhir anāvṛtam*; *anāvṛtam*, not supported by *dik* (*dik* means "sides").

And this way, when your energy of God consciousness becomes *nirāśraya* (*nirāśraya* means, without any support), when your God consciousness is support-less, it remains support-less, that God consciousness reveals to you Her[324] real nature (*svarūpaṁ darśayet tadā*).

This is *śāktopāya*. This can't be *āṇavopāya* because you have to concentrate on your body, that your body is only a void, nothing else.

---

324 *Citiḥ śaktiḥ*, the energy of consciousness.

Dhāraṇā 68

किञ्चिदङ्गं विभिद्यादौ
तीक्ष्णसूच्यादिना ततः ।
तत्रैव चेतनां युक्त्वा
भैरवे निर्मला गतिः ॥९३॥

kiñcidaṅgaṁ vibhidyādau
tīkṣṇasūcyādinā tataḥ /
tatraiva cetanāṁ yuktvā
bhairave nirmalā gatiḥ / / 93 / /

Kiñcid aṅgaṁ vibhidyādau: *ādau*, at first, *tīkṣṇa sūcyādinā*, there must be a needle which is very sharp, with some sharp needle, [and] *kiñcid aṅgaṁ*, let some limb of your body be stuck with a sharp needle (*tīkṣṇa sūcyādinā*). Just give it a prick.

By giving it a prick, it is *āṇavopāya*. And when you concentrate on that pain of that prick, that is the *śāmbhava* state. That will lead you to *śāmbhava* because there is only pain, there is no body consciousness; body consciousness is over.

With some sharp needle (*tīkṣṇa sūcyādinā*; *tīkṣṇa* means "sharp"; *sūcyādinā* means "needle"), with some sharp needle, *ādau*, at first, you should *vibhidya*, pierce, *kiñcid aṅgam*, some part of your body. *Tataḥ*, and afterwards, *tatraiva cetanāṁ yuktvā*, adjust your consciousness in that pain. [Then] *bhairave nirmalā gatiḥ*, you will enter in that Bhairava state without any interruption (*nirmalā gatiḥ*).

This is *śāmbhava* with slight touches of *āṇava*.

Dhāraṇā 69

चित्ताद्यन्तःकृतिर्नास्ति
    ममान्तर्भावयेदिति ।
विकल्पानामभावेन
    विकल्पैरुज्झितो भवेत् ॥९४॥

cittādyantaḥkṛtirnāsti
mamāntarbhāvayediti /
vikalpānāmabhāvena
vikalpairujjhito bhavet / / 94 / /

Just imagine that, "The three internal organs (mind, intellect, and ego) are not existing in me." When you contemplate in this way, then after[wards] the functioning of these three internal organs ceases to be, [their] function ceases for good–the mind does not work, the intellect does not work, and so the ego does not work.

Just put your imagination[325] and then contemplate on this imagination, then they won't function. The functioning of these three internal organs will cease, and then you achieve the thought-less state of *śāmbhava*.

This is *śāktopāya*.

---

325 "The "super-mind" is imagining [this]. There is something more than the mind in your body!" *Vijñāna Bhairava*, additional audio (USF archives).

Dhāraṇā 70

माया विमोहिनी नाम
कलायाः कलनं स्थितम् ।
इत्यादिधर्मं तत्त्वानां
कलयन्ना पृथग्भवेत् ॥९५॥

māyā vimohinī nāma
kalāyāḥ kalanaṁ sthitam /
ityādidharmaṁ tattvānāṁ
kalayannā[326] *pṛthagbhavet / / 95 / /*

Kalayan, when you imagine and think that the functioning of *māyā* is to put you in illusion, and the functioning of those five coverings (*kalāyāḥ*, the five-fold coverings[327]) is also functioning in its own way, [and that], "I have nothing to do with that, I have no concern with these six elements; *māyā* has nothing to do with me and those five coverings (*kalā*, *vidyā*, *rāga*, *kāla*, and *niyati*[328]), they also have nothing to do with me, I am separate from these; *ityādi dharmaṁ tattvānām*, this is their own work, let them function in their own way, what have I to do? I have nothing to do with them, I am absolutely separated from these six elements", when you think this way, *nā*, that *sādhaka* (*nā* means, the individual being) *pṛthag bhavet*, becomes absolutely void of all these worldly aspects. So he is liberated from *māyā*, he is liberated from *kalā*, he is liberated from *vidyā*, he is liberated from *rāga*, and he is liberated from all these limited aspects of *māyā*.

This is *śāktopāya* also.

---

326 Swamiji corrected "*kalayana*" to read "*kalayannā*".
327 *Kañcukas*.
328 See Appendix for an explanation of the *kañcukas*.

Dhāraṇā 71

झगितीच्छां समुत्पन्ना-
मवलोक्य शमं नयेत् ।
यत एव समुद्भूता
ततस्तत्रैव लीयते ॥९६॥

jhagitīcchāṁ samutpannām-
avalokya śamaṁ nayet /
yata eva samudbhūtā
tatastatraiva līyate // 96 //

When any desire comes in your mind, let it come, let it flow out. As soon as this desire flows out, put an end to it at once. Don't let it function at all. As soon as it begins to function, let this functioning be seized by your force of concentration, awareness. And then, wherefrom this desire had risen, it is dissolved in that point again, and then you enter in that desire-lessness.

DEVOTEE: Is that desire to be resisted, sir?

SWAMIJI: Not resisted–abolished, because it is that point of beginning. It must flow out. That energy, when it flows out, at the point when it flows out–it has not [yet] flown–it begins to flow and then stop it, at that very moment.

This is *śāmbhavopāya*. This is not *śāktopāya*. This is *śāmbhavopāya* because, at that very first start of desire, you enter in the desire-less state, the thought-less state of God consciousness.

DEVOTEE: This is why it is called "*icchopāya*".

SWAMIJI: *Icchopāya*, it is *śāmbhavopāya*.

Dhāraṇā 72

यदा ममेच्छा नोत्पन्ना
ज्ञानं वा कस्तदास्मि वै ।
तत्त्वतोऽहं तथा भूत-
स्तल्लीनस्तन्मना भवेत् ॥९७॥

yadā mamecchā notpannā
jñānaṁ vā, kastadāsmi vai /
tattvato'haṁ tathā bhutas-
tallīnastanmanā bhavet / / 97 / /

"In fact, I have no desire and I have no cognition of any object."

When desire and cognition cease to be, cease to function, then where is that individual being also? The individual being also ceases to function as an individual being. The individual being is limited I-consciousness.

"In fact, I am like that. I am neither an individual being, nor the individual state of cognition, nor the individual state of desire. I am without desire and without cognition and without the state of the individual state. I am deprived, I am separated, from these three states." Although it seems that I am one with these three–I have got desire, I have got knowledge, and I have got a limited soul, but [I] must imagine that, "The limited soul is not existing, and its desire and its cognition are not existing. In fact, my formation of consciousness is like that."

Tat līnas tan manā bhavet, when one sentences his mind in this way, his individual consciousness is absorbed in God consciousness, and he enters in That.

DEVOTEE: What is this "*tathā bhūtaḥ*"?

SWAMIJI: *Tattvato ahaṁ tathābhūtaḥ*. *Tathābhūtaḥ* means, without these three states–without desire, without knowledge, and without individuality. Individuality is finished, desire is finished, and knowledge is finished. And, by meditating in this way, one enters in the state of God consciousness.

DEVOTEE: There are only two, *yadām–icchā* and *jñānam*. Where is the third?

SWAMIJI: *Tadā asmi. Asmi kaḥ? Tadā asmi kaḥ?* Then where is *asmi*, where is I-consciousness, where is that individual "I"? Individual "I" also expires in nothingness. *Asmi* means here "I", [individual] I-consciousness.

This is *śāktopāya*.

Dhāraṇā 73

इच्छायामथवा ज्ञाने
जाते चित्तं निवेशयेत् ।
आत्मबुद्ध्यानन्यचेता-
स्ततस्तत्त्वार्थदर्शनम् ॥९८॥

icchāyāmathavā jñāne
jāte cittaṁ niveśayet /
ātmabuddhyānanyacetās-
tatastattvārthadarśanam / / 98 / /

Concentrate your mind on your will when it is about to flow out; not when it has flown out, when it is about to flow–*icchāyām*. Or, concentrate your mind on your knowledge when it is about to flow out. When it has flown out, then nothing will come, nothing will happen, you won't achieve anything. Just at that very point when it flows out, put your awareness there, let your awareness be fixed there. When your awareness is fixed on that very first start of desire and knowledge, by your own thought-less intellectual awareness, *ātma buddhya ānanya cetā*, then the essence of truth is revealed (*tatas tattvārtha darśanam*; *tattvārtha* means "truth", the essence of truth is *darśanam*, revealed).

This is *śāktopāya* with touches of *śāmbhava*.

DEVOTEE: Where is the touch of *śāmbhava*?

SWAMIJI: *Śāmbhava*–[at the] first start. When you fix your awareness at the first start, when desire is about to flow out–it has not flown out, it is [about] to flow out–that is *śāmbhava*, that is *śāmbhavopāya*. When knowledge is [about] to flow out, then it is *śāmbhavopāya*.

DEVOTEE: When knowledge is to flow out?

SWAMIJI: Is to flow out. When it has flown out, not then.

DEVOTEE: So this is an alternative. These are two meditations here–either on *icchā* or on *jñāna*?

SWAMIJI: Yes, or it is only one.

DEVOTEE: Is this two *dhāraṇās*?

SWAMIJI: No, it is only one.

DEVOTEE: But how do you move from meditation on *nirvikalpa* in *icchā* and then on to *jñāna*?

SWAMIJI: No, you can do only on one, one energy at a time–either on desire, the start of desire, or the start of knowledge.

DEVOTEE: But how are they one *dhāraṇā* if they come into different *upāyas*?

SWAMIJI: It is one *dhāraṇā*. This is one *dhāraṇā*. This is not to be done successively. Either put awareness on *icchā* or put awareness on *jñāna* at its first start[329].

---

329 *Prathamābhāsa.*

Dhāraṇā 74

निर्निमित्तं भवेज्ज्ञानं
निराधारं भ्रमात्मकम् ।
तत्त्वतः कस्यचिन्नैत-
देवंभावी शिवः प्रिये ॥९९॥

nirnimittaṁ bhavejjñānaṁ
nirādhāraṁ bhramātmakam /
tattvataḥ kasyacinnaitad-
evaṁbhāvī śivaḥ priye / / 99 / /

It is the next process.

This objective cognition (*jñānam* means, objective cognition), this field of objective cognition, has no cause to rise. How it rises, it is a wonder. This field of objective cognition is *nirādhāram* (baseless), it has no support, it is without support. So how it rises? It is a wonder. Hence, it is *bhramātmakam*[330]. It is only [that] you feel the rise of this cognition, but objective cognition does not rise at all. The field of objective cognition is rising in you–in the daily routine of your life, objective cognition rises in you always–but in fact, it does not rise at all because it is *nirnimittam*, it has no cause to rise. How it rises? It has no support. If it is there, so it is an illusion (*bhramātmakam*), it is only an illusion. The rise of cognition of the objective field is an illusion. It is an illusive perception if this perception is not a real perception.

This is what He says in this process.

In fact, *kasyacit na etat*, in fact, for those who are not realized souls and for those who are realized souls, for both these classes, this objective consciousness, the question of objective consciousness, does not [actually] arise.

GANJOO: For both of them?

SWAMIJI: For both of them.

GANJOO: In reality?

330 Confusion, perplexity, error, mistake.

SWAMIJI: In reality, in fact.

Evaṁbhāvī, in this way, when you contemplate and put your awareness like that, you become one with Śiva, one with that universal God consciousness, I-consciousness.[331]

This is *śāktopāya*. This can't be *śāmbhavopāya*.

331 "You have put this illusive I-ness on this objective consciousness. From your birth to innumerable births, you have created this perception of objectivity. Objective perception is not at all established there. I-consciousness is to be taken in God consciousness, and God consciousness will be diluted and merged in universal I-consciousness. There, you are at home." *Vijñāna Bhairava*, additional audio (USF archives).

Dhāraṇā 75

चिद्धर्मा सर्वदेहेषु
विशेषो नास्ति कुत्रचित् ।
अतश्च तन्मयं सर्वं
भावयन्भवजिज्जनः ॥ १०० ॥

ciddharmā sarvadeheṣu
viśeṣo nāsti kutracit /
ātaśca tanmayaṁ sarvaṁ
bhāvayanbhavajijjanaḥ / / 100 / /

Sarva deheṣu, in all the bodies, [in the body] of an insect, a tiny, feeble insect, and in the body of Brahma–in the body of an insect (*kīṭa*) and in the body of Brahma–from an insect to Brahma, in all the bodies, the state of consciousness is the same, without any difference. *Viśeṣo nāsti kutracit*, there is no difference in *caitanya* (consciousness) in that small [creature], that tiny ant, or germ, or worm, or in the body of Brahma, or in the body of the sun.

So, this way, when any *sādhaka* puts awareness that *cetanā* is the same in each and every object, he conquers the duality of the objective world; he rises from duality to the monistic state of God consciousness.

This is also *śāktopāya*.

Dhāraṇā 76

कामक्रोधलोभमोह-
मदमात्सर्यगोचरे ।
बुद्धिं निस्तिमितां कृत्वा
तत्तत्त्वमवशिष्यते ॥ १०१ ॥

kāmakrodhalobhamoha-
madamātsaryagocare /
buddhiṁ nistimitāṁ kṛtvā
tattattvamavaśiṣyate / / 101 / /

When the fire of sex rises in you and the fire of wrath rises in you–when the fire of *kāma*[332] rises in you and the fire of wrath (*krodha*)–and the fire of *lobha*, . . .

Lobha is . . .

DEVOTEE: Greed.

SWAMIJI: Yes, greed.

. . . and the fire of confusion (when you are confused, absolutely confused, totally confused), and when you are absolutely intoxicated (*mada*), and when your body is full of hatred towards the person who is sitting before you (*mātsarya gocare*)–do you know what to do there?–*buddhiṁ nistimitāṁ kṛtvā*, put the awareness of your intellect the same in all these; *buddhiṁ nistimitāṁ kṛtvā*, the same and without any interruption of agitation. Don't let your mind be agitated by these (*buddhiṁ nistimitāṁ kṛtvā*; *nistimitām* means, motionless, without agitation). Your mind must remain in an un-agitated state.

DEVOTEE: Within excitement.

SWAMIJI: [With the] rise of excitement, not in the excitement; when the excitement is [about] to rise, at the point of rising; when *krodha* is just [about] to start, [when]

332 Swamiji is using "*kāma*" here in the sense of *kāma tattva*, or the rise of the sexual impulse (see verse 91).

the fire of *krodha* is [about] to rise.[333] When it has risen, then [the *yogi*] is lost; then he is lost and he can't control his mind, he can't control his intellect, he can't control his ego–he is finished! He has ruined all the states of these internal organs. These are internal organs: mind, intellect, and ego. These are also organs. The ego is also an organ.

It is why saints are broad-minded just like the sky, saints are broad-minded just like the ocean. Big tides do not agitate them. Big tides of the ocean do not agitate them. Big flows of these–wrath, *kāma*, *lobha*, *moha*[334]–do not agitate them. They are the same, they remain the same.

> *kāma krodha lobha moha*
> *mada mātsarya gocare /*
> *buddhiṁ nistimitām kṛtvā*
> *tattattvamavaśiṣyate / / 101 / /*

When [the *yogi*] puts his un-agitated consciousness on the point of [the rising of] these states, that supreme Lord is revealed (*tat tattvaṁ avaśiṣyate*, that supreme Lord is revealed to him).

This is *śāmbhavopāya*. This can't be *śāktopāya* because it is just at the rise of *krodha*–the rise.

DEVOTEE: There is no thought here.

SWAMIJI: There is no thought.

DEVOTEE: Only awareness.

SWAMIJI: This is the thought-less field.

DEVOTEE: Only awareness?

SWAMIJI: Only awareness, so it is *śāmbhava*.

---

333 *Prathamābhāsa*.

334 *Krodha* (wrath), sexual impulse (*kāma*), greed (*lobha*), illusion (*moha*).

Dhāraṇā 77

इन्द्रजालमयं विश्वं
न्यस्तं वा चित्रकर्मवत्
भ्रमद्वा ध्यायतः सर्वं
पश्यतश्च सुखोद्गमः ॥१०२॥

indrajālamayaṁ viśvaṁ
nyastaṁ[335] *vā citrakarmavat /*
bhramadvā dhyāyataḥ sarvaṁ
paśyataśca sukhodgamaḥ / / 102 / /

This whole universe is a world of magic. This is a magician's world, this is not the real world. *Indrajāla mayaṁ viśvam*, just imagine that this whole universe is only magic, a magic trick, [that] it has no substance in it, no substance of its own, except God consciousness. This *viśva*[336] is only just a magician's trick.

Do you know who is the great magician? The Lord Himself is the great magician. He has put this trick and placed this trick before us, and we are differentiated in [this universe] although we are undifferentiated. It seems that we are differentiated from each other.

DEVOTEE: Although undifferentiated.

SWAMIJI: Although we are undifferentiated. In fact, we are undifferentiated.

DEVOTEE: But also, in fact, we are differentiated because it's His Self-expression.

SWAMIJI: We are expanded, we are not differentiated. This is only the expansion of one's [undifferentiated] Self, this is not the differentiated-ness of one's Self.[337]

---

335 Swamiji corrected "*vyastaṁ*" to read "*nyastaṁ*".

336 Universe.

337 "Appearance in expansion, not differentiated-ness. This is Shaivism. This whole universe is the *vikāsa* (expansion) of your own Self. This is not *māyā*, this is not an illusion. This is only the expansion of your own nature." *Vijñāna Bhairava*, additional audio

So this expansion, if you perceive [it] as differentiated, in a differentiated formation, that is *indrajāla*[338], that is only the trick played by Lord Śiva to get you confused. You are confused, you don't know what to do there. You think that he is your enemy, he is your friend, she is your daughter, he is your son, he is your . . . , and you are lost in that magician's trick.

Or, imagine that this is only a painting in one's own Self, [that] this whole universe is only a painting of one's own Self (*nyastaṁ vā citrakarmavat*; *nyastaṁ*, it is a very well-drawn painting).

Brahmat vā dhyāyataḥ sarvaṁ, or just imagine that this whole universe is not stationary, [that] it is moving. It is moving from one point to another point, from one point to another point. It is moving (*bhramat*; *bhramat* means, it is moving). It is in its move. It is not destroyed. When one is dead, don't say that he is destroyed. He has moved from one point to another point. When one is young–a boy, a child–and he becomes [a youth], he moves from childhood to youth, from youth to old age, from old age to death, from death to the next birth. It is movement. So it is only a movie, a great movie, a movie picture.

When one perceives and contemplates this way, then the state of real bliss takes place (*dhyāyataḥ paśyataśca sukhodgamaḥ*, the rise of bliss takes place).

This is *śāktopāya*.[339]

DEVOTEE: Is this perceived by the mind or by the "I"?

SWAMIJI: You mean the perceiver, who is the perceiver? The perceiver is thought, not mind. Perceiving is the functioning of the mind, but the perceiver is thought. Mind is that individual being who has got differentiated perception.

(USF archives).

338 The net (*jāla*) of illusion.

339 "First *dhyāna* and then *sākṣātkāra* (realization), because there are two states. It is why it is *śāktopāya*. If it was only *dhyāna* and [the simultaneous realization of] *sukhodgamah*, then it would be *śāmbhavopāya*. [It is *śāktopāya*] because it is first *dhyāna*, you have just to contemplate on it, and then perceive it in your perception, and then that real state of bliss will rise." *Vijñāna Bhairava*, additional audio (USF archives).

Thought is the desire-less state of that mind. Thought is just nearing that *ātmā*, the state of *ātmā*. That is the difference between thought and the mind. Thought is *nirvikalpa*, the mind is *savikalpa*.[340]

340 Thought is thought-less (*nirvikalpa*) and the mind is thought-full (*savikalpa*). "*Vṛtti parāmarśa** is the mind and *śakti parāmarśa* is thought. *Vṛtti parāmarśa* goes [away] when your *parāmarśa* is developed in full awareness, then it takes the formation of *śakti parāmarśa*. When that awareness [of *śakti parāmarśa*] is trodden down, then it takes the formation of *vṛtti parāmarśa* and you are in the mind, you are roaming in the mind then. Otherwise, you are shining in thought, not roaming in thought. [Either] you are shining in thought [or] you are roaming in the mind (or wandering in the mind)." *Vijñāna Bhairava*, additional audio (USF archives). **Parāmarśa* literally means, seizing or pulling; remembrance, recollection, or reflection. In Kashmir Shaivism, it is used in the sense of "awareness" (viz., *vimarśa*). So, *vṛtti parāmarśa* (viz., the mind) is the awareness of the flux (*vṛtti*) of thoughts and *śakti parāmarśa* (viz., thought) is the awareness of the energy (*śakti*) behind the flux.

Dhāraṇā 78

न चित्तं निक्षिपेद्दुःखे
न सुखे वा परिक्षिपेत् ।
भैरवि ज्ञायतां मध्ये
किं तत्त्वमवशिष्यते ॥ १०३ ॥

na cittaṁ nikṣipedduḥkhe
na sukhe vā parikṣipet /
bhairavi jñāyatāṁ madhye
kiṁ tattattvamavaśiṣyate / / 103 / /

Bhairavī, O Pārvatī, don't put Your mind or awareness in pain or in pleasure. *Na cittaṁ nikṣiped duḥkhe*, don't put Your mind in *duḥkha* (in pain). *Na sukhe vā parikṣipet*, don't put Your mind in *sukha* (in pleasure).

Then where to put it? We have to put our mind somewhere.

Jñāyatāṁ madhye, You know that the mind must be put in-between these two, where there is the center of pain and pleasure. Where the pain is risen and pleasure has ended, when pleasure has risen and pain has ended, there You must put Your mind, there You must put Your awareness. Then You will see what reality of truth will be revealed to You (*bhairavi jñāyatāṁ madhye kiṁ tattvam avaśiṣyate*).

First do practice between pain and pleasure. Then, if you are not successful, do it again, do it again, do it again–one hundred times, one thousand times, in two lives, in four lives, in ten lives, in innumerable lives. DO IT! But do it now, begin it from now.

This is *śāktopāya*.

Dhāraṇā 79

विहाय निजदेहास्थां
सर्वत्रास्मीति भावयन् ।
दृढेन मनसा दृष्ट्या
नान्येक्षिण्या सुखी भवेत् ॥ १०४ ॥

vihāya nijadehāsthāṁ
sarvatrāsmīti bhāvayan /
dṛḍhena manasā dṛṣṭyā
nānyekṣiṇyā sukhī bhavet / / 104 / /

Take away the I-consciousness of the body (*vihāya nija deha āsthām*; *āsthām* means, I-consciousness of *nija deha*, of your own body). Take away the I-consciousness of the body and perceive (*bhāvayan*[341]), and perceive, *dṛḍhena manasā*, with a firm mind, and *nānyekṣiṇyā dṛṣṭyā*, and one-pointed knowledge, perceive with a firm mind and one-pointed knowledge, that, "I am everywhere (*sarvatrāsmi*). I am not only in my body."

Take away the I-consciousness of your body by imagination. It is just to imagine that the I-consciousness of your body is taken away from your body. Take away the I-consciousness from your body, that "I am this body." *Sarvatrāsmi iti bhāvayan*, and then perceive that, "I am everywhere, and in each and every body, I am existing."

And, by this one-pointed knowledge of a firm mind, one becomes blissful.[342]

It is *śāktopāya*.

---

341 Or, regard or imagine.

342 "Blissful with *sat*, *cit*, and *ānanda* from the Vedānta point of view, and filled with *svātantrya śakti* from the Shaiva point of view." *Vijñāna Bhairava*, additional audio (USF archives).

Dhāraṇā 80

घटादौ यच्च विज्ञान-
मिच्छाद्यं वा ममान्तरे ।
नैव सर्वगतं जातं
भावयन्निति सर्वगः ॥१०५॥

ghaṭādau yacca vijñānam-
icchādyaṁ vā mamāntare /
naiva sarvagataṁ jātaṁ
bhāvayanniti sarvagaḥ / / 105 / /

Ghatādau yacca vijñānam icchādyaṁ vā mamāntare. This is a pot. This is a bottle. This bottle is situated in [itself]. This bottle is not situated in my consciousness because, if this bottle would have been situated in my consciousness, then I would perceive this bottle always, [but] I perceive this bottle only when I see this bottle. So, this bottle is [only] this bottle–this bottle is there–and that perception of this bottle is [only] in me. *Ghaṭādau yacca vijñānam*, in this pot, this *ghaṭa*[343] is there. And *icchādyam* is in me; *icchādyam* (thinking of this, desiring for this, making use of this) is existing in my consciousness. The actual existence of this object is there [in the object itself], and this using of this object, or misusing of this object, or perceiving of this object, is in my consciousness. [But] in fact, this [particular] object is not existing at all, and this [particular] desire for this object, or using of this object for some purpose, is not existing in me at all.

Then where is it?

This consciousness is everywhere (*sarva gataṁ jātam*). This consciousness of the objective world and this consciousness of the subjective world is not only in these two things–it is everywhere. Because, [if] this objective pot (e.g., this bottle) would be only there [in itself, we must account for the fact that] when I go to dream, I will see this bottle again. And [so] this bottle is there [in my dream], this bottle is in my

343 Pot.

bedroom also (I am perceiving that bottle also), so it is everywhere. This bottle is everywhere and this desire is also everywhere. Only this is a trick of that Magician that it has [been] put in only two places. The re-placement of these, from individuality to universality, is to be done by the *sādhaka*. We have to re-place it in its real way–I mean, in our consciousness. In our consciousness, we have to re-place this object in each and every object.

In the *prathamābhāsa* state, in the first start of this consciousness, there is no difference between [spectacles] and a bottle. And you have come to know, [according to] that *Pratyabhijñā*[344] school of philosophy of Shaivism, that there is no difference [between] specs, the formation of specs, and the formation of this bottle, in that point. So specs is a bottle, a bottle is specs. I am Dina Nath Ganjoo, Dina Nath Ganjoo is myself.

So, *sarva gataṁ jātam*, my individual consciousness is universal consciousness. Actually, individual consciousness is universal consciousness, and one object is the universal object. *Eka pramātā viśva pramātā*, all individuals are one universal Being. *Iti bhāvayan*, when you contemplate with full awareness in this way, you become all-pervading. Then you don't find your body only at one place. Your body is everywhere and your objective world is everywhere.

This is also *śāktopāya*.

344 The school or doctrine of recognition (*pratyabhijñā*).

ग्राह्यग्राहकसंवित्तिः
सामान्या सर्वदेहिनाम् ।
योगिनां तु विशेषोऽयम्
संबन्धे सावधानता ॥ १०६ ॥

grāhyagrāhakasaṁvittiḥ
sāmānyā sarvadehinām /
yoginām tu viśeṣo'yam[345]
saṁbandhe sāvadhānatā // 106 //

The mode of perception of objectivity and subjectivity is the same in each and every being. I mean, the mode, the way, in which we perceive, and the way in which this objective world is perceived, that way is the same in each and every being. *Grāhya grāhaka saṁvittiḥ*, the knowledge and the mode of knowledge of the objective world and the subjective world is the same in each and every being. Only there is one exception in *yogis*, in realized souls, that the contact of objectivity and subjectivity is different in them. The contact of objectivity and subjectivity in *yogis* is divine. They remain fully aware in each and every act of this daily routine of life, the daily routine of action, the daily routine of *vyavahāra*.

When you see your wife, you are excited. When you see your enemy, you are not excited; the flood of wrath begins to rise in your mind because you want to hate this [enemy], you want to remove that [person] from your sight. This *saṁbandha* (this contact) of objectivity with your subjectivity is inferior. And *yogis* have not this kind of contact. They have got divinity in each and every contact.

So this is not a *dhāraṇā*.

345 Swamiji corrected "*viśeṣo'sti*" to read "*viśeṣo'yam*".

Dhāraṇā 81

स्ववदन्यशरीरेऽपि
संवित्तिमनुभावयेत् ।
अपेक्षां स्वशरीरस्य
त्यक्त्वा व्यापी दिनैर्भवेत् ॥ १०७॥

svavadanyaśarīre'pi
saṁvittimanubhāvayet /
āpekṣāṁ svaśarīrasya
tyaktvā vyāpī divairbhavet // 107 //

Put your consciousness of feeling in other living beings also, in the same way [as for yourself]. As you would feel the prick of a needle in your body paining you, feel the prick of a needle in some other's body. Feel that way also, that way, too.

Don't laugh at that prick [upon another], don't weep at your own prick. If you get a prick on your body, you will weep. If you get a prick on some other's body, you will laugh, you will just enjoy. It is not to be done. Put your consciousness in each and every being just like you have put [it] in your own body.

Apekṣāṁ svaśarīrasya tyaktvā. What will be the fruit of this act? Do you know what will be the fruit of this act? The fruit of this act will be that you will lose, day by day, the I-consciousness of your body, and this universal consciousness, God consciousness, will get its rise day by day.

This is *śāktopāya*.

Dhāraṇā 82

निराधारं मनः कृत्वा
विकल्पान्न विकल्पयेत् ।
तदात्मपरमात्मत्वे
भैरवो मृगलोचने ॥ १०८ ॥

nirādhāraṁ manaḥ kṛtvā
vikalpānna vikalpayet /
tadātmaparamātmatve
bhairavo mṛgalocane // 108 //

Sit in some posture and see what your mind wants to do. And when it moves to function, don't give any place for its existence. Don't let it exist in any way. *Nirādhāraṁ manaḥ kṛtvā*, don't let your mind exist at all, in any way, while functioning.

Then what will happen?

Tadā–is this not *tadātma paramātmatve*?–*tadā ātma paramātmatve*, then *ātmā*, that individual being, *paramātmatve,* enters in universal Being. Hence, you are one with God consciousness, you enter in that Kingdom of the transcendental state of God consciousness, or Bhairava.

This is *śāmbhavopāya*. This is not *śāktopāya* because *nirādhāram*, you have not to give any place to the mind for its existence. Don't let it exist anywhere. Put it dispersed, then there won't be a seat for this mind to rest, where it would create confusion and all that bother. This is the *śāmbhava* state.

Dhāraṇā 83

सर्वज्ञः सर्वकर्ता च
व्यापकः परमेश्वरः ।
स एवाहं शैवधर्मा
इति दार्ढ्याद्भवेच्छिवः ॥१०९॥

sarvajñaḥ sarvakartā ca
vyāpakaḥ parameśvaraḥ /
sa evāhaṁ śaivadharmā
iti dārḍhyādbhavecchivaḥ // 109 //

In fact, Lord Śiva is all-full of knowledge, full of action, and all-pervading. In fact, Parāmeśvara is *sarvajñaḥ* (all-knowing), all-doing, and [all-]pervading.

Concentrate on that Lord Śiva for a while and, when after a while you are fully concentrated on that awareness of Lord Śiva, put that awareness in your own consciousness, in your own individual being. Think that your individual consciousness is one with that Lord Śiva, [who is] all-knowledge, all-action, and all-pervading. By this way, when your mind and awareness are firmly established, you become one with Śiva.

This is *śāktopāya* with some touch of *śāmbhavopāya*.

Dhāraṇā 84

जलस्येवोर्मयो वह्ने-
ज्वालाभङ्ग्यः प्रभा रवेः ।
ममैव भैरवस्यैता
विश्वभङ्ग्यो विभेदिताः ॥११०॥

jalasyevormayo vahner-
jvālābhaṅgyaḥ prabhā raveḥ /
mamaiva bhairavasyaitā
viśvabhaṅgyo vibheditāḥ // 110 //

[You must think]: "As waves and tides are one with the water of the ocean, as waves and tides are one with water (they are no other than water), as waves and tides are one with water, and the current of flames is one with fire, and as the rays [of the sun] are one with the sun–*jalasya iva ūrmayaḥ*, *vahner jvālā bhaṅgayaḥ*, *prabhā raveḥ*–in the same way, all the universal currents rise from me, *mamaiva bhairavasya*, who am one with Bhairava.

"As waves and tides are one with water, and the current of flames is one with fire, and the rays of the sun are one with the sun, in the same way, all the universal currents are one with me, rise from me, who am one with Bhairava."

This is *śāktopāya* ending in the *śāmbhava* state.

Dhāraṇā 85

भ्रान्त्वा भ्रान्त्वा शरीरेण
त्वरितं भुवि पातनात् ।
क्षोभशक्तिविरामेण
परा संजायते दशा ॥ १११ ॥

bhrāntvā bhrāntvā śarīreṇa
tvaritaṁ bhuvi pātanāt /
kṣobhaśaktivirāmeṇa
parā saṁjāyate daśā / / 111 / /

Go on walking and walking and wandering, moving and wandering, without any end. For instance, you go to Amarnath pilgrimage.[346] Go on walking on foot. *Bhrāntvā bhrāntvā śarīreṇa*, after moving and wandering for a considerable period–I don't mean walking for half an hour–[after] walking for about six hours without a stop, and then, when your body aches, you want to lie down somewhere, and you don't reach home, *tvaritaṁ bhuvi pātanāt*, just lie down on the ground at once, put your body absolutely motionless on the ground. *Kṣobha śakti virāmeṇa*, when that agitation of that *cañcalatā* (of moving) and perceiving [that agitation] is over, you will enter in the state of Lord Śiva–only when you are aware, *kṣobha śakti virāmeṇa*, when the agitating energy ends.

The agitating energy goes throughout your journey. That [strenuous activity] agitates all your limbs and body joints and everything and you want to take a rest [but] you have no room to rest. Just sit down on the ground there and then. Then enter in *samādhi*.

Actually, it happens to *yogis* when they are absolutely tired. They sit, close their eyes, and enter in that God consciousness.

This is *śāmbhavopāya*. This is a first class *upāya*. You have nothing to do. Only enter in God consciousness after resting. You rest and enter in That.

346 The Amarnath cave is a shrine located in Jammu and Kashmir, which houses a naturally-forming Shiva liṅgam made of ice.

Dhāraṇā 86

आधारेष्वथवाऽशक्त्या-
ऽज्ञानाच्चित्तलयेन वा ।
जातशक्तिसमावेश-
क्षोभान्ते भैरवं वपुः ॥ ११२ ॥

ādhāreṣvathavā'śaktyā-
'jñānāccittalayena vā /
jātaśaktisamāveśa
kṣobhānte bhairavaṁ vapuḥ / / 112 / /

Aśaktya is, not being capable of understanding those objects. Because, [for example], when you are blind, you want to perceive that object, but you can't perceive that, you can't see that object, but you have got curiosity to see it, but you can't see it. That is *aśakti*. Or, if you want to assimilate some point in some book, but *ajñānāt*, you can't understand it, you just roam in that ether of ignorance. You can't understand it. There is no understanding in you. That understanding power is gone. That is *ajñānāt*. *Aśaktyā* is, [for example], when you are blind, you cannot perceive that form, and you have got curiosity. And [*ajñānāt* is when] you want to assimilate that point in that book, but that [understanding] power is not there; only curiosity remains.

What happens in the end?

Go in that curiosity only. Just meditate on that curiosity in which you are floating without understanding anything. *Citta layena vā*, then your mind will not function.

And, at that time, what will happen next?

Jāta śakti samāveśa kṣobhānte (*śakti*, that is power; the power to know it but not knowing, the power to assimilate that but not assimilating–that is *śakti*), and that *śakti* diverts in[to] the internal vacuum of God consciousness, and you will get entry in God consciousness.

This is *śāktopāya*. This is another way how to get inside consciousness.

Dhāraṇā 87 and 88

संप्रदायमिमं देवि
    श्रृणु सम्यग्वदाम्यहम् ।
कैवल्यं जायते सद्यो
    नेत्रयोः स्तब्धमात्रयोः ॥११३॥

संकोचं कर्णयोः कृत्वा
    ह्यधोद्वारे तथैव च ।
अनच्कमहलं ध्याय-
    न्विशेद्ब्रह्म सनातनम् ॥११४॥

saṁpradāyamimaṁ devi
śṛṇu samyagvadāmyaham /
kaivalyaṁ jāyate sadyo
netrayoḥ stabdhamātrayoḥ // 113 //

saṁkocaṁ karṇayoḥ kṛtvā
hyadhodvāre tathaiva ca /
anackamahalaṁ dhyāyan-
viśedbrahma sanātanam // 114 //

These two *ślokas* refer to *śāmbhavopāya*. This is a very supreme way of going inside God consciousness, in the state of God consciousness.

Saṁpradāyam, this secret (*saṁpradāya*, secret trick), the technique of the pathway, O Devī, I am explaining to You vividly, perfectly.

Kaivalyaṁ jāyate sadyo netrayoḥ stabdhamātrayoḥ. Just keep Your eyes open [but] don't see anything. [If You] keep Your eyes wide open [but] don't see anything, You will get freedom from repeated births and deaths, You will achieve the state of *mokṣa*[347]. *Netrayoḥ stabdhamātrayoḥ*, don't move

347 Liberation.

the eyelids [and] go on looking but don't perceive anything.

This is one technique of *śāmbhavopāya*.

Another technique in the same way is: *saṁkocaṁ karṇayoḥ kṛtvā hyadhodvāre tathaiva ca. Hyadhodvāre* is the opening of the rectum. You squeeze it (*saṁkoca*; *saṁkoca* is just to squeeze it inside), and, at the same time, with your fingers, you close the opening of your ears–at the same time. Squeeze that organ of the rectum with the breath and close your ear openings with your fingers (*saṁkocaṁ karṇayoḥ kṛtvā*, that is closing your ears with your fingers, *hyadhodvāre tathaiva ca*, and–*adhodvāre* means, that rectum–you have to squeeze that rectum with the breath at the same time). *Anackam ahalaṁ dhyāyan*, and then go on meditating on that sound which is neither a vowel nor a consonant (*anackam* means "vowel-less"; *ahalam* means "consonant-less"). You just see. It is easy. It is a practical thing. That sound in continuity you hear.

GURTOO: Like a stream flowing.

SWAMIJI: Like a stream. But you can't utter it, you can't utter that sound. You have to meditate upon it [and] *viśed brahma sanātanam*, you will get entry in that supreme eternal Brahma[348].

This is *śāmbhavopāya*.

348 Brahman (Bhairava), not Brahma (the god of creation).

Dhāraṇā 89

कूपादिके महागर्ते
स्थित्वोपरि निरीक्षणात् ।
अविकल्पमतेः सम्यक्
सद्यश्चित्तलयः स्फुटम् ॥११५॥

kūpādike mahāgarte
sthitvopari nirīkṣaṇāt /
avikalpamateḥ samyak
sadyaścittalayaḥ sphuṭam // 115 //

This is another technique regarding *śāktopāya*. This is *śāktopāya*:

Kūpādike mahāgarte, just go and stand on the top of the well, *mahāgarte sthitvā*, which is a deep well. *Upari nirīkṣaṇāt*, put your sight down to the bottom of that well and don't think anything; *avikalpa mateḥ*, don't let any other thoughts get entry in your mind. *Sadyaḥ*, at that very moment, instantaneously, *citta layaḥ sphuṭam*, your mind will not function. You'll become un-minded and thus get entry in God consciousness.

This is *śāktopāya*.

Dhāraṇā 90

यत्र यत्र मनो याति
बाह्ये वाभ्यन्तरेऽपि वा ।
तत्र तत्र शिवावस्था
व्यापकत्वात्क्व यास्यति ॥ ११६ ॥

yatra yatra mano yāti
bāhye vābhyantare'pi vā /
tatra tatra śivāvasthā
vyāpakatvātkva yāsyati // 116 //

Or, there is another technique. I will tell you another technique.

That is, *yatra yatra mano yāti*, keep your mind loose, keep your mind absolutely loose; don't control it, don't put any effort to control it. Keep your mind loose [in the] outside objective world and [in the] inside objective world. The outside objective world is when you perceive all these outside objective objects, when you perceive outward objects. And there are inward objects also, that is, *sukha*, *duḥkha*, . . .

GURTOO: And *moha*.

SWAMIJI: . . . *moha*. *Sukha*, *duḥkha*, *moha*, *viṣāda*[349], all that, or excitement of sexual joy, that internal [excitement], those are internal objects. Keep your mind loose from both sides, internally and externally (*yatra yatra mano yāti bāhye vā abhyantare api vā*). *Bāhye* means, in the outside objective world. *Ābhyantare* [means], the inside objective world. The inside objective world is grief, sorrow, sadness, joy, etcetera–these are also objects.

Tatra tatra śivāvasthā, when you put [your mind] loose and see that this is only the expansion of God, the expansion of your own consciousness, and that your consciousness is pervading outside, in the outside objective world and the inside objective world, where that state of Śiva *bhāva* will go? It is there!

It is *śāmbhavopāya*.

349 Pleasure (*sukha*), pain (*duḥkha*), delusion (*moha*), and depression (*viṣāda*).

Dhāraṇā 91

यत्र यत्राक्षमार्गेण
चैतन्यं व्यज्यते विभोः ।
तस्य तन्मात्रधर्मित्वा-
च्चिल्लयाद्भरितात्मता ॥ ११७॥

yatra yatrākṣamārgeṇa
caitanyaṁ vyajyate vibhoḥ /
tasya tanmātradharmitvāc-
cillayādbharitātmatā // 117 //

Or, there is another technique. It is a technique concerned with *śāktopāya*.

Yatra yatrākṣa mārgeṇa, whatever you perceive through the channels of your perceptive organs, *yatra yatra vibhoḥ caitanyaṁ vyajyate*, from every side you will find the presence of *jñāna*, the presence of perception, pure perception (that is, *vibhoḥ caitanyam*; *vibhoḥ caitanyaṁ* means, the consciousness of the Lord). The consciousness of the Lord is found in each and every perception, through each and every channel of your organic world.[350]

Tasya tanmātra dharmitvāt, because, you must find out at that moment, when you perceive a pencil, when you perceive some object through your organs, when you perceive that, *bas*, just know that this perception exists on the basis of consciousness, on the basis of God consciousness. So, the [basis] of this perception is God consciousness. The aspect of perceiving smell, the aspect of perceiving the sensation of touch–*śabda*, *sparśa*, *rūpa*, *rasa,* and *gandha*–basically, the [basis] is *caitanyam*, the consciousness, God consciousness. God consciousness is handling in these perceptions. The basis is God consciousness.

350 Organic world refers to the five organs of cognition (*jñānendriyas*: smell, taste, sight, touch, and hearing), in the sense of the energy of seeing and the energy of hearing, etc., along with the three internal organs (*antaḥkaraṇas*: mind, ego, and intellect).

So, *cit layāt*, just dive deep in that consciousness. At the time of perceiving these objects, don't perceive [these objects]; go on, dive deep in that consciousness, which is the basis of all these perceptions, [and] *bharitātmatā*, you will become Bhairava, you will just become Bhairava.

This is *śāktopāya*.

Dhāraṇā 92

क्षुताद्यन्ते भये शोके
गह्वरे वा रणाद्द्रुते ।
कुतूहले क्षुधाद्यन्ते
ब्रह्मसत्ता समीपगा ॥ ११८ ॥

kṣutādyante bhaye śoke
gahvare vā raṇāddrute /
kutūhale kṣudhādyante
brahmasattā samīpagā[351] */ / 118 / /*

It is *śāmbhavopāya*. This is another technique of how to find the reality of God consciousness. This is *śāmbhavopāya*, the technique of *śāmbhavopāya*.

Kṣutādyante, just when you begin to sneeze and when you have sneezed already (*kṣuta ādi ante*, at the beginning of sneezing and at the end, when sneezing is over; *kṣuta ādi ante*, at the beginning and the end of sneezing), [or] *bhaye*, at the time when you are afraid, when you are extremely afraid of something happening, . . .

When Skylab was to fall and the time was fixed that it will fall at 4:00PM,[352] at that moment, that, there, everywhere there was *bhaya*, there was a threat, the fear [of] what will happen [in the] next five minutes. That is *bhaye*–at that stage.

. . . *śoke*, or at the time of the intensity of grief, sadness, [or] *gahvare* (*gahvare* means, when you are stuck), . . .

Gahvara means, for instance, you are climbing [and then] you descend, [but] when you descend, you don't find the way. You have lost the way of how to descend and there is no way to go down. Either you will fall and roll down and you will

---

351 Swamiji corrected "*brahmasattāmayī daśā*" to read "*brahmasattā samīpagā*".

352 Reference to the first U.S. Space Station which was re-entering the earth's atmosphere and was expected to crash at an undetermined location.

die . . . and there is no hope of your reaching safely down. That is *gahvara*. That is a place where there is *gahvara*. *Gahvara* is, a very difficult pathway to tread on. At that moment, what is the position of your mind? See the position of your mind at that moment. What to do? You can't move now–*gahvare*.

. . . *vā raṇād drute*, or there is a gang of those enemies [who] have come with [many] weapons and machine guns and they are just torturing you and *raṇād drute*, you are flying, you are running (just like flying), *kutūhale*, or when there is the intensity of curiosity, . . .

When there is intensity of curiosity, e.g., "What is this? I want to find out what this is." Sometimes that also happens. Curiosity comes.

. . . and *kṣudhādyante*, when there is hunger, [when] you have got an appetite, [when] you have got too much [of an] appetite (at the beginning of [having] too much appetite and at the end of [having] too much appetite), [in all these states], *brahma sattā samīpagā*, God consciousness is near in your hand. It is there. You find it out. This is *śāmbhavopāya*.

Dhāraṇā 93

वस्तुषु स्मर्यमाणेषु
दृष्टे देशे मनस्त्यजेत् ।
स्वशरीरं निराधारं
कृत्वा प्रसरति प्रभुः ॥ ११९ ॥

vastuṣu smaryamāṇeṣu
dṛṣṭe deśe manastyajet /
svaśarīraṁ nirādhāraṁ
kṛtvā prasarati prabhuḥ // 119 //

Whenever you get something in your memory, [when] you get something, [when] you remember something of the past (you are at present here and something comes in your memory of the past, that is *vastuṣu smarya māṇeṣu*), *smarya māṇeṣu vastuṣu*, when you memorize those past happenings now at the present (*vastuṣu smarya māṇeṣu*), *dṛṣṭe deśe manas tyajet*, just focus your mind to that, that space and that time.

Where?

DENISE: What you are remembering.

GURTOO: Which you have already seen.

SWAMIJI: [That] which you have already seen. Just focus your mind there. Don't sit here [in the present]. You just focus your mind to that past . . .

ERNIE: Event.

SWAMIJI: Yes, past event.

DENISE: As if you are reliving it.

SWAMIJI: Yes, as you are perceiving that. *Dṛṣṭe deśe manas tyajet*; *manas tyajet*, you should put that mind there. "*Tyajet*" does not mean you should leave that. Focus that mind [in the memory].

GURTOO: It means, focus it.

SWAMIJI: *Svaśarīraṁ nirādhāraṁ kṛtvā*–and what will happen?–your body, which is existing here in this present cycle, *nirādhāram*, it won't remain, it will remain without any basis. It will remain without any basis because it has gone there, it has gone there in the past . . .

Past what?

ERNIE: In the past experience.

SWAMIJI: . . . past space and past time–the past space which was fifty years before and the past time also. Your body and your mind, your everything, has gone there. So here, nothing is . . . it is only your phantom formation of your body here. It is equal to nothing. *Svaśarīraṁ nirādhāraṁ kṛtvā*, and you find that your body is not existing. Although it is existing here, but it is not existing. It is existing in the past eventful world, experienced world. *Prasarati prabhuḥ*, the fountain of God consciousness will appear at that moment.

This is *śāktopāya*. *Śāktopāya* [it] is because you have to take the help of the body.

Dhāraṇā 94

क्वचिद्वस्तुनि विन्यस्य
शनैर्दृष्टिं निवर्तयेत् ।
तज्ज्ञानं चित्तसहितं
देवि शून्यालयो भवेत् ॥१२०॥

kvacidvastūni vinyasya
śanairdṛṣṭiṁ nivartayet /
tajjñānaṁ cittasahitaṁ
devi śūnyālayo bhavet // 120 //

This is another technique of *śāktopāya*, this one hundred and twentieth *śloka*.

Kvacid vastūni vinyasya śanair dṛṣṭiṁ. Kvacit vastūni dṛṣṭiṁ śanair vinyasya, just on some object, put your sight on that object (*kvacid vastūni*, on some particular object, *dṛṣṭiṁ vinyasya,* you should put that sight on that), *śanair nivartayet*, and go on withdrawing that perception of that object slowly, slowly, slowly, in your own self (*śanair nivartayet*; *śanair* means, *śanaiḥ-śanaiḥ*).

GURTOO: Very slowly.

SWAMIJI: Very slowly you withdraw this perception from that object. This is a technique of *śāktopāya*.

Tat jñānaṁ, and [after removing] that knowledge of that object, *citta sahitam*, along with your mind, Devī, O Pārvatī, *śūnyālayo bhavet*, You will get entry in that voidness of God consciousness.

Dhāraṇā 95

भक्त्युद्रेकाद्विरक्तस्य
यादृशी जायते मतिः ।
सा शक्तिः शाङ्करी नित्यं
भावयेत्तां ततः शिवः ॥१२१॥

bhaktyudrekādviraktasya
yādṛśī jāyate matiḥ /
sā śaktiḥ śāṅkarī nityaṁ
bhāvayettām tataḥ śivaḥ / / 121 / /

There is another technique. That is, the intensity of love for God, the intensity [of devotion]–*bhakti udrekā*.

When there is the intensity of love, you can't understand anything else in this world. When there is the intensity of love for God, you won't recognize Viresh[353], you won't recognize John, you won't recognize your body, you won't recognize anything in this world. *Viraktasya*, *vairāgya* (detachment) appears from all sides except for that intensity of love of God.

Bhakti udrekāt, by the intensity of love for the Lord, *viraktasya*, when detachment rises in your mind, *yādṛśī jāyate matiḥ*, and that position of your intellectual cycle at that time, the state of that intellectual cycle of yours, is [no longer] intellectual, is [no longer] the element of intellect in you, *sā śaktiḥ śāṅkarī*, that is the energy of God consciousness. That intellect is transformed in the energy of God consciousness, and you should perceive that this energy is the real energy. [By] detachment, being detached from all sides because of the intensity of love towards the Lord, *bhāvayet*, you will find out that *tataḥśivaḥ*, you will become one with Śiva.

This is *śāmbhavopāya*, the technique of *śāmbhavopāya*.

353 The son of John and Denise Hughes.

Dhāraṇā 96

वस्त्वन्तरे वेद्यमाने
शनैर्वस्तुषु शून्यता।
तामेव मनसा ध्यात्वा
विदितोऽपि प्रशाम्यति ॥१२२॥

vastvantare vedyamāne
śanairvastuṣu śūnyatā /
tāmeva manasā dhyātvā
vidito'pi praśāmyati / / 122 / /

Vastvantare vedyamāne śanair vastuṣu śūnyatā. When you perceive something (e.g., you perceive this stand), at the time of the perception of this stand, don't think of this stand, think of what you have perceived before that (that is *vastvantara*; *vastvantara* is, another object which you have perceived already, before that). At the time of perceiving this present object, don't perceive this present object, go to that previous object. *Vastvantare vedyamāne śanair vastuṣu śūnyatā*, by doing this technique–what will happen?–you won't find, you won't perceive, anything in this world. You won't perceive anything. *Śanair vastuṣu śūnyatā*, all objects will melt in nothingness, by and by. *Tāmeva manasā dhyātvā*, and, through your mind, focus on that nothingness, how all these objects are dissolved in nothingness in the end.

Because, when I perceive Stephanie, [and] then I perceive Ellen, at the time of perceiving Ellen, I must perceive Stephanie. At the time I am perceiving Ernie, I must perceive Ellen. So it works like this, that everything becomes dissolved in nothingness. You don't perceive anything. When you perceive a pencil, you perceive this [previous object]; at the time of perceiving this, you perceive this; at the time of perceiving this, you perceive this. So you will neither perceive this, nor this, nor this. There will be only *śūnya*, nothingness. Nothingness will appear in you, in the cycle of the objective world–*śanair vastuṣu śūnyatā tāmeva manasā dhyātvā*.

[Then] *vidito'pi*, after going in the cycle of perception

also,[354] you will enter in the appeased position of God consciousness (*praśāmyati*; *praśāmyati* is the appeased state of God consciousness where there is nothing).

This is *śāktopāya*.

354 That is, even while beholding objects of perception.

Dhāraṇā 97

किंचिज्ज्ञैर्या स्मृता शुद्धिः
साऽशुद्धिः शंभुदर्शने ।
न शुचिर्ह्यशुचिस्तस्मा-
न्निर्विकल्पः सुखी भवेत् ॥ १२३ ॥

kiñcijjñairyā smṛtā śuddhiḥ
sā'śuddhiḥ śaṁbhudarśane /
na śucirhyaśuciśtasmān-
nirvikalpaḥ sukhī bhavet // 123 //

Kiñcit jñair . . .

This is another technique. this is *śāktopāya*.

. . . *kiñcit jñair yā smṛtā śuddhiḥ*, the purification which is observed by *kiñcit jñair* . . .

Kiñcit jñair means, the masters of other schools of thought, [other] than Shaivism, and they have proved that this is pure and this is impure, [that] this [action] is pure and this is impure.

. . . *sā'śuddhiḥ*, that impurity, *śaṁbhu darśane*, in Shaivism, in our Shaivism, that impurity is neither impure nor pure. If you go deep in the philosophy of Shaivism, then there you will find [that] it is neither pure nor impure. *Nirvikalpaḥ sukhī bhavet*, so you should leave aside all doubts of purity and impurity, and you will get the blissful state of God consciousness.

This is *śāktopāya*.

Dhāraṇā 98

सर्वत्र भैरवो भावः
सामान्येष्वपि गोचरः ।
न च तद्व्यतिरेकेण
परोऽस्तीत्यद्वया गतिः ॥१२४॥

sarvatra bhairavo bhāvaḥ
sāmānyeṣvapi gocaraḥ /
na ca tadvyatirekeṇa
paro'stītyadvayā gatiḥ / / 124 / /

This is *śāktopāya*. This is another technique of *śāktopāya*.

Sarvatra, you have to think *sarvatra bhairavo bhāvaḥ sāmānyeṣvapi gocaraḥ*, [that] in ordinary (*sāmānyeṣu* means, in ordinary, ignorant persons also), in ordinary, ignorant persons also, when they act in their daily routine of life (they talk with each other, confidentially, in public, and everything), whatever they talk, they talk on the basis of God consciousness.

"Where are you going?" "I will do that." This is the *gocarī bhāva* of God consciousness [that] they have, [that] they have possessed. They have possessed the perception of God consciousness at the time of their daily routine of *hānādān-ādi vyavahāra*, the daily routine of life. Because, in each and every point of your daily routine of activities, daily activities, God consciousness is not ignored. *Sāmānyeṣu api,* in ignorant persons also, it is *gocaraḥ*, it is known.

It is also said in Vedānta:

utainaṁ gopā adṛśannutainamudahāryaḥ /
utainaṁ viśvā bhūtāni sa dṛṣṭo mṛḍayāti naḥ / /[355]

God is realized by everybody. God is realized by ignorant people. God is realized by those who have nothing to do with God–they have realized that God. And those who are only

355 See *Vijñāna Bhairava*, *KSTS* vol. 8, p109.

engrossed in the activity of household activities (they know nothing else), they have also realized God. So, *dṛṣṭaḥ*, he is realized; from all sides he is realized. Let him elevate us.

In the same way, He says, *sarvatra bhairavo bhāvaḥ sāmānyeṣvapi gocaraḥ*, in ignorant persons also, this is realized. The Bhairava *bhāva* (the state of Bhairava) is realized by ignorant persons also.

Because you must dive deep in this [so] that *na ca tad vyatir-ekeṇa paro asti*, there is nothing existing outside that God consciousness. By realizing that, *advayā gatiḥ*, you'll get entry in that oneness of God consciousness.

This is *śāktopāya*.

Dhāraṇā 99

समः शत्रौ च मित्रे च
 समो मानावमानयोः ।
ब्रह्मणः परिपूर्णत्वा-
 दिति ज्ञात्वा सुखी भवेत् ॥ १२५ ॥

samaḥ śatrau ca mitre ca
samo mānāvamānayoḥ /
brahmaṇah paripūrṇatvād-
iti jñātvā sukhī bhavet // 125 //

This is another *śāktopāya* technique, that *samaḥ śatrau*, when you reside in sameness, the cycle of sameness, everywhere. If anybody shoots you, kills you, you laugh, [and] if anybody embraces you, you laugh. You laugh everywhere–*samaḥ śatrau*, in [the midst of an] enemy also, in [the midst of a] friend also. In the behavior of friendship, in the behavior of enmity, *samaḥ*, remain the same, [and] remain the same *mānāvamānayoḥ*, in honor and in dishonor, *brahmaṇaḥ pari*, because you are always full. If you are dishonored, you are full. If you are honored, you are full. If you are teased by enemies, you are full. If you are loved by friends, you are full. You are always in fullness. You exist, you live, in fullness because, in the real sense, the state of Brahman is always full in each and every movement of life.

In the *Utpalastotrāvalī* also [it is said]:

jayanto'pi hasantyete jitā api hasanti ca /[356]

If they get victory, they laugh, [and] if they are defeated, they laugh (*jayanto'pi hasantyete, jitā api hasanti ca*–if they are defeated, if they are conquered). If they conquer, they laugh, [and] if they are conquered, they laugh.

Iti jñātvā, if you understand this, *sukhī bhavet*, you will get entry in that blissful state of God.

This is *śāktopāya*.

356 *Festival of Devotion and Praise–Śhivastotrāvalī*, 16.3.

Dhāraṇā 100

न द्वेषं भावयेत्क्वापि
न रागं भावयेत्क्वचित् ।
रागद्वेषविनिर्मुक्तौ
मध्ये ब्रह्म प्रसर्पति ॥ १२६ ॥

na dveṣaṁ bhāvayetkvāpi
na rāgaṁ bhāvayetkvacit /
rāgadveṣavinirmuktau
madhye brahma prasarpati / / 126 / /
[not recited in full]

You should not be attached in any way to some particular subject [or] object–you must not be attached. You must not be detached from some particular object. Without detachment and attachment; you should remain without detachment [and attachment]. *Rāga dveṣa vinir muktaḥ*, without detachment and attachment if you remain, in the center this supreme Brahman will shine.

This is *śāktopāya*.[357]

357 "Śivopadhyāya has put this as *śāmbhava* state, but it is not *śāmbhava*, it is *śāktopāya*." *Vijñāna Bhairava*, additional audio (USF archives).

Dhāraṇā 101

यदवेद्यं यदग्राह्यं
यच्छून्यं यदभावगम् ।
तत्सर्वं भैरवं भाव्यं
तदन्ते बोधसंभवः ॥१२७॥

yadavyedyaṁ yadagrāhyaṁ
yacchūnyaṁ yadabhāvagam /
tadsarvaṁ bhairavaṁ bhāvyaṁ
tadante bodhasaṁbhavaḥ // 127 //

You see, the definition of *śāmbhava* is just when you put your mind, when you meditate, on nothingness, absolute nothingness. That is the *śāmbhava* state. When there is some object to be meditated upon, that will be *śāktopāya* or *āṇavopāya*. Here it is *śāmbhavopāya*; the one hundred and twenty-seventh *śloka* is the technique of *śāmbhavopāya.*

Yat avedyaṁ, that which is not an object, that which has not come in objectivity, [and] *yat agrāhyaṁ*, that which is not realized, perceived (that which is beyond perception, that is *agrāhyaṁ*), [and] *yat śūnyaṁ*, that which is void, it is nothing, [and] *yat abhāvagam*, [that] which has melted in absolute nothingness, *tat sarvaṁ bhairavam*, that is Bhairava, that is the state of Bhairava. In this way if you meditate, in the end you will attain the state of God consciousness.

This is the *śāmbhava* state, a *śāmbhava* technique.

Dhāraṇā 102

नित्ये निराश्रये शून्ये
व्यापके कलनोज्झिते ।
बाह्याकाशे मनः कृत्वा
निराकाशं समाविशेत् ॥ १२८॥

nitye nirāśraye śūnye
vyāpake kalanojjhite /
bāhyākāśe manaḥ kṛtvā
nirākāśaṁ samāviśet // 128 //

This is the state where you begin with *śāktopāya* and end in *śāmbhavopāya*. This technique, the one hundred and twenty-eighth [verse], is just to begin with *śāktopāya* and end in the *śāmbhava* state.

Nitye nirāśraye śūnye vyāpake kalanojjhite bāhyākāśe. This ether, just meditate upon the ether. Which ether? This *bāhyākāśa*[358], that blueish-ness [of the ether]. In fact, this blueish-ness also does not exist there. You feel that blueish-ness, but it is just nothingness. This [ether] is not a blue color. This is *nitya* (eternal), it is always eternal. It won't be affected by Skylabs[359]. *Nirāśraye*, it has no *ādhāra*, it is not based on some support, it is support-less (that is *nirāśraye*). *Śūnye*, it is void, absolutely void. *Vyāpake*, and it is all-pervading, everywhere you find the state of *ākāśa*. *Kalanojjhite*, and there is nothing to be perceived in that, in this *ākāśa*.

When you go on realizing and diving deep in the state of this *bāhyākāśa*, put[ting] your mind on this *bāhyākāśa*, a time will come [when] you will get entry in that *ākāśa* which is beyond this *bāhyākāśa*. That is the supreme voidness of God consciousness.

So, at the time of entering in the supreme void of God consciousness, that is the *śāmbhava* state. Till then, it is

358 Lit., external (*bāhya*) ether (*ākāśa*).

359 That is, it won't be affected by external phenomena.

śāktopāya because there is some support. In voidness, there is some support (i.e., that blueish-ness), but that blueish-ness also fades when you get entry in that supreme voidness of God consciousness.

Dhāraṇā 103

यत्र यत्र मनो याति
तत्तत्तेनैव तत्क्षणम् ।
परित्यज्यानवस्थित्या
निस्तरङ्गस्ततो भवेत् ॥ १२९ ॥

yatra yatra mano yāti
tattattenaiva tatkṣaṇam /
parityajyānavasthityā
nistaraṅgastato bhavet // 129 //

This also is the technique when you begin with *śāktopāya* and end in *śāmbhavopāya*.

Yatra yatra mano yāti, just leave your mind free, let it go wherever it goes. Wherever it wants to go, let it remain free (*yatra yatra mano yāti*). *Tat tat tenaiva tatkṣaṇaṁ parityajya*, for instance, if it goes to these [spectacles], your mind goes to the specs, at that very moment, don't let [your mind] perceive those specs, tell [your mind] to do something else. Then [when your mind] will go to a book, tell him to do something else. Don't let [your mind] stay at the perception of the book. Let [your mind] go to something else. *Parityajya*, you should just push it from that point. Wherever the mind moves, push it on[to] [an]other object. And from [the] other object, push it to another object. Just disperse it. Just don't let it remain at one point. *Tat tat tenaiva*, *tenaiva*, by that very mind, *tat kṣaṇam*, at that very moment [of perceiving an object], *parityajya*, you should let it abandon that [perception]. *Anavasthityā*, so you should keep your mind *anavasthita* (*anavasthita* means, you should not let it remain at any point, rested). You have to leave your mind free, but follow your mind. You have to follow your mind. If it goes to one point, just don't allow it to function there. Tell it to go somewhere else, tell it to go somewhere else, tell it to go somewhere else, so it will remain without any support. When it becomes support-less, *nistaraṅgastato*, [the *yogi*] will get entry in the state where there are no tides, the tide-less state of God consciousness where there are no waves. That is the *nirvikalpa* state, the *śāmbhava* state.

So this is . . . here, you have to begin with *śāktopāya* and end in the *śāmbhava* [state].

Dhāraṇā 104

भिया सर्वं रवयति
    सर्वगो व्यापकोऽखिले ।
इति भैरवशब्दस्य
    संततोच्चारणाच्छिवः ॥ १३० ॥

bhiyā sarvaṁ ravayati
sarvago vyāpako'khile /[360]
iti bhairavaśabdasya
saṁtatoccāraṇācchivaḥ // *130* //

Just find out the meaning of "*bhairava*". When you want to find out the meaning of "*bhairava*", you have to explain these three letters of "*bhairava*": "*bha*", "*ra*", and "*va*". "*Bha*" means, threat, fear. "*Ra*" means, screaming, crying. "*Va*" means, all-pervading, present–the presence of God consciousness. There you find the presence of God consciousness. When you scream [to God] in fear, God is there.

BRUCE: Does it mean the intensity of that experience?

SWAMIJI: The intensity of that fear. The fear that [causes one to scream], "O God, protect me! I am finished! I am ruined!"

BRUCE: Why is it at that moment that God consciousness is more accessible?

SWAMIJI: Because when you want It . . . when you scream, you want It. It means you are screaming for wanting the support of God. You just scream and God is there.

ERNIE: But then why wouldn't it be also available to you if you didn't cry, if you were afraid, but didn't . . . ?

SWAMIJI: But you don't want to have It. There, you don't want to have It. When you scream [for It], you want to have It. When you cry [for It], you want to have It. There is the urge for having That support. If you don't scream [for God], there is no urge for having that God to support you.

---

360 Swamiji corrected "*bhayā*" to read "*bhiyā*" and "*sarvado*" to read "*sarvago*".

ERNIE: So really, this is just about fear.

SWAMIJI: Fear, yes.

ERNIE: This technique is just about fear.

SWAMIJI: When you are afraid, He is your refuge.

BRUCE: But you don't . . . it's not a mental; you do not think that you want Him and then you scream. It's automatic.

SWAMIJI: No, it is just the explanation of "*bhairava*", what is the state of Bhairava. "*Bhairava*" means, when you are afraid and scream [to Him], He is there. *Vyāpakaḥ* means, He is pervading, He is there.

Iti bhairava śabdasya, when you find out and when you want to explain, discriminate, the state of Bhairava, this word "*bhairava*", *saṁtatoccāraṇāt*, in continuity, you will become Bhairava. When you become yourself Bhairava, what fear is there?

This is *śāktopāya*.

Dhāraṇā 105

अहं ममेदमित्यादि-
प्रतिपत्तिप्रसङ्गतः ।
निराधारं मनो कृत्वा
तद्ध्यानप्रेरणाच्छमी ॥१३१॥

ahaṁ mamedamityādi-
pratipattiprasaṅgataḥ /
nirādhāraṁ mano kṛtvā[361]
taddhyānapreraṇācchamī / / 131 / /

This is *śāktopāya* ending in the *śāmbhava* [state]. Ending in *śāmbhava* is, *tad dhyāna preraṇāt śamī*, when you get that blissful sound state of appeasement, perfect appeasement, where you have nothing to do–that is the perfect state of appeasement, that is the *śāmbhava* state.

Now, you have to begin with *śāktopāya*. That is, *ahaṁ mama idaṁ ityādi pratipatti prasaṅgataḥ*. "*Prasaṅgataḥ*" here [does not mean] "by *prasaṅgataḥ*", it [means] "in *prasaṅgataḥ*". *Prasaṅgataḥ* means, in all these *prasaṅgeṣu*, in all these happenings. Which happenings? "I am Lakshmanjoo", "Mine is Denise", "Viresh is my son", "Stephanie is my disciple", all these things. These (*pratipatti* means "perceptions"), all these perceptions, in the state of all these perceptions, when you keep your mind support-less (*nirādhāram*), . . .*

Without Viresh, without your friend, without your husband, without your wife, you should keep your mind away from these perceptions–"This is mine", "This is not mine". You have to remove personal I-ness from all these things: "This is mine", "This is not mine", "This is my money", "This is not my money", all those things.

ERNIE: Discrimination.

SWAMIJI: Discrimination, discriminating perceptions. And

361 Swamiji corrected "*nirādhāre mano yāti*" to read "*nirādhāraṁ mano kṛtvā*".

your mind, you have to keep your mind *nirādhāram*, without this attachment, without the *ādhāra*[362] of these discriminating perceptions.

*. . . *tad dhyāna preraṇāt*, by this way, *nirādhāraṁ manaḥ kṛtvā*, by this way, if you induce your mind to do this kind of perceiving, *śamī*, you will get the appeased state of the blissful state of God consciousness.

This is the *śāmbhava* [state].

362 Support or basis.

Dhāraṇā 106

नित्यो विभुर्निराधारो
व्यापकश्चाखिलाधिपः ।
शब्दान् प्रतिक्षणं ध्यायन्
कृतार्थोऽर्थानुरूपतः ॥ १३२ ॥

nityo vibhurnirādhāro
vyāpakaścākhilādhipaḥ /
śabdān pratikṣaṇaṁ dhyāyan
kṛtārtho'rthānurūpataḥ / / 132 / /

Nityo vibhuḥ nirādhāraḥ vyāpakaḥ ca akhilādhipaḥ. God is eternal, God is all-pervading, God is support-less, God is *vyāpakaḥ*, everywhere found, *akhilādhipaḥ*, He is the ruler of each and every object of this world (*akhilādhipaḥ*).

Just try to find out these things that I am speaking. I am speaking: "God is eternal, God is all-pervading, God is support-less, God is everywhere, and God is the ruler of each and every object." And these words, *pratikṣaṇaṁ dhyāyan*, just meditate upon [them]. You meditate in continuity on these words: eternity, all-pervading-ness, support-less, everywhere (being everywhere), and the ruler of each and every object.

Śabdān pratikṣaṇaṁ dhyāyan kṛtārtho'rthānurūptaḥ, by concentrating on its meaning in this way (*arthānurūpataḥ* means, when you concentrate on these words in this way), *kṛtārthaḥ*, a *sādhaka* gains his desired object and becomes purposeful.

You know "purposeful"?

The purpose, for that purpose he had come here, [and] it is done. With what purpose he was sent here in this field of repeated births and deaths, it becomes purposeful.[363]

This is *śāktopāya*.

---

363 *Kṛtārtha*: accomplished, successful, satisfied, contented.

Dhāraṇā 107

अतत्त्वमिन्द्रजालाभ-
मिदं सर्वमवस्थितम् ।
किं तत्त्वमिन्द्रजालस्य
इति दार्ढ्याच्छमं व्रजेत् ॥ १३३ ॥

atattvamindrajālābham-
idaṁ sarvamavasthitam /
kiṁ tattvamindrajālasya-
iti dārḍhyācchamaṁ vrajet / / 133 / /

There is another technique. This is a technique of *śāmbhava*. And that technique, the previous one, was *śāktopāya*. This is *śāmbhava* [*upāya*]. When there is nothingness, it is *śāmbhava*–I told you once, when there is nothingness. When there is some support for the time being, this is *śāktopāya*. When there is support, all-around support, up to the end, this is *āṇavopāya*. So you can find out yourself what is *śāmbhava*, what is *śākta*, and what is *āṇava*, if you keep your alertness, awareness there.

Idaṁ sarvaṁ avasthitam, whatever you find in this world, in the one hundred and eighteen worlds, whatever you see, whatever you perceive in these one hundred and eighteen worlds, it is *atattvam*, there is nothing, in fact. It is just a joke. *Atattvaṁ indra jālābham*; *indra jālābham*, it is just like the net of Indra (that is *māyā*; *māyā* means just [that] it has no substance in it). So, this way, you find [that] all these one hundred and eighteen worlds, the one hundred and eighteen worlds, it is a joke. There is no one hundred and eighteen worlds. In its place, there is only God consciousness always shining, and this God consciousness appears in the state of the one hundred and eighteen worlds.

Idaṁ sarvaṁ avasthitaṁ atattvaṁ, it has no basis to it. There is no substance in it. And *indra jāla*, it is just like *indra jāla*, the net of Indra. The net of Indra is just like *māyā*, [and] *māyā* is just a joke.

Kiṁ tattvaṁ indrajālasya, what do you mean by "*indra*

jāla"? Just find out what is *indra jāla*, just find out [that] these one hundred and eighteen worlds [are] just like *indra jāla*, and analyze that *indra jāla*, what is *indra jāla*. It will end in God consciousness if you meditate on it; it will make you achieve that blissful state of *śāmbhava*.

Dhāraṇā 108

आत्मनो निर्विकारस्य
क्व ज्ञानं क्व च वा क्रिया ।
ज्ञानायत्ता बहिर्भावा
अतः शून्यमिदं जगत् ॥१३४॥

ātmano nirvikārasya
kva jñānaṁ kva ca vā kriyā /
jñānāyattā bahirbhāvā
ataḥ śūnyamidaṁ jagat / / 134 / /

"I know it." "I don't know it." "I know it." For instance, I tell you to read it and explain it to him. Can you do that? [If] you won't do it, so it is not knowing, it is not knowing. I will tell Nilakanth Gurtoo to explain it. He will read and explain it. That is knowing. But, in fact, the soul, the nature of your Self, is *nirvikāra*, it is without changes, it has no changes (it has no *vikṛti*). So, actually there is neither knowledge nor lack of it. Here you find the lack of it [and] here you find knowledge, but it is all a joke. It is a kind of change in you. There is some change in you [when] you can't understand. There is some change in him [when] he can understand. So this is change. Wherever there is change, it is ignorance; as long as there is change, say, change of perception. When there is one-pointed perception, that is reality. That is neither knowledge nor ignorance. That is what He says here.

Ātmano nirvikārasya, the Self, the real Self, is *nirvikāra*, it has no *vikāra*, these changes. Because actually *jñāna* and *kriyā* are unnatural. They are not natural. It is not your nature. *Jñānāyattā bahir bhāvā*, these (knowledge and action) are adjusted only in outward objectivity, the outward world of the cycle of objectivity (*bahir bhāvā jñānāyattā*, they are adjusted with knowledge and action).

ERNIE: This is not a technique then. This is just information.

SWAMIJI: No, it is a technique. It is a technique through the mind, through perception. You have to find out what is knowledge [and] what is action. For instance, you can't understand anything. Just try to see that not-understanding state [and] you will get entry in God consciousness. When you understand and just find out how I have understood, you will get entry in God consciousness. This is a *śāmbhava* technique.

ERNIE: Because there is no support.

SWAMIJI: There is no support because it is *śūnya*; it is neither knowledge nor action.

Ataḥ śūnyam idaṁ jagat, so [the *yogi*] finds the whole universe dissolved in *śūnya*, voidness.[364]

It is *śāmbhava*.

364 *Mahā śūnyā*, supreme voidness.

Dhāraṇā 109

न मे बन्धो न मे मोक्षो
जीवस्यैता विभीषिकाः ।
प्रतिबिम्बमिदं बुद्धे-
र्जलेष्विव विवस्वतः ॥ १३५ ॥

na me bandho na me mokṣo
jīvasyaitā vibhīṣikāḥ /[365]
pratibimbamidaṁ buddher-
jaleṣviva vivasvataḥ // 135 //

"*Na me bandho*, I have no bondage." "*Na me mokṣo*, I am not liberated." "I am neither bound nor liberated." This liberation and bondage is just attributed to the *jīva*, the individual soul, and to him, these two perceptions (being in bondage and being liberated) are *vibhīṣikāḥ*, they make him terrified–he grumbles, he jumps.

ERNIE: Even the knowledge of liberation?

SWAMIJI: Yes, liberation. "I am liberated. I am liberated!" What is that? It is also bondage. It is also ignorance. Knowledge and liberation is attributed to those who are individuals; and they get change in bondage and in liberation.

Pratibimbam idaṁ buddher jaleṣviva vivasvataḥ. If you are bound in this cycle of the world, that is bondage, and [if] you are liberated from the cycle of the world, you are liberated. You should find out that this knowledge–being elevated and being liberated or being bound in this cycle of the world–this bondage and liberation is just a reflection in the limited intellect. It is a reflection in *buddher* ("*buddher*" is the limited intellectual element).

On the contrary, it is not a reflection in unlimited God consciousness. In the mirror of unlimited God consciousness, that reflection is something else–that is *śāmbhava*. When you

365 Swamiji corrected "*na me bandho na mokṣo me bhitasyaita vibhiṣikāḥ*" to read "*na me bandho na me mokṣo jīvasyaitā vibhiṣikāḥ*".

find out [that] this whole cycle of one hundred and eighteen worlds is reflected in God consciousness, that is something else. But when you find, when you perceive, this reflection of this world in your intellect, in your limited intellectual state, this terrifies you. Because, e.g., you will ignore Samdu's son and you won't ignore Viresh. This is the reflection of that in that limited cycle of *buddhi*, in the intellect (that is *buddhi*).

And that is *saṁvit*. What? Unlimited. The unlimited cycle of *jñāna* is *saṁvit*, God consciousness. When you find out it is a reflection in God consciousness, then there is neither attachment nor detachment for Viresh. Then you are *muktaḥ*, you become *jīvan muktaḥ*[366].

So, *pratibimbam idaṁ buddher*, this makes you sad when you find out this reflected in your limited intellect, not in unlimited *saṁvit* (knowledge).

Jaleṣu iva vivasvataḥ, just as in various pools or various streams of water, you find the reflection of the sun in varieties (e.g., somewhere you'll find the sun being cut if the water is flowing; if the water is stationary, you will find it stationary–the reflection of the sun), in the same way, these things happen in the individual reflection, in the individual cycle of the intellect. When there is the individual cycle of the intellect, it is bondage, it will give you fear. It will give whom fear? *Jīvasya*. *Jīvasya*, who is an individual.

So, you have to find out [that], "*Na me bandho na me mokṣo*, neither I am bound nor I am liberated."[367]

So this is *śāktopāya*.

---

366 Liberated while embodied.

367 "Become divine! Do not put limited shrunken thoughts in yourself. Try to keep your mind broad. That will make you divine!" *Vijñāna Bhairava*, additional audio (USF archives).

Dhāraṇā 110

इन्द्रियद्वारकं सर्वं
सुखदुःखादिसंगमम् ।
इतीन्द्रियाणि संत्यज्य
स्वस्थः स्वात्मनि वर्तते ॥ १३६ ॥

indriyadvārakaṁ sarvaṁ
sukhaduḥkhādisaṁgamam /
itīndriyāṇi saṁtyajya
svasthaḥ svātmani vartate / / 136 / /

This is the technique of *śāktopāya* ending in the *śāmbhava* [state].

Indriya dvārakaṁ sarvaṁ sukha duḥkhādi saṁgamam. When you find pleasure, you find pain. All these things happen in this world–pain, pleasure, sorrow, sadness, excitement, all those things. *Indriya dvārakam*, it is through your organs, it happens only through your organs. When your organs are functioning in a limited way, you find sometimes pleasure, sometime pain, sometime sorrow, sometime excitement, sometime ego, all this. *Iti indriyāṇi*, leave aside the functioning of your organs. Be above the organs, be above the state of the organs, [and then] *svasthaḥ svātmani vartate*, you'll remain in your real nature of God consciousness.

This is *śāktopāya* ending in *śāmbhava* [state]. This is also a technique of wisdom, not a technique of *sādhanā* [in activity].[368] This is a *sādhanā* in wisdom, in understanding, a practice in wisdom.

---

368 That is, it is a technique of knowledge (*śaktopāya*), not activity (*āṇavopāya*).

Dhāraṇā 111

ज्ञानं प्रकाशकं लोके
आत्मा चैव प्रकाशकः ।
अनयोरपृथग्भावात्
ज्ञानी ज्ञाने विभाव्यते ॥ १३७॥

jñānaṁ prakāśakaṁ loke
ātmā caiva prakāśakaḥ /
anayorapṛthagbhāvāt
jñānī jñāne vibhāvyate / / 137 / /[369]

Jñānaṁ prakāśakaṁ loke, in this world, knowledge is that thing which makes you understand things. *Jñānaṁ prakāśakaṁ loke*, knowledge is the only thing that makes you understand things in this world. *Ātmā caiva prakāśakaḥ*, but that individual soul is also that element which makes you understand things. So, there are two things: one is knowledge and one is the holder of knowledge (*ātmā* is the knowledge-holder, where knowledge is resting).

Where is knowledge resting?

GURTOO: In *ātmā*.

SWAMIJI: In *ātmā*.

So, there are these two substances: one is knowledge and one is *ātmā*. Knowledge makes you understand things in this world and *ātmā* also makes you understand these things.

So, in this way (this is also a technique of wisdom, a technique of understanding), you have to understand what is knowledge and what is *ātmā*. *Anayor apṛthag bhāvāt*, *ātmā* and knowledge are actually one. So, *jñānī jñāne vibhāvyate*, the *ātmā* you will find resting in knowledge and knowledge you will find resting in the *ātmā*–vice versa.

ERNIE: That's *śāmbhavopāya*?

---

369 Swamiji corrected this verse from that found in the original text, which reads: *jñānaṁ prakāśakaṁ sarvaṁ sarveṇātmā prakāśakaḥ / ekamekasvabhāvatvāt jñānaṁ jñeyaṁ vibāvyate //* (*KSTS* vol. 8, pp121-122).

SWAMIJI: No, because it is wisdom. You have to find out, so it is *śāktopāya*.

ERNIE: But last time it was wisdom.

SWAMIJI: No. [The last technique was the] wisdom of nothingness. [Here] it is the wisdom of something.

ERNIE: This is knowledge and *ātmā*.

SWAMIJI: Yes.

Dhāraṇā 112

मानसं चेतना शक्ति-
रात्मा चेति चतुष्टयम् ।
यदा प्रिये परिक्षीणं
तदा तद्भैरवं वपुः ॥१३८॥

mānasaṁ cetanā śaktir-
ātmā ceti catuṣṭayam /
yadā priye parikṣīṇaṁ
tadā tadbhairavaṁ vapuḥ / / 138 / /

Mānasam (mind), *cetanā*, *śakti*, and *ātmā*–these four–*iti catuṣṭayam*, these are four substances. One is the mind. The mind is the organ of differentiated thoughts. The organ of the differentiated cycle of thoughts is the mind, when you have the differentiated cycle of thoughts. *Cetanā* is differentiated perception. Differentiated perception, *cetanā*, is a kind of intellect. *Śakti* is the energy of breath, breathing in and out. So, mind is the organ of differentiated thoughts, and the organ of differentiated perception [is *cetanā*], and the energy of breath [is *śakti*], and *ātmā* [is] the limited ego–*iti catuṣṭayam*, these are four.

These four have ruined the nature of a man. These four have actually destroyed and ruined everything that we have, the treasure we had. It is looted by these four substances. Which substances? Mind, differentiated perception (the intellect), and the energy of breath (when you breathe in and out, this is the ruining center), and *ātmā* (the limited ego).

Yadā priye parikṣīṇam, when You leave it aside, O dear Pārvatī (*yadā* [*priye*] *parikṣīṇaṁ*), *tadā tad bhairavaṁ vapuḥ*, then You will find the state of Bhairava shining all around. So, You have to leave these things–don't breathe!

In the technique of the *āṇava* cycle, the purpose of breathing in and out is just to ignore the breathing in and out, because the time will come when you breathe in and out, breathe in and out, [and then] the breath will stop. It stops and you get entry in that central vein.

And differentiated perception: when you put that one-pointedness in differentiated perception and make your intellect feel that differentiated perception is a wrong perception–it is a wrong notion, it is a wrong notion, wrong notion, wrong notion–[then] there will be undifferentiated perception. And undifferentiated perception is attributed to Śiva. And differentiated thoughts will become undifferentiated thoughts, only one thought of mind. So, the mind will become mind-less, differentiated perception will become undifferentiated (they will reside in the undifferentiated state), the energy of breath becomes breath-less, and *ātmā* (ego) becomes unlimited Being. That is the reality of the *śāmbhava* [state].

BRUCE: This practice is *śāmbhavopāya*?

SWAMIJI: *Śāmbhavopāya*, yes.

End of 112 *dhāraṇās*.

The techniques are finished. In the *Vijñāna Bhairava*, all techniques, one hundred and twelve techniques, are finished.

निस्तरङ्गोपदेशानां
शतमुक्तं समासतः ।
द्वादशाभ्यधिकं देवि
यज्ज्ञात्वा ज्ञानविज्जनः ॥ १३९ ॥

nistaraṅgopadeśānāṁ
śatamuktaṁ samāsataḥ /
dvādaśābhyadhikaṁ devi
yajjñātvā jñānavijjanaḥ // 139 //

This way I have explained to You, O Pārvatī, *upadeśa* (*upadeśa* means, these techniques), which are *nistaraṅga* techniques, techniques of the tide-less state (you know, where there are no tides, where there are no changes–*nistaraṅga upadeśa*). These are *upadeśas* of the *nistaraṅga* state. And these techniques I have explained to You–one hundred techniques plus twelve more (*dvādaśa abhyadhikam*, plus twelve more)–so, one hundred and twelve techniques I have explained to You, [and] *yat jñātvā*, by the knowledge of these techniques, You will become filled with knowledge.

अत्र चैकतमे युक्तो
जायते भैरवः स्वयम् ।
वाचा करोति कर्माणि
शापानुग्रहकारकः ॥ १४० ॥

atra caikatame yukto
jāyate bhairavaḥ svayam /
vācā karoti karmāṇi
śāpānugrahakārakaḥ // 140 //

In these one hundred and twelve ways that have been

already described, explained, any person attached to one of these processes (*atra ca ekatame yuktaḥ*, the person who is attached to one of these processes), only one out of one hundred and twelve, he becomes himself Bhairava, one with Bhairava. He and Bhairava are one. There is not the least difference between him and Lord Śiva.

Vācā karoti karmāṇi, he does things by speech, not by doing. He says [something] and that is done. Whatever he says, it is done (that is *vācā karoti karmāṇi*; *karmāṇi vācā karoti*, by speech he works).

Śāpānugraha kārakaḥ, and he becomes the giver of curses and the bestower of boons; *śāpa anugraha kārakaḥ*, he can curse and he can bestow boons also.

अजरामरतामेति
    सोऽणिमादिगुणान्वितः ।
योगिनीनां प्रियो देवि
    सर्वमेलापकाधिपः ॥ १४१ ॥

जीवन्नपि विमुक्तोऽसौ
    कुर्वन्नपि च चेष्टितं ।

ajarāmaratāmeti
so'ṇimādiguṇānvitaḥ /
yoginīnāṁ priyo devi
sarvamelāpakādhipaḥ / / 141 / /

jīvannapi vimukto'sau
kurvannapi ca ceṣṭitam[370] */ 142a*

Saḥ (he) achieves that state where there is neither birth nor death (*ajara amaratām eti*) and he becomes attached with all the eight great *yogic* powers (*aṇimādi guṇa anvitaḥ*; *guṇa* here means "powers")–*aṇimādi aṣṭa guṇa anvitaḥ*, *aṣṭa*

370 Swamiji corrected "*kurvannapi na lipyate*" to read "*kurvannapi ca ceṣṭitam*".

siddhi anvitaḥ.

Yoginīnāṁ priyo devi, O Devī, he becomes attached to *yoginīs*. The one who is beloved by *yoginīs*, loved by *yoginīs,* he becomes one with Lord Śiva. *Yoginīnām priyaḥ*, his life is filled with life.[371] He becomes totally attached to *yoginīs.*

Sarva melāpaka adhipaḥ, and he becomes the *adhipaḥ* (the chief director) of all the *melāpas* (spiritual gatherings, *sarva melāpa*). *Melāpa* means, spiritual gatherings that take place by *yoginīs* and *siddhas* in *samādhi*. In *samādhi*, you can experience this *melāpa* (the gathering) of *siddhas* and *yoginīs*. They gather before the *sādhaka* who is in *samādhi*; they gather before him and they bestow on him all the boons they can.

Kurvan api ca ceṣṭitam, although he is doing all his daily routine of life, he becomes absolutely *jīvan mukta*, liberated.

श्रीदेवी उवाच

śrīdevī uvāca

Now, Devī puts a question before the Lord:

इदं यदि वपुर्देव
  परायाश्च महेश्वर ॥ १४२ ॥
एवमुक्तव्यवस्थायां
  जप्यते को जपश्च कः ।

idaṁ yadi vapurdeva
  parāyāśca maheśvara / / 142b / /
evamuktavyavasthāyāṁ
  japyate ko japaśca kaḥ / 143a

371 On the contrary, Swamiji said, "*Devānām priyaḥ*, the one who is loved by the *devās*, that is death. [When the] *devās* call him back to their abode, his life is over." *Vijñāna Bhairava*, additional audio (USF archives).

O Lord, if this is the *svarūpa*, [if] this is the essence of supreme energy, then where recitation and the recited one will stand? There will be no recitation of any deity and no deity who is to be recited, whose name is to be sung, whose name is to be remembered.

So, there is neither recitation . . . not *japya*, not *japa*. *Japa* means "recitation", *japya* means recitation for whom . . .

GURTOO: . . . the recitation is done.

SWAMIJI: Then these two are gone. These two are not existing there, in this situation. If this is the real situation of supreme energy, [then] what have You put in these one hundred and twelve ways, one hundred and twelve processes?

ध्यायते को महानाथ
पूज्यते कश्च तृप्यति ॥१४३॥
हुयते कस्य वा होमो
यागः कस्य च किं कथम् ।

dhyāyate ko mahānātha
pūjyate kaśca tṛpyati / / 143b / /
hūyate kasya vā homo
yāgaḥ kasya ca kiṁ katham / 144a

Dhyāyate ko mahānātha, O My Lord, who can meditate?

Pūjyate kaśca, who can do worship?

Kaśca tṛpyati, and who can get satisfaction?

Hūyate kasya vā homaḥ, who is to be offered?

Kaḥ hūyate, who can offer the oblations in the sacrificial fire?

Kasya vā homaḥ, whose is the offering?

Neither there is offering nor is there anything to be offered.

Yāgaḥ kasya ca kiṁ katham, how can an oblation take place and whose is the oblation there? There is nothing of that sort there.

Now, Bhairava explains to Devī:

श्रीभैरव उवाच

एषात्र प्रक्रिया बाह्या
स्थूलेष्वेव मृगेक्षणे ॥ १४४॥
भूयो भूयः परे भावे
भावना भाव्यते हि या ।
जपः सोऽत्र स्वयं नादो
मन्त्रात्मा जप्य ईदृशः ॥ १४५॥

śrī bhairava uvāca

eṣātra prakriyā bāhyā
sthūleṣveva mṛgekṣaṇe / / 144 / /
bhūyo bhūyaḥ pare bhāve
bhāvanā bhāvyate hi yā /
japaḥ so'tra svayaṁ nādo
mantrātmā japya īdṛśaḥ / / 145 / /

I think you must put these two lines also attached with this *śloka*, with this one hundred and forty-fourth [verse]:

bhāvanā bhāvyate hi yā /
japaḥ so'tra svayaṁ nādo
mantrātmā japya īdṛśaḥ / / 145 / /

One and a half *ślokas* to be kept together.

O Devī, this is the outward tradition of *japa*, *dhyāna*, *pūjā*, worship, all, etc. This is the outward tradition meant only for gross *sādhakas* (*sthūleṣu eva sādhakeṣu vartate*; *sthūla* means "gross"), [for *sādhakas*] who have not that subtle strength of awareness, [of] maintaining that subtle strength of awareness. But [*sādhakas*] who have that strength of that subtlest awareness, for them, *bhūyo bhūyah pare bhāve bhāvanā bhāvyate hi yā*, contemplation which is done, *bhūyo bhūyaḥ*, in continuity, *pare bhāve*, in that supreme state, *yā bhāvanā bhāvyate*, the contemplation which is done there, that is real *japa*, that is their real recitation. And this way You should know the embodiment of the universal is Bhairava Himself. [That is the real] *mantra* to be recited.

Bhāvanā means, contemplation, meditation, in continuity. *Bhūyo bhūyaḥ* is not "again and again". *Bhūyo bhūyaḥ* means, just like in a chain-like way. "Again and again" [it is] not. When you put [contemplation] again and again, then there is a pause. There should not be a pause.

DEVOTEE: Chain-like.

SWAMIJI: Chain-like contemplation, just like the flame you see in movement of a candle, without any pause. In that way you should meditate. You should not meditate with pauses. If you meditate with pauses, everything is finished, nothing will be achieved.

That is real recitation where you get the flow of *nāda* yourself; *nāda*, automatic; automatic *nāda* flows out. *Nāda* means, the real I-consciousness.

And the *japya* (*japya* means, the deity for whom you are reciting) is *mantrātmā*, is the full[-ness] of universal "I"–*mantrātmā* (*mantra* means, universal "I").

Now, He puts what is *dhyāna*:

ध्यानं हि निश्चला बुद्धि-
निराकारा निराश्रया ।
न तु ध्यानं शरीराक्षि-
मुखहस्तादिकल्पना ॥ १४६ ॥

dhyānaṁ hi niścalā buddhir-
nirākārā nirāśrayā /
na tu dhyānaṁ śarīrākṣi-
mukhahastādikalpanā / / 146 / /

Meditation means when your intellectual awareness becomes one-pointed and attached to formlessness; not only formlessness but support-less-ness (*nirāśrayā*, without any support).

If you contemplate with support . . . for instance, to meditate with support is just to meditate between the two breaths, just to meditate between the two eyebrows, just to meditate between one point and another point. This is meditation with support. But you should meditate without any support. Just take hold of that–finished. Maintain awareness there. That is *nirāśrayā*.

That is *dhyāna*. That is the real meditation. That is real contemplation. *Na tu dhyānaṁ śarīrākṣi mukha hastādi kalpanā*, that is not meditation where you meditate on the body of the deity, or *akṣi*, the organs of the deity, or the *mukha*[372] and hands [of the deity], and so on. This is not *dhyāna*. *Dhyāna* is that when you are attached with *niścalā buddhi*, without form and without support.

And, what is *pūjā*, real worship?

पूजा नाम न पुष्पाद्यै-
र्या मतिः क्रियते दृढा ।

372 Face.

निर्विकल्पे परे व्योम्नि
सा पूजा ह्यादराल्लयः ॥ १४७॥

pūjā nāma na puṣpādyair-
yā matiḥ kriyate dṛḍhā /
nirvikalpe pare vyomni
sā pūjā hyādarāllayaḥ // 147 //

Pūjā nāma na puṣpādyair, worship is not done with flowers, with *ghee*[373], with all those things that you gather from the market and the garden. That way you can't do the real *pūjā*, the real worship.

Real worship is that where your intellect is firmly established (*kriyate dṛḍhā*, where your intellect is firmly established) in the supreme voidness of thought-lessness. And where that intellect is firmly established in the thought-less and supreme voidness, the supreme voidness of *cidākāśā* (consciousness), that is real *pūjā*, *hyādarāt layaḥ*, where one merges, one gets expired, with great respect, with great honor (*hyādarāt layaḥ*, you are expired with honor). You expire your everything, you lose your everything, not with dishonor, not with hatred, but with honor. With honor, you expire in that supreme thought-less state of *cidākāśā*.

अत्रैकतमयुक्तिस्थे
योत्पद्येत दिनाद्दिनम् ।
भरिताकारता सात्र
तृप्तिरत्यन्तपूर्णता ॥ १४८॥

atraikatamayuktisthe
yotpadyeta dinād dinam /
bharitākāratā sātra
tṛptiratyantapūrṇatā // 148 //

---

373 Clarified butter.

In these one hundred and twelve ways, anyone who is attached to one of these (*atra ekatama yuktisthe*), to him, any state, whatever is found to him, whatever is experienced by him, that state is filled with the Bhairava state. That is the real satisfaction you get from worship; *sātra tṛptir*, that is the real satisfaction of worshiping. And hence, this satisfaction is *atyanta pūrṇatā*, supreme fullness.

महाशून्यालये वह्नौ
भूताक्षविषयादिकम् ।
हूयते मनसा सार्धं
स होमश्चेतनास्रुचा ॥ १४९ ॥

mahāśūnyālaye vahnau
bhūtākṣaviṣayādikam /
hūyate manasā sārdhaṁ
sa homaścetanāsrucā / / 149 / /[374]

Mahā śūnyālaye, when in that *agni*, when in that fire, the fire which is situated or established in the great voidness, in the fire of the great voidness, in that fire, when all the five elements of your body, and all the sensual engagements of your body, and all your senses along with your mind, are offered in that fire, that is the real *homa*[375], that is the real *havan* (*yāga*), where awareness is the spoon, [where] awareness is the spoon of the offering.

You mean, "spoon"? That "*sruk*".

DEVOTEE: Sacrificial ladle.

SWAMIJI: Yes, ladle, sacrificial ladle.

374 While commenting upon this verse, Swamiji gave the reading of "*sa homaḥ sruk ca cetanā*" as an alternative. This reading is also found in *KSTS* vol. 8, p132, commentary, line 6.

375 Oblation or sacrifice.

यागोऽत्र परमेशानि
तुष्टिरानन्दलक्षणा ।

yāgo'tra parameśāni
tuṣṭirānandalakṣaṇā / 150a

And *yāga*[376] is there [meant], O Devī, the satisfaction of being united with that final beatitude, final bliss.

Now, what is *kṣetra*, *tīrtha*? [It is said that] you must go to a *tīrtha*[377] also for removing your sins.

क्षपणात्सर्वपापानां
त्राणात्सर्वस्य पार्वति ॥ १५० ॥
रुद्रशक्तिसमावेश-
स्तत्क्षेत्रं भावना परा ।

kṣapaṇātsarvapāpānāṁ
trāṇātsarvasya pārvatī / / 150b / /
rudraśaktisamāveśas-
tatkṣetraṁ bhāvanā parā / 151a

When you get the full trance in the energies of Bhairava, when you enter in the wheel of energies of Bhairava (*rudra śakti samāveśaḥ*, when you enter in the *śaktis* of *rudra*, of Bhairava–that is "*śakti samāveśa*"), when you get *śakti samāveśa*, that is *kṣetra*, that is the real *kṣetra* (*kṣetra* means, the sacred spot where worship and all spiritual things are done; that is *kṣetra*, *tīrtha*).

There are two [syllables] in "*kṣetra*": "*kṣa*" and "*tra*". "*Kṣa*" means, to destroy; "*tra*" means, to protect. What is destroyed and what is protected? All sins are destroyed (*kṣapaṇāt sarva pāpānām*). Where all sins are destroyed and where you get all-round protection from evils, that is the real *kṣetra*.

---

376 Oblation or sacrifice.
377 Place of pilgrimage.

Hence, this *kṣetra* is the supreme *bhāvanā*, the supreme state of *bhāvanā* (*bhāvanā* means, when you sentence your mind with awareness to one point).

अन्यथा तस्य तत्त्वस्य
का पूजा कश्च तृप्यति ॥ १५१ ॥

anyathā tasya tattvasya
kā pūjā kaśca tṛpyati / / *151b* / /

Otherwise, if this was not the real *kṣetra*, how can that supreme element–I would not call that an "element"–[how that] supreme state of Lord Śiva would be adored or would get satisfaction?

Adoration, satisfaction, only exists in this trance of *rudra śakti*, when you enter in the energies of Lord Śiva. When you enter in a *tīrtha* (e.g., in Khirbhavani, in Jvala), you enter only in duality and nothing is achieved there.[378]

Now, just see what is bath, bathing:

स्वतन्त्रानन्दचिन्मात्र-
सारः स्वात्मा हि सर्वतः ।
आवेशनं तत्स्वरूपे
स्वात्मनः स्नानमीरितम् ॥ १५२ ॥

svatantrānandacinmātra-
sāraḥ svātmā hi sarvataḥ /
āveśanaṁ tatsvarūpe
svātmanaḥ snānamīritam / / *152* / /

First, you must feel and experience that your own Self–which is not your individual self but it is universal because of its freedom, because of its felicity, blissfulness, and because of its consciousness–[is] filled with freedom, filled with bliss, filled with consciousness. And the essence of these three is

378 Khirbhavani and Jvalamukhi are two ancient shrines.

your Self. And that Self is the universal Self, that is not the individual self. And, that universal Self is found everywhere (*svātmā hi sarvataḥ vartate*). And in that *svarūpa*, when you enter in that *svarūpa*, and when you make yourself enter in that supreme *svarūpa*, when you make your individual being enter in that universal Self, that is really a "bath", that is really "bathing", that is really "taking a bath".

When you go to the bathroom and put the geyser on and take a bath, that is not a bath. That is only washing your material body.

यैरेव पूज्यते द्रव्यै-
स्तर्प्यते वा परापरः ।
यश्चैव पूजकः सर्वः
स एवैकः क्व पूजनम् ॥ १५३ ॥

yaireva pūjyate dravyais-
tarpyate vā parāparaḥ /
yaścaiva pūjakaḥ sarvaḥ
sa evaikaḥ kva pūjanam // 153 //

Take your garden where flowers are there. You cut these flowers just to offer them at the feet of your Lord; or you get *dhūpa*[379], *dīpa*[380], and *guggul*[381] from the market and offer it before the feet of the Lord. But actually, these things are the Lord themselves. That flower is the Lord, that [incense] is the Lord (that *agarbatti* is the Lord), everything is the Lord. And the adorer is the Lord. So the Lord is everywhere.

Kva pūjanam, where adoration will take place? Adoration is not possible. How can you adore the Lord if you are yourself the Lord? How can you offer the Lord anything, if anything, whatever you offer, is the Lord Himself? So there is no way of worshiping [because] He is the worshiper Himself.

---

379 Incense.

380 Light.

381 *Guggul* is a type of fragrant resin traditionally used in worship.

vrajetprāṇo viśejjīva
icchayā kuṭilākṛtiḥ /

Now, the essence of all these one hundred and twelve ways, He is putting here:

व्रजेत्प्राणो विशेज्जीव
इच्छया कुटिलाकृतिः ।
दीर्घात्मा सा महादेवी
परक्षेत्रं परापरा ॥ १५४ ॥

vrajetprāṇo viśejjīva
icchayā kuṭilākṛtiḥ /
dīrghātmā sā mahādevī
parakṣetraṁ parāparā / / *154* / /

When your breath flows out (*vrajet prāṇo*, when your breath flows out), [and] *viśet jīvaḥ*, when your ingoing, intaking breath, enters in, and *kuṭilākṛtiḥ*, in the way of crooked movement (because from the heart, [the breath] moves in the crooked way to this ether[382], [and] from here again, [the breath] moves in a crooked way, it does not move in a straight line–that is "*kuṭilākṛtiḥ*")–now what you have to do? He says–*dīrghātmā icchayā*, *icchayā dīrghātmā*, . . .*

There are three powers in the movement of breath [that are] functioning. One power is that of breath (that is called *prāṇa śaktiḥ*). Another power is that of the Lord (that is called *prabhu śaktiḥ*). One power is that of the Self (that is called *ātmā śaktiḥ*). *Prāṇa śaktiḥ*, *prabhu śaktiḥ*, and *ātmā śaktiḥ*.

Prāṇa śaktiḥ is that energy when you are asleep, when you are unaware of where you are. You go to bed and still this moving of breath takes place unconsciously. That is the energy of *prāṇa*, that is called "*prāṇa śaktiḥ*".

---

382 Here ether refers to *bāhya dvādaśānta*, the starting point of breath outside (*bāhya*) the body, twelve finger spaces from the center of the eyebrows.

Ātmā śaktiḥ is when you control the breath. You stop it, you stop it for some time. This energy is called "*ātmā śaktiḥ*".

And when, by the grace of the Lord, this *prāṇa* enters in your central vein (*madhyā nāḍi*), that is functioned by *prabhu śaktiḥ*. That is the energy of the Lord.

Among these three energies, you have to function . . . not *prāṇa śakti*. *Prabhu śaktiḥ* is out of the question; *prabhu śakti* is in the hands of Lord Śiva, so that thing is absolutely impossible [to function]. *Prāṇa śakti* is also there . . .

DEVOTEE: Automatic?

SWAMIJI: . . . automatic; but in an automatic way, you have not to breathe in and out.

* . . . He says "*icchayā*", by your *ātmā śaktiḥ*, by your *ātmā śaktiḥ* you have to breathe in and by *ātmā śaktiḥ* you have to breathe out. You have not to breathe out and in as it goes on [automatically]. *Dīrghātmā*, the moving of the breath must occupy more time (that is the meaning of "*dīrghātmā*"). That is the supreme *kṣetra*[383], and not [only] the supreme *kṣetra*– more supreme than supreme!

Parāparā means, more supreme than supreme.

अस्यामनुचरन् तिष्ठन्
महानन्दमयेऽध्वरे ।

asyāmanucaran tiṣṭhan
mahānandamaye'dhvare / *155-1a*

And this is the real *adhvara* (*adhvara* means, *yāga*, *havan*, sacrificial fire). In this supreme sacrificial fire, the one who is attached in continuity in the recitation of the breath, giving it more span of time, not span of space (duration of time, not space), . . .*

The space [of breath] will be shortened. The more time, the less space; the less time, the more space. When you are breathing violently, it will occupy more space–it will go up to

383 When you enter in the wheel of energies of Bhairava, that is the sacred spot where worship and all spiritual things are done; that is *kṣetra*.

this point [Swamiji demonstrates]. When you are breathing slowly, it will go to this place. So, more time, less space; less time, more space. You have to put . . .

DEVOTEE: More time, less space.

SWAMIJI: . . . less space. Thank you. You have understood it.

तया देव्या समाविष्टः
परं भैरवमाप्नुयात् ॥ १५५॥

tayā devyā samāviṣṭaḥ
paraṁ bhairavamāpnuyāt / / 155-1b / /

*. . . and, in this supreme *yāga*, he who is attached in continuation, he is actually married to that supreme energy of Lord Śiva (*samāviṣṭaḥ* means, married to the energy of Lord Śiva, the supreme energy of Lord Śiva). He is married, absolutely married.

Do you know what is "married"? *Ātmasāt*, he has become one with that energy. And the one who is married this way, he enters and he achieves the state of supreme Bhairava.

सकारेण बहिर्याति
हकारेण विशेत्पुनः ।
हंसहंसेत्यमुं मन्त्रं
जीवो जपति नित्यशः ॥ १५५। ।

sakāreṇa bahiryāti
hakāreṇa viśetpunaḥ /
haṁsahaṁsetyamuṁ mantraṁ
jīvo japati nityaśaḥ / / 155-2[384]

384 This verse, although not found in the *KSTS*, is referred to in the *Śiva Sūtra Vimarśinī* of Kṣemarāja, in the commentary on *sūtra* 27 of the Third Awakening. It is accepted by Swamiji in his revelation of the *Śiva Sūtra Vimarśinī* (see *Shiva Sutras–The Supreme*

By [breathing] out, he utters '*sa*'; by [breathing] in, he utters '*ha*'. In the same way, he recites the mantra of '*haṁsa*', i.e., '*so'haṁ*', '*so'haṁ*', '*so'haṁ*'. This *ajapa gāyatrī* is always existing for him, day and night.

षट् शतानि दिवा रात्रौ
सहस्राण्येकविंशतिः ।
जपो देव्याः समुद्दिष्टः
प्राणस्यान्ते सुदुर्लभः ॥ १५६ ॥

ṣaṭ śatāni divā rātrau
sahasrāṇyekaviṁśatiḥ /
japo devyāḥ samuddiṣṭaḥ
prāṇasyānte sudurlabhaḥ // 156 //

And this *japa* is . . . this automatic recitation of breath in twenty-four hours takes place twenty-one thousand and six hundred times–*śaṭ śatāni*, six hundred, *divā rātrau*, in the day and night, *sahasrāṇi ekaviṁśati*, and twenty-one thousand. Twenty-one thousand and six hundred times, this [automatic] recitation is done, in twenty-four hours.[385]

Japo devyāḥ samuddiṣṭaḥ, and this recitation of the supreme energy is available to everybody. *Prāṇasyānte sudurlabhaḥ*, but, when it is being recited the way I have taught to You, O Devī (I mean, to give it more time and less space), then it is *sudurlabhaḥ*, it is very *durlabha*[386] (*prāṇasyānte sudurlabhaḥ*), i.e., this *japa*.

DEVOTEE: What is "*prāṇasyānte*"?

SWAMIJI: *Prāṇasyānte* means, when the breath is

Awakening, 3.27). The same verse has been included by Jaideva Singh in his edition of the *Śiva Sūtras*, which was prepared under the guidance of Swamiji. A slightly different version of the last line of this verse is also found in the *KSTS*, vol. 9. In light of Swamiji's unique interpretation of verses 154-156, the inclusion of this verse is important to complete the flow of meaning.

385 Among all humans.

386 'Rare' or 'difficult to obtain'.

disconnected with one *tuṭi*. *Prāṇasyānte* means "on the *tuṭi* of *prāṇa*."

We have classified the space of [one normal] breath in sixteen *tuṭis*. One *tuṭi* is two finger spaces and one quarter. And, in these thirty-six finger spaces, there are sixteen *tuṭis*. *Prāṇasyānte* means, when one *tuṭi* is abolished. When [one] *tuṭi* is shortened, when [one] *tuṭi* is lessened, only fifteen *tuṭis* are there, then that *japa* is *durlabha*. So, when you breathe in a lengthy way, then it is *durlabha japa*. Otherwise, everybody recites for twenty-four hours and nothing has happened, nothing is happening. But, when you breathe in fifteen *tuṭis* only, [when] you give it more duration of time and less space, then it will be real *japa*. And afterwards, what you have to do? You have to lessen again another *tuṭi*. Go on with fourteen *tuṭis*, and afterwards, only on thirteen *tuṭis*. Lessen the span of space. That is real *japa*. And then you will see, after one or two weeks, you will be born anew, you will get some substantial progress. That is real *japa*.[387] Otherwise, everybody is breathing in and out, day and night–like asses, dogs, bears, beasts.

इत्येतत्कथितं देवि
परमामृतमुत्तमम् ।
एतच्च नैव कस्यापि
प्रकाश्यं तु कदाचन ॥ १५७॥
परशिष्ये खले क्रूरे
अभक्ते गुरुपादयोः ।
निर्विकल्पमतीनां तु
वीराणामुन्नतात्मनाम् ॥ १५८॥

ityetatkathitaṁ devi
paramāmṛtamuttamam /

387 This practice is described in more detail in *Self Realization in Kashmir Shaivism*, 2.42-43, and also in the *Tantrāloka*, 7th *āhnika*.

etacca naiva kasyāpi
prakāśyaṁ tu kadācana // 157 //
paraśiṣye khale krūre
abhakte gurupādayoḥ /
nirvikalpamatīnāṁ tu
vīrāṇāmunnatātmanām // 158 //

Ityetat kathitaṁ devi param āmṛtam uttamam. O Devī, I have put before You the supreme way where You will get Yourself nectarized. This is the supreme nectar I have put before You. You should never reveal this nectar to anybody–not to those who are *paraśiṣya* (the one who is a follower of other schools is *paraśiṣya*), to him You should not reveal this way of thought, not to those who are *khale*, the one who is mischievous, not to those who are *krūre*, the one who is hard-hearted, and not to those who are *abhakte gurupādayoḥ*, the one who is not attached to the feet of the master, who is not devoted to the feet of the master–but to those who doubtlessly surrender before the master, to them You must reveal this nectar, . . .*

Nirvikalpamatīnām: *vikalpa* means, doubt; *nirvikalpa* means, who are doubt-less, who don't put their own reasoning in between. Don't put questions. Whatever comes from the lips of your masters, don't put your reason there.

DEVOTEE: Total surrender.

SWAMIJI: Total surrender. That is "*nirvikalpamatīḥ*". When you have come to any master and given to him everything, then there is no questioning, then there is complete surrender.

DEVOTEE: But it's a big mistake to make that surrender before you know who is this person.

SWAMIJI: Yes, that is quite true. But once you have surrendered, there is no way out–finished!

*. . . and those who are *vīras* (*vīras* means, [those] who don't go into detail, [into] these limited details, of the here-and-there doings of [their] masters–those are *vīras*), to them, You must reveal this nectar, . . .*

You should not go in details of the acts of your masters. Whatever he is acting, in which way he acts, consider it divine, then you will rise. Otherwise, you will fall and fall and fall and fall.

*. . . and [to those who are] *unnatātmanām*, . . .*

You should expand your mind. You should have vast vision in your mind (*unnatātmanām*). Your *ātma* must become *unnata* (*unnata* means "expanded").

भक्तानां गुरुवर्गस्य
दातव्यं निर्विशङ्कया ।

bhaktānām guruvargasya
dātavyaṁ nirviśaṅkayā / 159a

*. . . *bhaktānām guruvargasya*, and to those also who are devotedly attached to masters, You must reveal to them this nectar that I have already explained to You, without any hesitation (*nirviśaṇkayā*). Otherwise, . . .

ग्रामो राज्यं पुरं देशः
पुत्रदारकुटुम्बकम् ॥ १५९ ॥
सर्वमेतत्परित्यज्य
ग्राह्यमेतन्मृगेक्षणे ।

grāmo rājyaṁ puraṁ deśaḥ
putradārakuṭumbakam / / 159b / /
sarvametatparityajya
grāhyametanmṛgekṣaṇe / 160a

. . . *grāmo*, if You have to abandon Your own town, Your own kingdom, Your own body, Your own space, Your own place, Your own son, Your own wife, Your own . . . , all that You must abandon, but You must protect this supreme nectar that I have told You.

किमेभिरस्थिरैर्देवि
स्थिरं परमिदं धनम् ॥१६०॥

kimebhirasthirairdevi
sthiraṁ paramidaṁ dhanam // 160b //

Kimebhir asthirair devi, those are already to be detached in the end; you will be detached, you will be separated, from your wife, you will be separated from your body, you will be separated from your house, you will be separated from your property, bank balance, everything, in the end. What is there in it? You must protect, you must have, *this* bank balance, this supreme . . .

DEVOTEE: Imperishable.

SWAMIJI: . . . money of nectar.

प्राणा अपि प्रदातव्या
न देयं परमामृतम् ।

prāṇā api pradātavyā
na deyaṁ paramāmṛtam / 161a

If you have to surrender your life also, you must surrender that, but you must not be disconnected from this supreme nectar.

श्रीदेवी उवाच

śrīdevī uvāca

Now, Pārvatī says:

देवदेव महादेव
परितृप्तास्मि शंकर ॥१६१॥

devadeva mahādeva
paritṛptāsmi śaṁkara // 161b //

O Lord, I am fully satisfied now.

रुद्रयामलतन्त्रस्य
सारमद्यावधारितम् ।
सर्वशक्तिप्रभेदानां
हृदयं ज्ञातमद्य च ॥ १६२ ॥

rudrayāmalatantrasya
sāramadyāvadhāritam /
sarvaśaktiprabhedānāṁ
hṛdayaṁ jñātamadya ca // 162 //

Adya rudrayāmala tantrasya sāram avadhāritam. Today I have understood the essence of the *Tantra* of *Rudrayāmala.* The essence of the *Rudrayāmala Tantra* I have today understood. And *sarva śakti prabhedānāṁ hṛdayam*, and I have understood the heart and the essence of all the processes, all one hundred and twelve ways. And I have not only understood, *adya ca*, I have gained also, I have achieved That.

इत्युक्त्वानन्दिता देवी
कण्ठे लग्ना शिवस्य तु ॥ १६३ ॥

ityuktvānanditā devī
kaṇṭhe lagnā śivasya tu // 163 //

And, in this way, Pārvatī was filled with bliss, and She embraced Lord Śiva and became one with Lord Śiva.

So, there ends the language of transcendental love. This is the language of transcendental love.

Jai Guru Dev!

APPENDIX

The *mantra "sauḥ"*

To begin with, you must understand that in the field of *mantras*, in the field of sacred words, the *mantra* that digests these thirty-six elements in its body is "*sauḥ*". It is the supreme *mantra*. It is not a creative *mantra*, it is a destructive *mantra*. Why? Because it winds up the complete cycle of the thirty-six elements. This *mantra* shows you the trick of how to wind up . . . these thirty-six elements and, in the end, rest in the element of Śiva. So it is not expansion, it is winding up. And this winding up is not actually destruction, it is contraction, just as a giant tree is contracted in a seed.

In this way, the entire universe consisting of thirty-six elements resides in the *mantra* "*sauḥ*". This *mantra* is called "the heart*mantra*" because it is the essence of all *mantras*. How is this so? In the same way that a clay bowl or a clay plate are only produced by changing earthen clay, the essence of this bowl or plate continues to be clay. Or, just as ice and vapor, which are produced by watery substances, are actually water.

So, in the realm of the supreme *mantra* "*sauḥ*", if you go into the depth of the thirty-one elements from *pṛthivī* (earth) to *māyā*, you will find that existence (*sat*) is the reality of these elements. All these elements are all existing externally.

After this, you must ascertain that, residing in the second part of the *mantra* "*sauḥ*" is the letter '*au*', which is superior to '*sa*', and which contains the elements *śuddhavidyā*, *īśvara*, and *sadāśiva*. These three elements are the essence of knowledge (*jñāna*) and action (*kriyā*). They are the embodiment of *śakti*.

Greater than the letter '*au*', and residing in the third part of the *mantra* "*sauḥ*", is the letter '*aḥ*', a creative energy which is twofold. This twofold creative energy is comprised of a higher cre-ative energy and a lower creative energy. The higher creative energy is of Śiva and the lower creative energy is of Śakti. This two-part creative energy, above and below, are the two points of the Sanskrit *visarga* (:).

The first part of the *mantra* "*sauḥ*", '*sa*', is in the cycle of *nara*, the second part of the *mantra* "*sauḥ*", '*au*', is in the cycle of *śakti*, and the third part of the *mantra* "*sauḥ*", '*aḥ*', combining both of the creative energies, is in the cycle of Śiva. So, the Trika system of Kashmir Shaivism is the combination of *nara*, Śakti, and Śiva.

In this way, this seed *mantra* "*sauḥ*" is the supreme *mantra*. It is above all other *mantras* including the blessed *mantras* "*ahaṁ*", "*oṁ*", and "*so'ham*". This supreme *mantra*, which is both universal (*viśvamaya*) and transcendent (*viśvottīrṇa*), is the essence of Trika.

Self Realization in Kashmir Shaivism, 3.67-69.

Krama mudrā

In the *Krama Sūtra*, it says that a *yogi* first enters *krama mudrā* in the introverted state. Then, owing to the intensity of *krama mudrā*, he emerges from the introverted state and enters into the outer, external cycle of consciousness.

First, from outside, he goes inside, and then from inside he goes outside. This movement of going in and coming out and then again going in and coming out takes place by the force of the absorption (*samāveśa*) of *krama mudrā*, not by the effort of the *yogi*.

Where the *yogi* travels from outside to inside and then from inside to outside, just to come to the understanding that outside and inside are not different aspects but one, that is *krama mudrā*.

There is one more thing for you to understand. The one who experiences this state of the absorption (*samāveśa*) of *krama mudrā* experiences this whole universe melting into nothingness in the great sky of God Consciousness (*cidgagana*). Although he opens his eyes and perceives that everything is melting into that state, yet, when he strives to come out of that state, it becomes very difficult for him. As it is very difficult for us to enter into that state, in the same way, it is very difficult for that *yogi* to come out of it.

But why does he want to come out? He wants to come out for the fun of it, but he cannot come out. The intensity of God

Consciousness does not let him come out. Yet he struggles to come out. Then for a moment he rises up, and after that he again, filled with intoxication, rests inside. Then, again, he strives to come out. He continues trying to come out and he gets out briefly but then again he is united inside. This happens again and again and this called "*krama mudrā*".

Self Realization in Kashmir Shaivism, 5.114.

This is an automatic process. It does not come by functioning it. You can't function it . . . *Krama mudrā* is no *mudrā*; *krama mudrā* is automatic . . . [*Krama mudrā* is] just to observe that state of *samādhi* in [the external world] also. When it is not so clearly found outside, go again in *samādhi* and pull it out with that *samādhi* and see in external world again. And again and again, again and again, you have to [experience] this way of *krama mudrā* until [you gain] entry in *jagadānanda*. When *jagadānanda* takes place, then everything is divine, no [more] *krama mudrā*.

Tantrāloka 3.263-264, (USF archives).

When you are established in the process of *krama mudrā*, then you experience that ecstasy in action. When you eat, you are in that bliss. When you talk, you are in that bliss. When you walk, you are in that bliss. Whatever you do, you remain in that Universal state. This is the state of "*jīvanmukti*", liberated in life. This state is experienced, not by ordinary *yogins*, but only by great *yogins*. This is the real state of *cit kuṇḍalinī*.

In the actual rise of *cit kuṇḍalinī*, you will only get a glimpse of it and then come out. The full rise of *cit kuṇḍalinī* takes place only by the grace of your master and by the grace of your own strength of awareness. The experience of establishing the full rise of *cit kuṇḍalinī* through the process of *krama mudrā* can take place in one day, one life, or one hundred lifetimes.

Kashmir Shaivism–The Secret Supreme, 17.120.

The establishment of *krama mudrā* is called *jagadānanda*, which means "universal bliss" This is the seventh and last state of *turya*. In this state, the experience of the universal transcendental Being is never lost and the whole of the universe is experienced as one with your own transcendental I-consciousness.

Kashmir Shaivism–The Secret Supreme, 16.114.

Pramiti, pramātṛ, pramāṇa, prameya bhava

Pramiti bhava is the supreme subjective state, *pramātṛ bhava* is the pure subjective state, *pramāṇa bhava* is the cognitive state, and *prameya bhava* is the objective state.

There is difference between *pramātṛ bhāva* and *pramiti bhāva*. *Pramātṛi bhāva* is that state of consciousness where objective perception is attached. When that state of *pramātṛ bhāva* is attached with objective perception, that is pure state of *pramātṛ bhāva*. When it moves to the state where there is no objective perception, there is no touch of objective perception, it is beyond objective perception, that is *pramiti bhāva*.

Tantrāloka 4.124, commentary, USF archive.

[*Pramiti bhāva* is an] objectless-subjective state. It is residing in only pure subjective consciousness. It has nothing to do with the object. When there is the objective state also attached to the subjective state, that is not *pramiti bhāva*, that is *pramātṛ bhāva*. And when that objective state is connected with the cognitive state, that is *pramāṇa bhāva*. When that objective state is completely a pure objective state, that is *prameya bhāva*. And *pramiti bhāva* is complete subjective consciousness without the slightest touch and trace of this object. In the long run, everything resides in *pramiti bhāva*; *pramiti bhāva* is the life of all the three. This is pure consciousness. . . . And that *pramiti bhāva* is absolutely one with *svātantrya śakti* . . . it is one with Lord Śiva.

Tantrāloka 11.72-73a, (USF archive).

In fact, this *pramiti bhāva* is the real source of understanding anything. Whatever you see, it must touch the state of *pramiti bhāva*, otherwise you won't understand it. For instance, you see [an object]. You'll only know [that object] when this sensation of [that object already] resides in *pramiti bhāva*, in that super state of subjective consciousness. And the super state of subjective consciousness is not differentiat From that undifferentiated point of *pramiti bhāva*, the differentiated flow of *pramātṛ bhāva* and *pramāṇa bhāva* flow out.

Tantrāloka 11.62, (USF archive).

It is *nirvikalpa*, it is a thoughtless state. And in that thoughtless state, it [i.e., all knowledge] must reside, otherwise it is not known. It will be unknown for . . . eternity.

Ibid. 11.68-69.

For instance, when you are [giving a lecture while] reading your book, your consciousness is *with* an object. When you are giving a lecture without a book, without any support, your consciousness is *without* an object, it flows out . . . this is the state of *pramiti bhāva*.

Tantrāloka 6.180, (USF archive).

Thirty six elements (*tattvas*)[388]

Śuddha tattvas – Pure Elements

Śiva = I-ness (Being)
Śakti = I-ness (Energy of Being)
Sadāśiva = I-ness in This-ness
Īśvara = This-ness in I-ness
Śuddhavidya = I-ness in I-ness / This-ness in This-ness

(*Mahāmāyā tattva* = gap of illusion)[389]

---

388 In the successive explanation of *tattvas*, *mahāmāyā* and *guṇa tattva* are not nominated at all. This is the subtle understanding of Abhinavagupta that he had recognized *mahāmāyā tattva* in between *śuddhavidyā* and *māyā*, and also *guṇa tattva* in between *prakriti* and *buddhi*."

389 "It is the gap and power of delusion. Delusion, where you won't know that you are deluded. You will conclude that you are established on truth. But that is not truth, that is not the real thing. This is the abode of the *vijñānākalas*." *Tantrāloka* 8.337, (USF archives).

Ṣaṭ kañcukas **– Six Coverings**

Māyā = illusion of individuality
Kalā = limitation of creativity/activity
Vidyā = limitation of knowledge
Rāga = limitation of attachment
Kāla = limitation of time
Niyati = limitation of place

Puruṣa = ego connected with subjectivity
Prakṛti = nature

(Guṇa tattva = manifest guṇas)[390]

Antaḥkaraṇas **– Three Internal Organs**

Buddhiḥ = intellect
Ahaṁkāra = ego connected with objectivity
Manas = mind

Pañca jñānendriyas **– Five Organs of Cognition**

Śrotra = ear, organ of hearing
Tvak = skin, organ of touching
Cakṣu = eye, organ of seeing
Rasanā = tongue, organ of tasting
Ghrāṇa = nose, organ of smelling

Pañca karmendriyas **– Five Organs of Action**

Vāk = speech
Pāṇi = hand
Pāda = foot
Pāyu = excretion
Upastha = procreative

---

390 ". . . in Shaivism, we have put another element, more than thirty-six elements. And that is the element of *guṇa*. *Guṇa tattva* is another *tattva*, another element. . . . But in *prakṛiti guṇa tattva* is not existing, *guṇa tattva* is not visible, it is the mixture of the three *guṇas*, . . . i.e. where from *guṇa*s will come out. . . . The un-agitated state of the *guṇas* is *prakṛti*, and the agitated state of the *guṇas* is *guṇa tattva*." *Tantrāloka* 9.215, 223, (USF archives).

***Pañca tanmātras* - Five Subtle Elements**

Śabda = sound
Sparśa = touch
Rūpa = form
Rasa = taste
Gandha = smell

***Pañca mahābhūtas* - Five Great Elements**

Ākāśa = ether
Vāyu = air
Tejas = fire
Jala = water
Pṛthvī = earth

For a full explanation of the 36 *tattvas* see *Kashmir Shaivism–The Secret Supreme*, chapter 1.

Kuṇḍalinī

Kuṇḍalinī śakti is the revealing and the concealing energy of Lord Śiva. On the one hand, it is the revealing energy and on the other hand, it is the concealing energy. It reveals and it conceals. This *kuṇḍalinī śakti* is not different from the existence of Lord Śiva, just as the energy of light and the energy of heat are not separate from the fire itself. *Kuṇḍalinī*, therefore, in the true sense, is the existence of Śiva. It is the life and glory of Śiva. It is Śiva Himself.

In our Trika Shaivism, *kuṇḍalinī*, which is that internal ser- pent power existing in the shape of a coil, is divided in three ways.

a) *Parā kuṇḍalinī–kuṇḍalinī* functioned by Lord Śiva.
b) *Cit kuṇḍalinī–kuṇḍalinī* functioned in consciousness.
c) *Prāṇa kuṇḍalinī–kuṇḍalinī* functioned in breath.

The supreme *kuṇḍalinī* is called *parā kuṇḍalinī*. This *kuṇḍalinī* is not known or experienced by *yogins*. It is so vast and universal that the body cannot exist in its presence. It is only experienced at the time of death. It is the heart of Śiva. This whole universe is created by *parā kuṇḍalinī*, exists in *parā kuṇḍalinī*, gets its life from *parā kuṇḍalinī*, and is consumed in *parā kuṇḍalinī*. When this *kuṇḍalinī* creates the universe, Śiva conceals His real nature and is thrown into the universe. When the universe is created, He becomes the universe. There is no Śiva left which is separate from the universe.* This is His creative energy. And when *kuṇḍalinī* destroys the universe, Śiva's nature is revealed. So, the creative energy for the universe is the destructive energy for Śiva, i.e., it is the revealing energy for the universe and the concealing energy for Lord Śiva. And the destructive energy for the universe is the creative energy for Śiva, i.e., it is the concealing energy for the universe and the revealing energy for Lord Śiva.

Parā kuṇḍalinī is the supreme *visarga* of Śiva. As you know from studying the theory of *mātṛkācakra*, *visarga* (:) comprises two points. These points are said to be Śiva and Śakti. In the real sense, however, these points are not Śiva and Śakti, they are the revealing point and the concealing point.

Cit kuṇḍalinī is experienced by *yogins* by means of concentrating on the center between any two breaths, thoughts, or actions; between the destruction and creation of any two things. The happiness and bliss that you experience here [in *cit kuṇḍalinī*] cannot be described. It is ecstasy beyond ecstasy, just like sexual bliss. In comparing sexual happiness with the happiness experienced in *cit kuṇḍalinī*, however, you will find that sexual happiness is one millionth part of the happiness experienced in *cit kuṇḍalinī*. In addition, simultaneously with the experience of ecstasy, you also realize the reality of Self. You recognize your real nature and you know, "I am only bliss (*ānanda*) and consciousness (*cit*)." In the actual rise of *cit kuṇḍalinī*, you will only get a glimpse of it and then come out. The full rise of *cit kuṇḍalinī* takes place only by the grace of your master and by the grace of your own strength of awareness.

Prāṇa kuṇḍalinī also comes about through the process of centering. *Prāṇa kuṇḍalinī*, however, is only experienced by those *yogins* who, along with their attachment to spirituality, also have attachments to worldly pleasures. If your desire and attachment is only for spirituality, then *cit kuṇḍalinī* takes place. Whether you experience the rise of *kuṇḍalinī* as *cit kuṇḍalinī* or as *prāṇa kuṇḍalinī* depends on your attachments. If you have attachment for spirituality and also for worldly pleasures, then the rise of *kuṇḍalinī* takes place in the form of *prāṇa kuṇḍalinī*. If you do not have attachments for worldly pleasures and are only attached to spirituality, then the rise of *kuṇḍalinī* takes place in the form of *cit kuṇḍalinī*. There is nothing you can do to determine how the rise of *kuṇḍalinī* will take place. It rises in its own way, depending on your attachments.

Kashmir Shaivism–The Secret Supreme, 17.117-121.

The Seven Perceivers

The first state is called *sakala*. The *sakala* state is that state where perception takes place in the objective world and not in the subjective world. In other words, I would call this state the state of *prameya*, the state of the object of perception. It is realized by its *pramātṛ*, the observer who resides in this state, in the field of objectivity and its world.

The second state is called *pralayākala*. This is the state of negation, where the whole world is negated. And the one who resides in this world of negation is called *pralayākala pramātṛ*, the observer of the *pralayākala* state. And this *pramātṛ*, this perceiver, does not experience the state of this voidness because it is actually the state of unawareness. This state would be observed at the time of *mūrcchā*, when one becomes comatose, which is like unnatural and heavy sleep, like deep sleep devoid of dreams. And the observer, *pralayākala pramātṛ*, resides in that void of unawareness.

These two states function in the state of individuality, not in the state of your real nature. These are states of worldly people, not spiritual aspirants.

The third state is called *vijñānākala pramātṛ*. This state is experienced by those who are on the path of *yoga*. Here, the *yogi* experiences awareness at times but this awareness is not active awareness, and at other times his awareness is active but he is not aware of that active awareness. This *vijñānākala pramātṛ*, therefore, takes place in two ways: sometimes it is full of action (*svātantrya*) without awareness and sometimes it is full of awareness without action.

The fourth state of the observer is called *śuddhavidyā* and its observer is called *mantra pramātṛ*. In this state, the observer is always aware with *svātantrya*.

The next state is called *īśvara* and its observer is called *man-treśvara pramātṛ*. The word *mantreśvara* means "the one who has sovereignty on *mantra* (*ahaṁ*–I)". This state is like that of *mantra pramātṛ*, full of consciousness, full of bliss, full of will, full of knowledge, and full of action, however, this is a more stable state. The aspirant finds more stability here. The *mantra* for this state is "*idaṁ-ahaṁ*". The meaning of this *mantra* is that the aspirant feels that this whole universe is not false. On the contrary, he feels that this whole universe is the expansion of his own nature. In the state of *mantra pramātṛ*, he felt that the universe was false, that he was the [only] truth of this reality. Now he unites the state of the universe with the state of his own consciousness. This is actually the unification of *jīva*, the individual, with Śiva, the universal.

The next state is the state of *sadāśiva*. The observer of this state is called *mantra maheśvara*. In this state, the observer finds himself to be absolutely one with the universal transcendental Being. He experiences this state to be more valid, more solid, and deserving of confidence. Once he enters into this state, there is no question at all of falling from it. This is the established state of his Self, his own Real nature. The *mantra* of this state is "*ahaṁ-idaṁ*". The meaning of this *mantra* is, "I am this universe". Here, he finds his Self in the universe, while in the previous state of *mantreśvara*, he found the universe in his Self. This is the difference.

The seventh and last state is the state of Śiva and the observer of this state is no other than Śiva Himself. In the other six, the state is one thing and the observer is something else. In this final state, the state is Śiva and the observer is also Śiva. There is nothing outside Śiva. The *mantra* in this state is "*ahaṁ*", universal-I. This-ness is gone, melted in His I-ness. This state is completely filled with consciousness, bliss, will, knowledge, and action.

Kashmir Shaivism–The Secret Supreme, 8.51-54.

Unmīlanā samādhi and *nimīlanā samādhi*

Nimīlanā samādhi is internal subjective *samādhi.* In your moving through these six states of *turya*, this *samādhi* becomes ever more firm. With the occurrence of *krama mudrā*, *nimīlanā samādhi* is transformed into *unmīlanā samādhi*, which then becomes predominant. This is that state of extroverted *samādhi*, where you experience the state of *samādhi* at the same time you are experiencing the objective world. And when *unmīlanā samādhi* becomes fixed and permanent, this is the state of *jagadānanda.* The establishment of *krama mudrā* is called *jagadānanda*, which means universal bliss. This is the seventh and last state of *turya.* In this state, the experience of universal transcendental Being is never lost and the whole of the universe is experienced as one with your own transcendental I-consciousness."

Kashmir Shaivism–The Secret Supreme, 16.114-115.

Seven States of Ānanda (*turya*)

[Paraphrase from *Kashmir Shaivism–The Secret Supreme*, 16.107.]

The practical theory of the seven states of *turya*, also known as the seven states of *ānanda* (bliss), was taught to the great *Śaivite* philosopher Abhinavagupta by his master Śaṁbhunātha.

The first state of *turya* is called *nijānanda* which means "the bliss of your own Self." When you concentrate in continuity with great reverence, with love, affection, and devotion, then your breath becomes very fine and subtle. Automatically, you breathe very slowly. At that moment, you experience giddiness. It is a kind of intoxicating mood. And when the giddiness becomes firm and stable, this is the second state of *turya* known as *nirānanda* which means "devoid of limited bliss." Here the aspirant falls asleep at once and enters that gap or junction which is known to be the start of *turya.* At that moment the aspirant hears hideous sound and sees furious forms. For example, he may experience that the whole house has collapsed upon him, or he may experience that there is a fire burning outside and this fire will burn everything including himself. He may actually think that he is going to die, but these thoughts are wrong thoughts and he must ignore them. When the aspirant desires to move from individuality to universality, all of these experiences occur because individuality has to be shaken off.

If you continue with tolerance, breathing and internally reciting your mantra according to the instructions of your master, then these terrible sounds and forms vanish and pulling and pushing in your breathing passage begins to occur and you feel as if you are choking, that you cannot breathe. At that point you must insert more love and affection for your practice, and then after some time, this choking sensation will pass.

This state of hideous sounds and forms, followed by the sensation that you are choking and that your breathing is about to stop, is called *parānanda*, which means "the *ānanda* (bliss) of breathing." Here, your breathing becomes full of bliss and joy, even though you are experiencing terrible forms and sounds. If you maintain your practice continuously with intense devotion, your breath stops at the center of what we call *lambikā sthāna*, which in English is known as the "soft palate." This *lambikā sthāna* is found on the right side near the pit of the throat. Here the aspirant experiences that his breath is neither moving out nor coming in. He feels that his breath is moving round and round, that it is rotating at one point. This state is called *brahmānanda*, which means, "that bliss which is all-pervading."

Here, as his breathing has stopped, the *yogi* must put his mind on his mantra and only his mantra with great devotion to Lord Śiva. If he continues this practice with great devotion, then a myriad of changes take place on his face and the apprehension of death arises in the mind of this *yogi*. He feels now that he is really dying. He is not afraid, he is apprehensive. This is the kind of death which takes place when individuality dies and universality is born. It is not a physical death, it is a mental death. The only thing the *yogi* must do here is shed tears of devotion and pray for the experience of universal "I." After a few moments, when the whirling state of breath becomes very fast, moving ever more quickly, you must stop your breath at once. You must not be afraid. At this point, it is in your hand to stop it or to let it go.

When you stop your breathing, then what happens next is,

the gate of the central vein (*madhyanāḍī*) opens at once and your breath is "sipped" down and you actually hear the sound of sipping. Here, your breath reaches down to that place called *mūlādhāra*, which is near the rectum. This state of *turya* is called *mahānanda* which means, "the great bliss."

After *mahānanda*, no effort is required by the aspirant. From this point on, everything is automatic. There is however one thing that the aspirant should observe and be cautious about, and that is that he should not think that "everything is now automatic." The more he thinks that everything will be automatic, the more surely he will remain at the state of *mahānanda*. This is why masters never tell what will take place after *mahānanda*.

From the *Śaiva* point of view, from *mahānanda* onwards, you must adopt *bhramavega* which means "the unknowing force." Here you have to put your force of devotion, without knowing what is to happen next. You cannot use your mantra because when your breath is gone, your mind is also gone, as the mind has become transformed into the formation of consciousness (*cit*). Here, breathing takes the form of force (*vega*). It is this *vega* which pierces and penetrates *mūlādhāra cakra* so that you pass through it.

When the penetration of *mūlādhāra cakra* is complete, then this force rises and becomes full of bliss, full of ecstasy, and full of consciousness. It is divine. You feel what you are actually. This is the rising of *cit kuṇḍalinī*, which rises from *mūlādhāra cakra* to that place at the top of the skull known as *brahmarandhra*. It occupies the whole channel and is just like the blooming of a flower. This state, which is the sixth state of *turya*, is called *cidānanda*, which means, "the bliss of consciousness."

This force then presses the passage of the skull (*brahmarandhra*), piercing the skull to move from the body out into the universe. This takes place automatically, it is not to be "done." And when this *brahmarandhra* is pierced, then at once you begin to breathe out. You breathe out once for only a second, exhaling from the nostrils. After exhaling, everything is over and you are again in *cidānanda* and you again experience and feel the joy of rising, which was already present. This lasts only for a moment and then you breathe out again. When you breathe out, your eyes are open and for a moment you feel that you are outside. You experience the objective world, but in a peculiar way. Then once again, your breathing is finished and your eyes are closed and you feel that you are inside. Then again your eyes are open for a moment, then they close for a moment, and then they again open for a moment. This is the state of *krama mudrā,* where transcendental "I" consciousness is beginning to be experienced as one with the experience of the objective world.

The establishment of *krama mudrā* is called *jagadānanda,* which means "universal bliss." This is the seventh and last state of *turya.* In this state, the experience of Universal Transcendental Being is never lost and the whole of the universe is experienced as one with your own Transcendental "I" Consciousness.

All of the states of *turya* from *nijānanda* to *cidānanda* comprise the various phases of *nimīlanā samādhi. Nimīlanā samādhi* is internal subjective *samādhi.* In your moving through these six states of *turya,* this *samādhi* becomes ever more firm. With the occurrence of *krama mudrā, nimīlanā samādhi* is transformed into *unmīlanā samādhi,* which then becomes predominant. This is that state of extraverted *samādhi,* where you experience the state of *samādhi* at the same time you are experiencing the objective world. And when *unmīlanā samādhi* becomes fixed and permanent, this is the state of *jagadānanda.*

In terms of the process of the seven states of the perceiver, the *sakala pramātṛ,* or the waking state, is the first state of *turya,* which is the state of *nijānanda. Vijñānākala* is the state of *nirānanda. Śuddhavidyā* is the state of *parānanda. Īśvara* is the state of *brahmānanda. Sadāśiva* is the state of *mahānanda. Śiva* is the state of *cidānanda.* And *Paramaśiva* is the state of *jagadānanda.*

In respect of the above experiences, Swamiji once wrote the following poem.

There is a point twixt sleep and waking
Where thou shalt be alert without shaking.
Enter into the new world where forms so hideous pass;
They are passing—endure, do not be taken by the dross.
Then the pulls and the pushes about the throttle,

All those shalt thou tolerate.
Close all ingress and egress,
Yawnings there may be;
Shed tears—crave—implore, but thou will not prostrate.
A thrill passes—and that goes down to the bottom;
It riseth, may it bloom forth, that is Bliss.
Blessed Being, Blessed Being,
O greetings be to Thee.

For the full explanation of the seven states of *ānanda* (*turya*) see *Kashmir Shaivism–The Secret Supreme*, 16.107.

In the fifth āhnika of Tantrāloka (5.43-45) Abhinavagupta explains God consciousness and the states of *turya* in relation to the five subtle *prāṇas*: *prāṇana, apānana, samānana, udānana* and *vyānana*.

Nijānanda is no state. It is the beginning point of putting awareness on subjective consciousness, *pramātṛi bhāva*. The first state is *nirānanda*, i.e. when you go inside, inside, inside, inside. But this is not the point to be maintained. You have to rise from that (*nirānanda*). And the rising point is from *parānanda*.

When this *prāṇana* takes place, that is the state of *spanda*. When awareness resides in *śūnyatā* (voidness), then the rise of *prāṇana* takes place and then he enters in another world. And that is the world of *apānana vṛtti*.[391]

> Just close your eyes tightly, just close your eyes tightly–tightly, squeeze it–and you will hear that sound from inside. Don't you hear . . . ? In sexual intercourse also that sound is there. That is the sound of *apānana* that gives you joy, happiness and entire bliss.

Apānana vṛtti is the supreme *ānanda* (bliss); that is the next state of yoga called *parānanda*, the absolute state of

391 *Vṛtti* means the 'established state'. *Prāṇana vṛitti* is that kind of state of breath which is not moving, i.e., breath without movement. For instance, *prāṇana vṛtti* means the establised state of *prāṇa*, and *apānana vṛtti* means the establised state of *apāna*, etc.

happiness. There, you feel that you have drowned in the sound of that bliss. In this state of *apāna vṛtti* you feel that breathing in and out is gathered in one point. Not only breath. All differentiated perceptions of the organic field and objective field are also gathered and balled in one point. It is why he sees that this whole universe has fallen down and is shattered to pieces; this whole world, all mountains have fallen down on him, in that *apānana vṛtti*. And it takes place on the right side here just below *tālu* (the soft palate). And when you establish your awareness in *apāna vṛtti* then those fearful forms, fearful apparitions, and fearful impressions that take place in your awareness, they subside.

Now, when you find that everything is completely balled inside peacefully, and there is no breathing in and out, and all the objective and cognitive world is balled inside in one pointedness without fear, then what happens next?

That yogi is absolutely filled with the state of joy, with the state of bliss, and that is the state of *samānana vṛtti* which is the state of *brahmānanda*.

Then that fourth state of *udānana vṛtti* takes place, where the yogī finds this ball is melted in that sound of bliss.

"Shsssssssssssssssssssssssssssssssssss!"

This very long sound is produced there and this ball is melted inside. Finished. There is no breath; this breathing process is finished. This is the state of *mahānanda*. And that sound that is not only, *"Shsssssssssssssssss,"* sound; sexual joy appears there with that sound.

When you are fully established there, and have settled your awareness fully there, then, in that supreme *tejas*, supreme light, he gets dissolved, he gets melted. He melts for good.

In the process of rising through these state, *prāṇa vṛtti* travels to *prāṇana vṛtti, apāna vṛtti* travels to *apānana vṛtti, samāna vṛtti* travels to *samānana vṛtti, udāna vṛtti* travels to *udānana vṛtti,* and *vyāna vṛtti* has to travel to *vyānana vṛtti*.

And when *vyāna vṛtti* travels to *vyānana vṛtti*, this is the fifth state of *ānanda* called *cidānanda*. This is the state of *mahāvyāpti*, the great pervasion, where you pervade this whole universe. But, you don't pervade this whole universe only. You pervade the negation of this whole universe also. When the state of *cidānanda* takes place nothing is excluded, nothing remains outside, *cidānanda* includes everything in its being.

Now the sixth state of *ānanda* is called *jagadānanda*. This is that universal state which shines in the whole cosmos, and which is strengthened and nourished by that supreme nectar of God consciousness, which is filled with knowledge which is beyond knowledge. Here there is no entry, there is no acceptance of remaining in *samādhi* or remaining in awareness and so on. That is the state of *jagadānanda*.

Abhinavagupta concludes by saying, "this state of *jagadānanda* was explained to me by my great master Śambhunātha."

The fifth āhnika of Tantrāloka also explains God consciousness and the states of *turya* in relation to the five activities of Lord Śiva (creation, *sṛṣṭi*; protection, *stithi*; destruction, *saṁhāra*; concealing, *tirodhāna*; and revealing, *anugraha*-grace).

Creation of God consciousness is in the state of *nirānanda*. Protecting God consciousness is in the state of *parānanda*. Destroying God consciousness (it is not destroying God consciousness, it is destroying differentiated God consciousness), is *brahmānanda*. Concealing of God consciousness is *mahānanda*, and revealing God consciousness is *cidānanda*. And *jagadānanda* is *anākhyā*[392], where God consciousness is not felt; it becomes your nature.

Nirvikalpa

In reality, everything, whatever exists, it is in the *nirvikalpa* state [where] you can't define anything . . . you can define only in the *vikalpa* state, in the cycle of *vikalpa*, e.g., when you say, "This is a specks cover". But it is not a specks cover in the real sense, in the state of God consciousness. It is just *nirvikalpa*. You can't say what it is, but it is! *Saṁketādi smaraṇam*, when you understand, "This is mine", "O, this was in my house and this is mine", this memory takes place in the

392 The literal meaning of *anākhyā* is unspeakable. Here *anākhyā* is being used in the sense of "the absolute void which is known in the state of the unknown. It is unknown and at the same time it is known." *Tantrāloka* 11.86, (USF archives).

vikalpa state, not the *nirvikalpa* state. And that *vikalpa* state cannot exist without *anubhavam*, the *nirvikalpa* state.

Nirvikalpa is the cause of all *vikalpas*; the undifferentiated state is the cause of all *vikalpas*. . . . It is not something foreign [to *vikalpas*]. It is their life. It is the life of all *vikalpas*.

Parātrīśikā Vivaraṇa (USF archives).

Kañcukas **(lit., coverings)**

Directly, universal consciousness can never travel to individual consciousness unless universal consciousness is absolutely disconnected. *Māyā* is the disconnecting element from God consciousness. *Kalā* (limited action) is the connecting element to that dead being in some limited thing. So he does something by *kalā*. When he does something, then individuality shines. Otherwise, direct from God consciousness, individual consciousness would never come in existence.

Tantrāloka 9.175-6, USF archive.

Kalā, *vidyā*, *rāga*, *kāla*, and *niyati* are the limiting connecting rods [between the individual and God].

Swami Lakhmanjoo, Tantrāloka 9.257, USF archive.

For a further explanation of the *ṣaṭ kañcukas* (the six coverings), see *Kashmir Shaivism–The Secret Supreme*, 1.7-8.

[The five pure states of Lord Śiva] take the formation of *ṣaṭ kañcuka* in the individual. Because, whatever is manifested in the universe, it is not manifested [as] other than Śiva. The same thing has come out in manifestation; the same thing what existed in Paramaśiva, that same thing is manifested outside also."

Tantrāloka 6.41, USF archive.

Kalā, *vidyā*, *rāga*, *kāla*, and *niyati*, these five elements are just offsprings of, offshoots of, *māyā*. *Kalā* means, "the capacity of doing something", *vidyā* means "the capacity of knowing something", *rāga* means "the capacity of some attachment (not universal attachment)", *niyati* means "the capacity of the limitation of space", *Kāla* means "the limitation of time".

Tantrāloka 9.41, USF archive.

These [*kañcukas*] are pertaining to the individual being. It is why [the grammarian] Pāṇini has also accepted these, the representatives of these [*kañcukas* as the letters] *ya*, *ra*, *la*, *va*; these letters as *antaḥstha*. . . . And all these [subtle] energies are found, not outside the individual being, but inside the individual being, inside the thought of the individual being, inside the perception of the individual being. So they are named, nomi-nated, by the grammarian [Pāṇini], as "*antaḥstha*". *Antaḥstha* means "that which is residing inside of the individual being". . . . We say that it is not *antaḥstha*, it is *dhāraṇā* [lit., the bearing or support] because it gives *life* to individual being. The individual being is created, the individual being is glorified, by these five elements ("five" means the five coverings); the glory of his own place, not the glory of Śiva; glorified with his own . . . that limited sphere.

Shiva Sutra Vimarśinī, USF archive.

In [Śaiva] *tantras*, they are nominated as "*dhāraṇā*". These five elements (*kalā*, *vidyā*, *rāga*, *kāla*, *niyati*, with *māyā*) are called "*dhāraṇā*" because they give life to the individual being; the individual being lives in these five elements. Without these five elements, there was no life to individual being, there was only the sphere of Lord Śiva. If these five elements would not be there, there was no question of the individual being to exist. The individual being lives only on the basis of these five elements. So they are nominated as *dhāraṇā*. *Dhāraṇā* means, that which gives you life to exist.

Śiva Sūtra Vimarśinī, USF archive. See also *Kashmir Shaivism–The Secret Supreme*, 1.7.

ABBREVIATIONS

KSTS	Kashmir Series of Texts and Studies
p	page
pp	pages
vol.	volume
v	verse

Bibliography

Swami Lakshmanjoo – Published text

Bhagavad Gita in the Light of Kashmir Shaivism (with original video), Swami Lakshmanjoo, ed. John Hughes (Universal Shaiva Fellowship, Los Angeles, 2013), xxi, 683.

Kashmir Shaivism – The Secret Supreme, Swami Lakshmanjoo, ed. John Hughes (Universal Shaiva Fellowship, Los Angeles, 1985-2003).

Paramārthasāra of Abhinavagupta, with the commentary of Yogarāja, translation and commentary by Swami Lakshmanjoo (original video recording, USF archives, Los Angeles, 1990).

Self Realization in Kashmir Shaivism – The Oral Teachings of Swami Lakshmanjoo, ed. John Hughes (State University of New York Press, Albany, 1995).

Śivastotrāvalī of Utpaladevācaryā – With the Sanskrit commentary of Kṣemarāja, edited with Hindi commentary by Rājānaka Lakṣmaṇa (Swami Lakshmanjoo) (Chowkhamba Sanskrit Series 15. Varanasi, 1964).

Festival of Devotion and Praise – Śhivastotrāvalī, Hymns to Shiva by Utpaladeva, Swami Lakshmanjoo, ed. John

Huges, (Universal Shaiva Fellowship, Los Angeles, 2014).

Shiva Sutras – The Supreme Awakening, Swami Lakshmanjoo, ed. John Hughes (Universal Shaiva Fellowship, Los Angeles, 2002).

Vijñāna Bhairava – The Manual for Self Realization, Swami Lakshmanjoo, ed. John Hughes (Universal Shaiva Fellowship, Los Angeles, 2007).

Swami Lakshmanjoo - Unpublished texts (USF archives)

Bhagavad Gitartha Samgraha of Abhinavagupta, translation and commentary by Swami Lakshmanjoo (original audio recording, USF archives, Los Angeles, 1978).

Interview on Kashmir Shaivism, Swami Lakshmanjoo with John Hughes (original audio recordings, USF archives, Los Angeles 1980).

Janmamaraṇavicāragranthaḥ, Janma Maraṇa Vicāra of Bhaṭṭa Vāmadeva, Swami Lakshmanjoo (original audio recording, USF archives, Los Angeles, 1980).

Kashmir Shaivism, The Secret Supreme, Swami Lakshmanjoo (original audio recording, USF archives, Los Angeles, 1972).

Parātriśikā Laghuvṛtti with the commentary of Abhinavagupta, translation and commentary by Swami Lakshmanjoo (original audio recording, USF archives, Los Angeles, 1982).

Parātriśikā Vivaraṇa with the commentary of Abhinavagupta, translation and commentary by Swami Lakshmanjoo (original audio recording, USF archives, Los Angeles, 1982-85).

Śivastotrāvalī of Utpaladeva, translation and commentary by Swami Lakshmanjoo (additional audio recording, USF archives, Los Angeles, 1975-80).

Spanda Kārikā of Vasugupta with the Nirṇaya (commentary) of Kṣemarāja, translation and commentary by Swami

Lakshmanjoo (original audio recording, USF archives, Los Angeles, 1975).

Spanda Saṁdoha of Kṣemarāja, translation and commentary by Swami Lakshmanjoo (original audio recording, USF archives, Los Angeles, 1981).

Stava Cintāmaṇi of Bhaṭṭanārāyaṇa, translation and commentary by Swami Lakshmanjoo (original audio recording, USF archives, Los Angeles, 1980-81).

The Tantrāloka of Abhinavagupta, Chapters 1 to 18, translation and commentary by Swami Lakshmanjoo (original audio recording, USF archives, Los Angeles, 1972-1981).

Vātūlanātha Sūtras of Anantaśaktipāda, translation and commentary by Swami Lakshmanjoo (original audio recordings, USF archives, Los Angeles, 1979).

Additional sources – Books

Bhagavadgītārthasaṁgraha: Śrimad Bhagavad Gītā with the commentary of Mahāmāheśvara Rājānaka Abhinavagupta, ed. Pandit Lakshman Raina Brahmachari (Swami Laksmanjoo), Kashmir Pratap Steam Press, Srinagar, 1933.

Śivastotrāvalī of Utpaladeva with the commentary (*-vivṛiti*) *of Kṣemarāja*, ed. Rājānaka Lakṣmaṇa (Swami Lakshmanjoo), Chowkhamba Sanskrit Series 15, Varanasi, 1964.

Tantrāloka of Abhinavagupta with the commentary (*-viveka*) *of Rājānaka Jayaratha*, ed. Mukunda Rāma Śāstrī, *KSTS* 1, Allahabad, Bombay, and Śrinagar, 1918-38.

Vijñāna Bhairava with the commentary partly by Kṣemarāja and partly by Śivopādhyāya, ed. Pandit Mukunda Rāma Śāstrī. *KSTS* 8, Bombay, 1918.

Yoga and the Luminous: Patañjali's Spiritual Path to Freedom, Christopher Key Chapple, Albany State University of New York Press (2008).

Mahārthamañjarī of Maheśvarānanda, with the commentary of the Author, with ed notes by Paṇḍit Mukunda Rāma Śāstrī, *KSTS* vol 11, Bombay, 1918.

Abhinavagupta 295–297
abhyāsa 64, 102
absolute 14, 171, 176, 233, 289
action 7, 21, 92, 207, 210, 228, 245–246, 275, 277, 283–284, 292
ādhāra 234
adhva 108–109
āgama 19
agni (fire) 99, 262
aḥ 51, 180, 183, 275–276
ahaṁ (I consciousness) 9, 15, 31, 109, 172, 191, 240, 276, 284
ahaṁkāra (ego) 99
ajapa 269
akāra 180–181
ākāśa (ether) 155, 168–169, 234
āmṛtam 271
anackam 9–10, 215
anāhata 68–69
ānanda (bliss) 24, 132, 137–138, 144, 282, 285–286, 289–291
ananta 171
āṇava 159, 172, 187, 243, 252
āṇavopāya 1–3, 33–35, 39–40, 43–44, 48–49, 51, 53–54, 64–66, 70–71, 76, 78, 80–81, 83, 92, 99, 101, 118, 121, 123, 128–130, 157–159, 163–164, 167, 186–187, 233, 243
anupāya 154
anuttara 56
apāna 121, 290–290
aparā 8, 13–14, 20
ardhacandra 8–9, 20, 78
ardhendu 77
ascending 50
ātma (soul) 193, 202, 209, 250–253, 266–267, 272
attachment 282–283, 292
attention 117, 128, 139, 159
au 76, 275–276
auṁ 8, 77–78
āveśa 137, 264
avikalpa 216
awareness 2, 34, 50, 54, 58, 62, 64, 70, 73–74, 82, 87, 91–92, 105, 116–117, 138–139, 145–146, 152, 158, 172, 190, 193–194, 196–199, 203, 206, 210, 243, 258, 260, 262, 264, 277, 282–283, 289–291
bahir 34, 121, 153, 245
bāhya 32, 121, 145, 170, 258
bathing 264–265
Being 277, 284, 292–293
Bhagavad 295–296
bhairava 6, 8, 16–17, 20, 23–26, 30, 32, 34, 36, 41–43, 168–171, 173, 175, 177, 211, 213, 233, 238–239, 252, 254, 258, 296
bhairavī 23–24, 152–154, 156
bhakti (devotion) 225
bhāva 24–25, 47, 97, 217, 229–230,278, 279, 289
bhāvana 28, 70–71, 87, 116, 118, 258–259, 263–264
bhrūmadhya 44–47, 49
bhutas 191
bhuvanādhva 107
bīja 155–156

bindu 8, 20, 65–67, 77–78, 163, 183
bliss 45, 93, 122–123, 127, 132, 137–141, 201, 204, 228, 231, 240–241, 244, 263–264, 274, 277, 282, 284–290
bondage 247–248
brahma 45, 49, 68, 137, 215, 221, 232, 287
brahmāloka 172–174
brahmaṇa 156, 231
brahmarandhra 42, 44–45, 49, 53, 60, 287
breath 2, 8–9, 32–34, 36–40, 42–43, 51–54, 59, 64, 93, 102–104, 115, 118, 123–124, 126–128, 130, 133, 153, 215, 252–253, 266–267, 269–270, 281, 285–287, 290
breathing 2, 9, 54, 68, 102, 104, 115, 129–130, 163, 252, 267–270, 286–288, 290
buddhi (intellect) 99, 198–199, 248, 260
caitanya 197, 218
cakra 11, 20, 42, 44–48, 129, 287
cakrodaya 44, 105, 106, 145
candra (moon) 8, 20, 77
center 53, 65, 77, 84, 93–94, 102, 114–115, 118, 130, 147, 163, 172, 203, 232, 252, 282, 286
centering 65, 125, 128, 282
central 36, 42–43, 62, 125, 252, 267, 287
cetanā 163, 187, 197, 252
cidākāśa 75, 167, 261
cidānanda 132, 287–288, 290–291
cintanā 50, 58–59
cit 41–45, 52, 61, 116, 129, 152, 219, 277, 281, 282–283, 287
citi 186
citta 51, 128, 131, 193, 203, 216, 224
cognition 134, 170, 191, 195
cognitive 84, 125–126, 278, 290
concealing 17, 281–282, 291
concentrate 33, 53, 56–57, 59, 62, 66–68, 70, 80, 83, 85–86, 88, 92, 98, 103, 114, 142, 158, 163, 167, 186–187, 193, 242, 285
concentration 52–54, 59, 67, 102, 130, 159, 190
conscious 60, 63, 104, 147, 206, 210, 218, 238, 291–292
Consciousness 1, 276–277
consonant 76–77, 215
contemplate 65, 69–70, 81, 88, 165, 176, 179, 188, 196, 201, 206, 260, 259–260
coverings 7, 111, 189, 292–293
creation 112, 282, 291
cycle 11, 13, 15, 24, 173, 223, 225–226, 231, 245, 247–248, 252, 275–276, 291
daśā 153, 212
death 101, 201, 214, 242, 255, 282, 286
deep sleep 283

deha (body) 15, 39, 80, 87, 88, 119, 142, 166, 197, 204
deity 257, 259–260
deśa (space) 23, 29, 272
desire 14, 26, 45, 46, 190–191, 193–194, 202, 205–206, 242, 282, 286
destruction 275, 282
deva 4, 6, 20, 62–63
devi 18, 166, 168, 180, 214, 224, 254–256, 270–271, 273
devī 26, 30–31, 145, 151, 274
devotion 225, 285–287
dhāma 61, 66, 125–128
dhāra 41, 49, 51
dhāraṇā 42, 82, 88, 95–96, 107–108, 116–118, 134, 148, 152, 162–163, 168, 178, 181, 194, 207, 293
dharma 27, 128, 189
dhyāna 19, 50–51, 59, 240–241, 258, 260
dhyātvā 96, 101–102, 108–109, 114, 138, 177, 226
differentiated 15, 19, 27, 29, 200–201, 252–253, 279, 290–291
dīrghātmā 266–267
disciple 58–59, 240
divine 45, 47–48, 153–154, 207, 271, 277, 287
doubt 5, 16, 228, 271
dṛḍha 90–91, 261
dream 18, 96, 101–102, 104, 153, 170–171, 205
dreaming 101, 103–105, 145–146, 147, 153, 170–172, 283
dṛṣṭe 64–65, 111, 113, 138–139, 156, 160, 222,224
duality 170, 197, 264
duḥkha 203, 217, 249
durbalāṁ 101–102, 105, 270
dvādaśa 49, 50, 101, 102, 254
dvādaśānta 32–33, 37, 42, 44–46, 66–67, 90–93, 102, 121
dviṣaṭkānte 41–42
dvitaya 32–33
ear 55–56, 64, 102, 179, 215, 280
earth 98–99, 111, 275, 281
eat 21, 140, 153, 277
ecstasy 24, 141, 277, 282, 287
effort 37, 217, 276, 287
ego 168, 188, 199, 249, 252–253, 280
element 98–99, 189, 225, 247, 250, 262, 264, 275, 279, 292–293
elevated 21, 125–126, 130, 143, 151, 154–155, 247
embodiment 12, 73, 169, 259, 275
energy 2–3, 4, 7, 8, 9, 12, 20, 27–29, 32, 34, 36–38, 53, 56, 58–59, 73, 83, 102–103, 125–126, 128, 130–132, 139, 145, 186, 190, 194, 212, 225, 252–253, 257, 263–264, 266–269, 275, 276, 281–282, 293
enlightenment 47, 151
entry 86, 105, 173, 213, 215–216, 224, 230–231,

234–236, 246, 252, 277, 291
essence 4, 6, 17–18, 25, 193, 257, 264, 266, 274–276
establishment 9, 20, 183, 277, 285, 288
eternal 215, 234, 242, 279
ether 34, 49–50, 89, 148, 213, 234, 281
excitement 131–133, 198, 217, 249
existence 13, 24, 96, 205, 209, 275, 281, 292
eyebrows 53–54, 65, 90–91, 93, 102–103, 121, 260
eyes 55, 56, 60, 64–66, 80, 89, 112, 128, 149, 152–153, 160, 175, 177–178, 179, 212, 214, 276, 280, 287–289
fire 27–28, 51, 60–61, 95–96, 99, 198–199, 211, 257, 262, 267, 281, 285
force 37, 49, 73, 190, 276,
formlessness 260
fullness 33, 155, 231, 262
fully 60, 143, 158, 207, 210, 274, 290
gandha 218
gandharva 18–19
gap 97, 104, 134, 168, 279, 285
gāyatrī 269
giddiness 103, 285
gocarī 229
God 1, 276, 291
grace 267, 277, 282, 291
grāhaka 207
greed 198
grief 217, 220
guṇa 255
guru 151, 271
hakāreṇa 268
haṁ 34
haṁsa 269
hand 25, 64, 74, 85, 143, 221, 280–281, 286
havan 19, 262, 267
head 60, 64–65, 67, 119, 129, 280
heart 32–33, 35, 37–38, 42–46, 49, 56–59, 66–67, 84, 89–91, 93, 102–103, 105, 121, 143, 266, 274, 282
homaḥ 257
hṛdaya (heart) 32, 55–56, 66–67, 89, 101, 103–105, 143, 274
hrīṁ 70
hūṁ 70
I-consciousness 278
icchā 2, 131, 133, 192–194, 205, 266–267
icchopāya 190
idaṁ 17, 240, 243, 246–248, 256, 284
ignorance 213, 245, 247
illusion 189, 195, 279–280
imagination 60–61, 96–97, 148–149, 160, 169, 188, 204
impressions 80, 85, 128, 290
individual 1, 6, 28, 62, 99–100, 119, 125–126, 140, 156–157, 168, 186, 189, 191–192, 201, 206, 209–210, 247–248, 250, 264–265, 284, 292–293
Indra 243–244
indrajālamayaṁ 200
inferior 1, 40, 50–51, 164, 166, 207

intellect 19, 21, 91, 188, 198–199, 225, 247–248, 252–253, 261, 280
intellectual 193, 225, 247 –248, 260
intercourse 184,
intoxication 198, 277
īśvara 7, 99, 275, 284
jaḍa 11
jagadānanda 132, 277, 285, 288, 291
jagat 96, 98, 119, 122, 185, 245–246
jāgrat 100, 105, 171
jala 99, 243–244
janma 296
janmāgra 49, 51
japa 257–259, 269–270
jīva 32, 33, 247, 248, 255, 256, 266, 268, 284
jñāna 28, 109, 131, 133–134, 150–152, 192, 193–194, 195, 218, 224, 245, 248, 250
jñānendriyas 99, 280
journey 6, 8, 18, 20, 26, 31, 107–108, 212
joy 132, 137–138, 217, 286 –287, 289–290
jvālā 211
jyoti 50–52
kaivalyaṁ 214
kalā 6–7, 189, 292–293
kāla 7, 189, 292–293
kalādhva 107
kālāgnirudra 95
kāma 131, 184, 199
kañcukas 7, 99, 280
kanda 49
kaṇṭha 49, 274
kapāla 31, 60
karaṅkiṇī 151–152, 156
karmendriyas 99, 280
Kashmir 1–2, 276–278, 281, 283–284, 295–296
kevalaṁ 19, 27, 131
khecarī 154–156
kingdom 89, 109, 117–118, 144, 272
kiraṇa 29, 41–42, 43
knower 14, 26, 88
knowledge 2–3, 7, 14, 109, 118, 131–134, 150–151, 181, 191, 193–194, 204, 207, 210, 224, 245–248, 250–251, 254, 275, 279–280, 284, 291
known 14, 24, 29, 31, 81, 88, 229, 279, 281, 285–287
krama 20, 43, 49, 74, 77, 132, 152, 276–277, 285, 288
kriyā 2, 245, 275
krodha 151–152, 198–199
kṛṣṇa 175
krūre 271
Kṣemarāja 295–297
kṣetra 263–264, 267
kṣobha 66, 212
kumbhakā 37, 39, 54, 133
kuṇḍalinī 41–42, 44–45, 47, 52, 61, 126–129, 152, 277, 281–283, 287
Laghuvṛtti 296
Lakshmanjoo 295–297
lalāṭa 49
laughing 93, 123–124, 129, 184, 208, 231
laya 50, 66–67, 112, 139, 216, 261
lelihāna 154, 156
letter 11, 33, 38, 50, 180, 183–184, 275
letters 6, 7, 10–11, 15, 50, 79, 238, 293

liberation 102, 173, 247
light 28–29, 148–149, 178, 281
lobha 198–199
lotus 62, 89
love 225, 274, 285–286
madhyā 36, 46, 62, 65, 114, 125–128, 131, 153, 163, 203, 232, 267
mahādeva 273
mahādevī 266
mahān 180–181, 257
mahāśūnyālaye 262
maheśvara 256, 284
mahodayaḥ 44–45, 48, 108–109
mala 15
manaḥ 53–54, 92–93, 158, 160–161, 209, 234, 241
manas 99, 144, 222
maṇḍala 55–56
mantra 2, 7–8, 11, 18, 28, 34–36, 47, 51, 59, 68, 70, 72–73, 76–77, 118, 123, 150–152, 157, 163, 167, 180, 259, 269, 275–276, 284, 286–287
mantrātmā 258–259
mantreśvara 47, 284
marriage 162, 133, 268
marrow 87–88
marut 34, 36
master 3, 162, 228, 271–272, 277, 282, 285–286, 287, 291
mātṛkā 11
mātsarya 198–199
matter 97
māyā 7, 18, 99, 189, 243, 275, 292–293
meḍhra 49
meditate 42, 66, 68, 93, 96, 118, 176–179, 191-194, 213, 215, 233–234, 242, 244, 257, 259–260
melāpa 150, 152–154, 256
mind 2, 12, 19, 24–25, 39, 53–54, 60, 62, 74–75, 78, 80, 85–86, 90–94, 107, 110, 115, 127, 131–134, 138, 141–142, 144–145, 158, 161, 167–168, 183–184, 188, 190–191, 193, 198–199, 201–204, 207, 209–210, 213, 216–217, 221–226, 233–234, 236, 240–241, 246, 252–253, 262, 264, 272, 280, 286–287
moha 199, 217
moment 29, 85–86, 112, 123, 128, 135, 138–140, 144–146, 154, 166, 168, 177, 190, 216, 218, 220–221, 223, 236, 238, 277, 285, 287–288
motionless 198, 212
mouth 21, 64, 152–153, 163, 179–181
movement 8–12, 20, 32, 50–53, 93, 101–102, 125–127, 129, 134–135, 151–152, 154, 156, 160, 167–168, 201, 231, 259, 266, 276
mudrā 43, 132, 151–155, 156, 180–182, 276–277, 285, 288
mukha 12, 29, 31, 260
muktaḥ 232, 248, 256
muktvā 49–50
mūla 49, 51, 82, 84
mūlādhāra 41–46, 287

mūlaśūnyaṁ 82, 84
music 141–142
muṣṭitrayaṁ 44–45
nābhī 42, 43, 49
nāda 6, 8, 20, 78, 141, 259
nādānta 8–9, 77, 78
nāḍī 62, 267
nagara 18–19
nature 11, 14, 41, 45, 47–48, 91, 158, 172, 186, 245, 249, 252, 280, 282–284, 291
navātma 6–8, 28
navel 44–46, 49, 91
nectar 153, 271–273, 291
netrayoḥ 214
netre 177
night 148, 153, 175, 269–270
nimīlanā 129, 132, 147, 171, 285, 288
nirādhāraṁ 160–161, 165, 183–184, 195, 209, 222–223, 240–241
nirmalā 187
nirodhikā 8, 9, 20, 52
niruddhā 116
nirvikalpa 25, 54, 84, 86–87, 97, 133, 135, 139, 150, 194, 202, 228, 237, 271, 279, 291–292
niṣkala 15
nitya 225, 234
niyati 7, 292–293
nose 55–56, 179, 280
nostrils 64, 163, 287
objective 24, 33, 36, 84, 107, 116–118, 173, 195, 197, 205–207, 217, 226, 233, 245, 278, 280, 283, 285, 288, 290
oṁ 70, 72, 276
oneness 9, 121, 152, 179, 230
organs 55, 180, 188, 199, 218, 249, 260
pain 187, 203, 249
palate 49, 286, 290
pañcakam 56, 149
para 50, 75, 107
parā 8, 12–14, 20, 25–27, 31–32, 41–43, 63, 98, 145, 156–157, 212, 263, 281–282
parādevī 25, 30–31
paraṁ 68, 89, 109, 153,209,268, 271
parāmarśaḥ 172
paramaśiva 39
parameśvara 4, 180–181, 210
parānanda 144, 286, 288–289, 291
parāparā 8, 12–14, 20, 266
Parātrīśikā 292
paravyoma 75
pārvatī 263
path 21–22, 26, 29, 36, 47, 62, 108, 283
pathway 11–12, 15, 42–44, 74, 173, 214, 221
pātra 58–59, 68
peace 14, 38, 144, 163
peacock 55
perceive 13, 24, 26, 55, 66, 88–89, 110, 114, 117, 137, 155–156, 178, 201, 204–205, 207, 213, 215, 217–219, 225–226, 233–234, 236, 243, 248, 276, 283, 288
perception 8, 117–118, 135, 195, 201, 205, 207, 218–219, 224, 226, 229,

233, 236, 240–241, 245–246, 247, 252–253, 278, 283, 290, 293
pervading 54, 108, 156, 206, 210, 217, 234, 238–239, 242, 286
piṇḍa 76–77
pipīla 125, 127, 129
possessed 46, 229
posture 60, 80, 103–104, 151–152, 154, 159, 209
pot 85, 111–112, 114, 116, 178, 205
power 46–47, 52, 103–104, 143, 151, 213, 255, 266, 281
prabhā 211
prabhu 222–223, 266–267
practice 10, 37–38, 46–47, 51, 53–54, 60, 64, 102–105, 114, 118, 142, 156, 163, 172, 178, 203, 249, 253
prājña 171–173
prakāśa 65, 122, 169–172, 250
prakriyā 108–109, 258
prakṛti 6–7, 99
pralaya 51
pralayākala 283
pramātā 206
pramātṛ 47, 63, 278–279, 283–284, 288
prameya 278, 283
pramiti 24–25, 278–279
prāṇa 32, 33, 37–39, 41–42, 44–45, 53, 102, 121, 125–130, 266–267, 270, 273,283, 290
prāṇaḥ
praṇava 70
prathamābhāsa 134, 206
pratibimbam 247, 248
praticakraṁ 44
pratikṣaṇa 92–93, 242
prayer 144
prayoga 123
priyaḥ 17, 29, 195, 252,255–256
process 21, 32, 34, 36, 38, 40, 46, 50–51, 60, 65, 70–71, 73, 76, 80, 82–83, 88–89, 97, 99, 131, 137–139, 150, 178, 195, 277, 282, 288, 290
protect 238, 263, 272–273
pūjā 2, 93, 258, 260–261, 264, 265
puṁbhāvaḥ 96–97
puṁsaḥ 96–97
punaḥ 12–13, 170–171, 173
puraṁ 95, 272
pūraṇam 24
pure 1, 7, 24, 56, 64–65, 69, 71, 87, 91, 109–110, 113, 144, 167–168, 181, 184, 218, 228, 278, 292
purī 104–106
purification 228
pūrṇā 157
pūrṇatā 262
puruṣa 7, 97, 99
pūrvakāle 73
rāga 7, 142, 189, 232, 292–293
rainfall 175–176
Rājānaka 295
randhra 45, 49, 287
rasa 140, 218
rāśi 6, 18, 20
rātrau 269
rays 29, 41–43, 211
reality 4–6, 8, 24, 47, 52, 90, 114, 179, 195–196,

203, 220, 245, 253, 275, 282, 284, 291
realization 40, 47, 51–52, 127, 137
rebirth 102
recitā 37
recitation 2, 33–34, 36, 68, 72–73, 77–78, 123, 151–152, 180, 257, 259, 267, 269
reciting 8, 72–73, 78, 259, 286
recognize 77, 139, 225, 282
rectum 49–50, 215, 287
reflection 112, 247–248
reveal
revealed 34, 38, 50, 58–61, 63, 84, 95–96, 109, 114–115, 123, 127, 159, 179, 186, 193, 199, 203, 271–272, 281–282, 291
revelation 129
rise 29, 42, 45–46, 52, 78, 121, 127, 129, 131–132, 138, 143, 152, 157, 181, 195, 198–199, 201, 207–208, 211, 271, 277, 282–283, 289
rodhanāt 65
ruddha 64–65
rudra 263–264
rudra śakti samāveśas 263
rudrayāmala 4, 274
śabda 6, 18, 20, 58, 68–69, 218
sadāśiva 7, 38–39, 99, 109, 275, 284
sādhaka 45–47, 74, 91, 93, 189, 197, 206, 242, 256
sādhanā 123, 136, 249
sādhu 17
sahasā 180–181
sahasrāra 45–46
saints 136, 150–152, 154, 199
śaivadharmā 210
sakala 13, 15, 283, 288
sākṣātkāratayā 31
śākta 59, 150, 154, 161, 243
Śakti 275–276, 282
śakti 2, 8–12, 20, 27–29, 36–38, 41–43, 49, 53, 78, 99, 102, 125–126, 128, 130, 136–137, 212–213, 252, 263–264, 267, 274–276, 278, 281
śāktopāya 1–3, 33–36, 39–40, 43, 48, 54, 56, 59–60, 63, 66, 68–69, 71, 84, 86–89, 91–92, 95, 97, 99, 107–110, 112, 114–115, 118, 120, 122–123, 130–132, 134–135, 139–140, 142–143, 149, 157–159, 161, 165, 167–169, 172, 176, 178–181, 186, 188–190, 192–193, 196–197, 199, 201, 203–204, 206, 208–211, 213, 216, 218–219, 223–224, 227–237, 239–240, 242–243, 248–249, 251
samādhi 65, 85, 87, 89, 107, 137, 139, 142, 147–148, 153, 158, 173, 212, 256, 277, 285, 288, 291
samanā 8–9, 20, 78
sāmānyā 207
samāveśa 67, 213, 263, 276
saṁbandha 207

śāmbhava 2, 75–76, 134, 142, 145, 150, 154–155, 161, 163–165, 168, 172, 187–188, 193, 199, 209, 211, 233–234, 237, 240–241, 243–244, 246–247, 249, 253
śāmbhavopāya 1–3, 33, 36, 40, 43, 48, 54, 59, 62–63, 70, 73, 75–76, 78, 80–83, 86, 88, 92, 95, 99, 101, 107, 110–113, 115, 119, 128, 130, 134–135, 139, 142, 145, 147, 155–157, 159, 161, 165, 168–169, 176, 181–182, 185, 190, 193, 196, 199, 209–210, 212, 214–215, 217, 220–221, 225, 233–234, 236, 250, 253
śaṁbhu 228
Saṁdoha 297
saṁghaṭṭa 121
saṁkocaṁ 214–215
saṁpradāya 214
saṁvit 151, 207, 248
śānta 38, 50, 131
śarīra 83
sarvaṁ 4, 21–22, 54, 81, 87, 96, 119, 122, 125, 169, 197, 200–201, 205–206, 233, 238, 243, 249, 274
sarvottīrṇā 155
śāstras 1, 151
saubhāgyam 89
sauḥ 72, 155–156, 275–276
savikalpa 135, 202
sensation 13–14, 56–57, 127, 186, 218, 278, 286
sense 18, 231, 281–282, 291
senses 55, 57, 125–126, 128, 262
sex 131–133, 136–138, 155, 184, 198, 217, 282, 289
Shaivism 2, 276–278, 281, 283–284, 295–296
siddha 150, 154
siddhi 151, 256
śikhā 67
śikhānte 66
sin 144, 263
Śiva 2–3, 49–50, 77, 79, 99, 225, 275–276, 281–282, 284
Śivastotrāvalī 295–296
sky 276
sleep 105, 145–147, 153, 171–172, 283, 288
so'ham 276
soul 6, 21, 143, 152, 168, 186, 191, 195, 207, 245, 247, 250
sound 9, 68–70, 74–75, 102–104, 141–142, 154, 172, 175–176, 215, 240, 281, 285, 287, 289–
soundless 9, 176, 184
sovereignty 284
space 23, 29, 31, 52, 163, 169, 222–223, 267–270, 272, 292
spanda 11, 50–52, 289, 296–297
sparśa 127, 129, 218
speech 255, 280
spirituality 282–283
śrīdevī 256, 273
sthitiḥ 32, 64–65
sthūla 50, 77, 258
subjective 24, 84, 117, 205, 207, 278–279, 280, 283, 285, 288–289

subtle 36, 41–43, 50, 59, 62, 66, 77–78, 98–99, 107, 161, 258, 285, 289, 293
śuddha 184
śuddhavidyā 7, 99, 275, 284
sukha 137, 141, 203, 217, 249
sūkṣma 50, 98, 107
sūkṣmāgni 66
sun 29, 148, 197, 211, 248
śūnya 56, 71, 75, 77, 79, 110, 149, 168, 226, 246
śūnyapañcakam 55–56
śūnyoccārāt 79
supreme 2, 7, 9, 13–14, 25–27, 32, 40, 45, 50, 54, 56–57, 60–61, 63, 65, 70, 75, 96, 108–110, 118, 120, 122–123, 127, 132, 137–138, 140, 144–145, 156–157, 163, 179, 181, 184, 199, 214–215, 232, 234–235, 257, 259, 261–262, 264–265, 267–269, 271–273, 275–276, 278, 281–282, 289–291, 295–296
surrender 271, 273
suṣumnā 36, 43, 62, 125–127
suṣupti 100, 171
Sūtra 276, 297
svadeham 165
svapna 100, 103–104, 171
svaras 50, 141–142
svarūpa 9, 12, 14–15, 20, 34, 38, 73, 86, 168–170, 257, 265
svātantrya 101, 103–104, 278, 283–284
Swami 295–297
taijas 171, 173
tālu 49, 290
tanmātra 99, 218, 281
Tantrāloka 277, 297
tāraka 65
taste 22, 56, 140, 154, 281
tattva 90–91, 104–106, 131, 184, 279–280
tattvādhva 107
technique 43–44, 88, 143, 214–218, 220, 224–226, 228–229, 231, 233–234, 236, 239, 243, 245–246, 249–252, 254
tejas 148, 169, 171, 290
terrifying 21, 181–182
thought 2, 4–5, 7, 10, 24, 40, 58, 72, 80–81, 84, 86, 89, 97, 103, 112–113, 116–117, 119, 125–126, 128, 130, 139, 150, 155, 161, 165, 170, 188, 190, 193, 199, 201–202, 228, 253, 261, 271, 293
tickling 123
time 10, 23–24, 31, 37–38, 43, 53, 57, 77, 93, 103, 116–117, 125, 147, 149, 153, 155–156, 159, 161, 184, 194, 213, 215, 219–220, 222–223, 225–226, 229, 234, 243, 251–252, 267–270, 280, 282–283, 285–286, 288, 292
tīrtha 263–264
tongue 55–56, 163, 280
trance 79, 263–264
transcendental 1, 25–26, 71, 171, 209, 274, 277–278, 284–285, 288
transcends 107
trick 123, 200–201, 206, 214, 275

Trika 276, 281
triśiro 8, 20
triśūlāṅka 30–31
tṛptir 262
truth 25, 193, 203, 284
turya 104, 147, 277, 285, 287–289, 291
tuṭi 270
uccāra 79, 163
undifferentiated 28–29, 200, 253, 279, 292
united 118, 132, 136, 141, 263, 277
universal 1, 7, 9, 20, 24, 26, 28, 49–50, 108, 112, 119, 127, 156–157, 171, 196, 206, 208–209, 211, 259, 264–265, 276–277, 281, 284–286, 288, 291–292, 295–296
universe 23, 96, 98, 108–110, 119, 122, 149, 200–201, 246, 275–276, 278, 282, 284–285, 287–288, 290–292
unlimited 173–174, 247–248, 253
unmanā 78
unmīlanā 171–172, 285, 288
unmukta 24, 23
unnata 272
upadeśa 254
upādhi 184
upāya 1, 33, 43, 60, 128, 139, 172, 212, 243
ūrdhva 42, 44–46, 61, 67
Utpaladeva 296
vācā 254–255
vacuum 60, 80–82, 110–112, 155, 158–159, 177–178, 186, 213
vahni 131
vairāgya 225
Varanasi 295
varṇa 15, 77, 183
vāyu 99
vein 36, 42–43, 62, 125, 252, 267, 287
vicintayet 88, 95, 110
vidyā 7, 189, 292–293
vijñāna 121, 205, 296
vikalpa 10, 19, 24–25, 96, 182, 271, 291–292
vimalaṁ 23, 168
vimarśa 122
vinyasya 224
vīras 143, 271
viṣa 131
visarga 33, 51, 76, 163, 180–181, 183–184, 276, 282
viṣaya 141
visualize 93–94
viśva 24, 171, 173, 206, 229
viśvapūraṇam 23
viśvottīrṇa 73, 276
vivarjitā 31
void 34, 56, 59, 71, 73, 75, 80, 84, 86–88, 176, 179, 186, 189, 233–234, 283
voidness 56, 58–59, 70–71, 73, 79–82, 84–86, 89, 91, 176, 179, 224, 234–235, 246, 261–262, 283, 289
vowel 10, 50, 76–77, 215
vṛtti 113, 128
vyāpakaḥ 210, 242
vyāpinī 8–9, 20, 49, 51, 78, 131, 156
vyavahāra 207, 229
vyoma 75, 186
wakefulness 104–105, 145–146, 153, 170–172

water 211, 248, 275, 281
waterfall 68–69, 113
wheel 9–10, 12, 20, 44, 263
will 1–3, 275, 277, 279, 282–284
wisdom 249–251
words 10–11, 24, 26, 79, 143, 155, 242, 275, 283
world 2–3, 6–7, 57, 98, 107, 118, 125, 127, 155, 170–171, 173, 197, 200, 205–207, 217–218, 223, 225–226, 242–243, 245, 247–250, 277, 283, 285, 288–290
worship 2, 257–258, 260–263
wrath 152, 198–199, 207
yāga 257, 262, 267–268
yatra 58, 92–93, 144, 217–218, 236
yoga 37, 151, 173, 283, 289
yogi 14, 46–47, 56, 59, 70, 88, 90–91, 107, 110, 121, 132, 141–142, 163, 168–169, 172, 175–176, 178–179, 181, 199, 236, 246, 276, 283, 286, 290
yogic 255
yoginī 150, 153–154

Teachings of Swami Lakshmanjoo published by The Lakshmanjoo Academy

Bhagavad Gita – In the Light of Kashmir Shaivism

Hymns to Shiva – Utpaladeva's *Shivastotravali*

The Manual for Self Realization
112 Meditations of The Vijñāna Bhairava Tantra

Revelations on Grace and Spiritual Practice

Shiva Sutras – The Supreme Awakening

Kashmir Shaivism – The Secret Supreme

Self Realization in Kashmir Shaivism,
The Oral Teachings of Swami Lakshmanjoo

Essence of the Supreme Reality
Abhinavagupta's *Paramārthasāra*

Lakshmanjoo ACADEMY

The teachings of Swami Lakshmanjoo are a response to the urgent need of our time: the transformation of consciousness and the evolution of a more enlightened humanity.

The Universal Shaiva Fellowship and its educational branch, The Lakshmanjoo Academy, a fully accredited non-profit organization, was established under Swamij's direct inspiration, for the purpose of realizing Swamiji's vision of making Kashmir Shaivism available to the whole world. It was Swamiji's wish that his teachings be made available without the restriction of caste, creed or color. The Universal Shaiva Fellowship and the Lakshmanjoo Academy have preserved Swamiji's original teachings and are progressively making these teachings available in book, audio and video formats.

This knowledge is extremely valuable and uplifting for all of humankind. It offers humanity a clear and certain vision in a time of uncertainty. It shows us the way home and gives us the means for its attainment.

For information on Kashmir Shaivism or to support the work of The Universal Shaiva Fellowship and the Lakshmanjoo Academy and its profound consciousness work,

visit the Lakshmanjoo Academy website or
email us at info@LakshmanjooAcademy.org.

www.LakshmanjooAcademy.org

Instructions to download audio files

1. Open this link to download the free audio . . .
https://www.universalshaivafellowship.org/ManualForSelfRealization

   It will **direct** you to "**Manual for Self Realization - Vijñāna Bhairava Audio**".

2. Select "**Add to basket** " which will send you to the next page.

3. Copy "**Manual**" into the "**Add Gift Certificate or Coupon"** box

4. Click "**Checkout**" and fill in your details to process the free downloads.

   If you have any difficulties please contact us at:
   www.LakshmanjooAcademy.org/contact

CPSIA information can be obtained
at www.ICGtesting.com
Printed in the USA
LVHW020748301221
707517LV00003B/21

9 780981 622828